Restaurant
Calra Nara Trattoria

Walking and Eating in Tuscany and Umbria

REVISED EDITION

JAMES LASDUN and **PIA DAVIS**

PENGUIN BOOKS

PENGUIN BOOKS

Published by the Penguin Group

Penguin Group (USA) Inc., 375 Hudson Street, New York, New York 10014, U.S.A.
Penguin Group (Canada), 90 Eglinton Avenue East, Suite 700, Toronto,
Ontario, Canada M4P 2Y3 (a division of Pearson Penguin Canada Inc.)
Penguin Books Ltd, 80 Strand, London WC2R 0RL, England
Penguin Ireland, 25 St Stephen's Green, Dublin 2, Ireland (a division of Penguin Books Ltd)
Penguin Group (Australia), 250 Camberwell Road, Camberwell,
Victoria 3124, Australia (a division of Pearson Australia Group Pty Ltd)
Penguin Books India Pvt Ltd, 11 Community Centre, Panchsheel Park, New Delhi – 110 017, India
Penguin Group (NZ), cnr Airborne and Rosedale Roads,
Albany, Auckland 1310, New Zealand (a division of Pearson New Zealand Ltd)
Penguin Books (South Africa) (Pty) Ltd, 24 Sturdee Avenue,
Rosebank, Johannesburg 2196, South Africa

Penguin Books Ltd, Registered Offices: 80 Strand, London WC2R 0RL, England

First published in Penguin Books (U.K.) 1997
Published in Penguin Books (U.S.A.) 1997
This updated edition published 2004

10   9   8

Copyright © James Lasdun and Pia Davis, 1997, 2004
Illustrations copyright © Susan Lasdun, 1997
Photographs copyright © Ron Davis, 1997
All rights reserved

LIBRARY OF CONGRESS CATALOGING-IN-PUBLICATION DATA

Lasdun, James.
Walking and eating in Tuscany and Umbria / James Lasdun and
Pia Davis.—2005 ed.
p.   cm.
Includes bibliographical references and index.
ISBN 0-14-100900-4
1. Walking—Italy—Tuscany—Guidebooks.   2. Walking—Italy—Umbria—
Guidebooks.   3. Tuscany (Italy)—Guidebooks.
4. Umbria (Italy)—Guidebooks.   I. Davis, Pia.   II. Title
DG732.L37 2005
914.5'50493—dc22   2004053429

Printed in the United States of America
Set in Bembo

To Violet and Leo: troopers

Maps : Chianti; Progetto
Integratto Esclurisionisme
H maps covering Chianti Lamole
is in map ≡. Tavola 2 #3.

Contents

THE WALKS

TUSCANY

CONTENTS

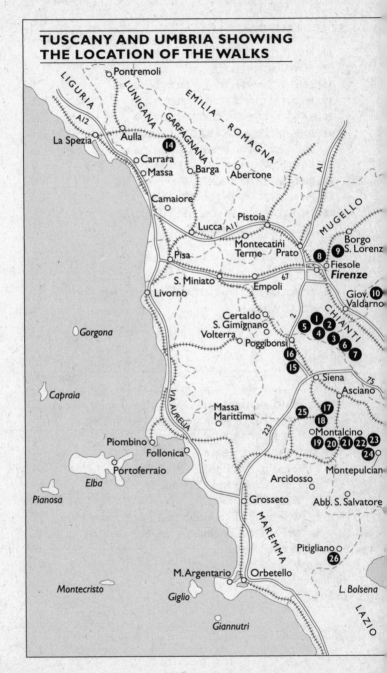

TUSCANY AND UMBRIA SHOWING THE LOCATION OF THE WALKS

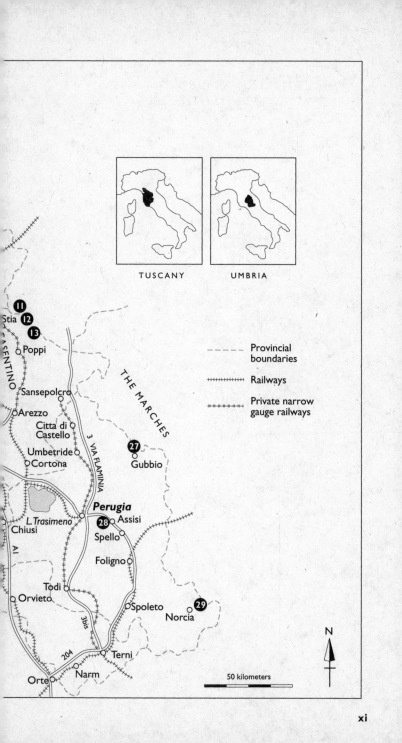

TUSCANY   UMBRIA

Provincial
boundaries

Railways

Private narrow
gauge railways

11
Stia **12**
13
Poppi
CASENTINO
Sansepolcro
Arezzo
Citta di
Castello
THE MARCHES
Umbetride
Cortona
3 VIA FLAMINIA
27
Gubbio
L. Trasimeno
Chiusi
Perugia
28 Assisi
Spello
AI
Foligno
Todi
Orvieto
Spoleto
Norcia **29**
3bis
204
Terni
Orte
Narm

N

50 kilometers

Acknowledgments

Our warmest thanks to Susan Lasdun for her drawings. To Max and Michael Hofmann for their stalwart help in Chianti. To Chris Shaw and Martha Kearney for keeping us company in Pitigliano. To Sally Greene and Charlotte Greene for sharing life *a castello.* To Monica Zatkova for her limitless resourcefulness with our kids. And to our editors, Sarah Manges and David Cashion, for their patience, flexibility and encouragement.

We are also extremely grateful to the people who have written to us over the years with feedback and updates. Your stories have been a source of great pleasure, and your updates have helped many others.

Non-Liability

The authors and the publishers have taken great care to point out potential hazards that may confront walkers in certain places described in this book. Under no circumstances can they accept any liability for any mishap, loss or injury sustained by any person venturing into any of the places described in this book.

Updating

We would greatly appreciate any corrections or comments you may have. Please write to us at our Web site **www. walkingandeating.com** or care of Penguin Books, 375 Hudson Street, New York, New York 10014 or 27 Wrights Lane, London W8 5TZ.

Introduction to the Revised Edition

Having, with some trepidation, given our e-mail address in the first edition of this book (1997), we very soon found ourselves at the receiving end of a large and steady volume of responses from our readers. For a long time, these were almost uniformly enthusiastic, with useful tips (a new restaurant here, a newly marked CAI trail there) which we were able to incorporate in subsequent printings of the book. As the years went by, however, the enthusiasm was increasingly tempered by odd notes of frustration, even exasperation: some of our directions no longer seemed to work; formerly abandoned farmhouses had been reoccupied, their new, non-Italian owners blocking access to old trails; pathways had become overgrown, farmers had reconfigured their fields so that the terrain no longer conformed with our maps; whole walks were on the verge of becoming unnavigable, readers were getting lost in the *campagna*.

As these weren't the kind of problems we could fix from a distance, we were faced with a choice: either we had to retire the book or else we had to go back to Italy and redo all the offending walks. We were loath to let the book go—not least because there is still nothing quite like it available for people who want to walk in Tuscany and Umbria. But our lives had changed since we wrote it: we had no children then; now we have two. From the logistical point of view, the idea of redoing the book *en famille* was daunting, to put it mildly. But with the encouragement of Penguin, and with several groups of friends lined up to keep us company, we decided to take the plunge. We went back to Italy in May 2003, and over the next two months, we rewalked and remapped the larger part of our original itineraries, eating at all our old restaurants and a great many new ones too, as well as adding brand new walks from areas we hadn't previously explored.

Knowing it would be impossible in our new circumstances to redo every walk, we decided to concentrate on those which—thanks to readers—we knew had changed. In the event, we ended up redoing the entire chapter of which that walk was a part, hence, most of the book. We did not revisit Assisi (see that walk's new introduction), nor the areas covered in the chapters "Around Florence," "The Casentino" and "North of Lucca," the latter two of which lie within parks (a national and regional, respectively) and have been generally very well signed by CAI. In the case of these three chapters, the walk directions and maps remain as in the original edition, and we have done our best to thoroughly update the Logistics sections of those walks. The result is an extensively revised, updated, and—we hope—improved book.

Along the way, it became clear that certain walks were no longer viable. As a friend of ours who joined us remarked, these walks are about finding a kind of "parallel geography"—a secret world set amid the roads and buildings of the modern world, but miraculously separated from it. The ways into that world are often delicate in the extreme—a gap in a hedge that brings you into a network of old mule trails; a forgotten track leading straight into quiet countryside from the back of one of the magnificent but busy hilltowns that you would otherwise have had to exit via noisy roads and ugly sprawl—and they are acutely vulnerable to new development. A few trees cut down, a path fenced off, can make all the difference. Then, too, we weren't interested in beautiful walks purely for their own sakes. They needed to be that, of course, but there had to be something extra: a monastery en route perhaps, an interesting town at the end, a good restaurant—at the very least the proximity of other places one might want to visit. Some of our old walks were already at the edge of acceptability on one count or another, and a couple of these have sadly gone beyond it. The Spoleto Railway walk is without a doubt our biggest loss (see the Umbria introduction for the reasons). The San Gimignano walk is also gone: altogether too spectacular for its own good, this is no longer a place you would want to go walking anywhere near.

On the other hand, we found splendid new walks and many improvements on our old ones. By relaxing our rule about setting off only from places accessible by public transport, we were able to include a stunning new ring walk from Badia a Passignano, in Chianti. More ring walks in general were requested by several readers, and we've added some of these (though we urge you to do the sequential walks as rings as well; see the How to Use This Book section for details). In place of our old Norcia ring walk, which was a trifle dull, with a reentry into the town along a busy road, we offer a spectacular two-day ring via the abbey at San Eutizio in the mountains above, returning to town along a route that miraculously avoids almost all the drabness that often surrounds the larger towns. Likewise in Radda, where we had spent days last time looking in vain for a pleasant final approach to the town, we finally found what we had been looking for—a tiny path that climbs up an embankment to a meadow, from which a series of farm tracks leads all the way up to the town: our equivalent of the Northwest Passage. And finally, with the addition of Pitigliano and its environs, far from the beaten track in southern Tuscany, we have broached altogether new and—to us—extraordinary territory.

Walking has become much more popular in Italy since we were last there. Walkers—independent or in guided groups—have started going there from all over the world, and the Italians themselves seem to have rediscovered their own countryside. There are many more marked trails than there used to be. And though these trails still have a habit of petering out in the middle of nowhere or not showing you which way to go at a crossroads, they are generally more reliable than they were nine years ago. Good maps have also become much easier to find, and there are one or two good new guidebooks in Italian (still very little in English).

Clearly things are going to go on changing. Many of the abandoned farmhouses that formed such forlornly beautiful sights along these walks have been bought and restored; some turned into *agriturismo* (a growth industry, with rather less of *agri* than *turismo* in many cases, but always pleasant places to stay), some into private vacation homes, complete with rottweilers and BMWs gleaming under the grape arbors. Doubtless those that remain will gradually be bought up, and this, along with all the other shifts and changes inevitable in a much-loved landscape, will have an impact on these walks. With that in mind, we are supplementing this new edition of the book with a Web site for new information, which we will keep as up to date as possible, and we invite readers to send in all possible comments, criticisms and suggestions.

Introduction to the 1997 Edition

On a clear day in the spring of 1993, we were looking out over the walls of the hill town of Montepulciano at a panorama of vineyards, olive groves and tiny hamlets that encircled the town and spread as far as the mountains on the horizon. We had been sightseeing in southern Tuscany for the previous week—the monastery at Monte Oliveto, on through the walled town of Buonconvento, Montalcino, the Abbey of Sant'Antimo, the little spa town of Bagno Vignoni, Pius II's unfinished Utopian town of Pienza— and a certain monotony had begun to creep into our daily routine. We both enjoy taking walks, and the countryside flashing by the windows of our buses and trains was be- ginning to seem at least as beguiling as the towns, muse- ums and churches that were then our destination. Once or twice we had wandered off down promising-looking lanes, but these had a habit of either leading to the town dump or turning into busy roads or else just giving out. How to get out into those hills with their astonishingly beautiful old farmhouses and dovetailing fields and woods? Was it even possible? Was the land all private? Were there rights- of-way, farm tracks, dirt roads you could walk along? And if so, how could you find out where they were?

The answers proved somewhat tantalizing at first. Yes, the entire countryside turns out to be crisscrossed with mule tracks, old cart roads, woodland paths, even remnants of Roman roads and medieval trade routes. Yes, even on private land the paths are generally open to the public. Furthermore a large number of them, particularly in the hillier regions, have been waymarked by the CAI (the Club Alpino Italiano), an indefatigable if also infuriatingly unsystematic organization dedicated to keeping the countryside open to walkers. On the other hand, aside from Curzio Casoli's useful but slim pamphlet about walking in Chianti, there isn't a single detailed walking guide in English. Nor is much of the region covered by walking maps on a useful (i.e., 1:25,000) scale. The Kompass series, allegedly for walkers, is 1:50,000 and only works well for the major mountain routes where the trails are usually well marked. The military maps are the right scale, but they are expensive, hard to get hold of and hopelessly out of date. And even the walking guidebooks written for Italians, though they were invaluable to us in our research, can be unreliable.

What we discovered, however, after a great deal of trial and error, is that there are plenty of walks out there, and that they are often spectacular, combining natural beauty, historical interest, physical exertion and the ubiquitously accessible amenities of good food, wine, coffee and sun. Forest trails connect great Benedictine monasteries of the medieval period; old trade routes call at abbeys and hermitages tucked along wild ridges of the Apennines. Footpaths wind through the high slopes of Umbria to remote farms with pitched-roof haystacks and bundles of kindling still tied together with strips of bark. Vineyards on the cutting edge of modern oenological methods give way to ancient fig orchards and olive groves where nothing appears to have changed since Roman times. From the austere Sibillini mountains to the green hills above Florence where Leonardo conducted his experiments with human flight, from spring-fed pools to Etruscan ruins, splendid walks await the visitor curious to explore the landscape framed by a car or bus window.

When we returned to Italy to research this book, we were able to repeat our entire itinerary of the previous year, from the monastery at Monte Oliveto to Montepulciano, this time *on foot*. Needless to say, the difference in the quality of our experience—not only of the countryside, but also of the towns themselves when we reached them—was immeasurable. It's one thing to hop on a bus, say, from Montalcino to the Abbey of Sant'Antimo; quite another to arrive there on foot, having left Montalcino early in the morning, walked through the Brunello vineyards surrounding it, the rolling farmland beyond with its quiet little villages, and then crossed the wooded ridge overlooking the Starcia valley to find the lovely Romanesque abbey directly below you in its setting of olive groves and pastures full of white heifers. The difference, as every walker knows, is something like that between being a spectator and being a participant. The abbey, just like almost every human artifact here, stands in a peculiarly delicate relationship with the landscape. Walking brings you into this relationship more intimately and pleasurably than a bus ride can begin to do. It is our hope that the walks in this book will enable you to experience this enormous pleasure as vividly as we did.

This is emphatically a *walking* book, rather than a "hiking" or "trekking" book. There are single-day or half-day walks, as well as sequential itineraries that stretch over several days, any part of which can be done on its own. With a few exceptions, we've concentrated on walks that offer maximum scenic beauty while remaining close enough to civilization to ensure a bed for the night and a restaurant meal at the end of the day. Since the satisfactions of walking are, for us at least, closely bound up with those of eating and drinking, we've tried to build as many of the walks as possible around the best restaurants we could find in every region. Bear in mind that neither Tuscany nor Umbria represents the most sophisticated side of Italian cooking. A simple style prevails, based in the old peasant traditions of *cucina povera:* pastas, plain grilled meats, seasonal vegetables, bread-based vegetarian dishes such as *ribollita* and *panzanella*. All of these are, of course, superb when done well, and on the whole they are. It's the places that offer a more elaborate menu that tend to be the most disappointing (with notable exceptions), and in general we recommend stick-

ing to the simpler establishments. We also list places where you can buy prepared food for picnics, often the best way of sampling local dishes and *prodotti tipici*.

Finally, this is by no means a comprehensive guide. Omissions include not only most of the higher mountain trekking routes, but also whole areas in each province where for one reason or another we were unable to find walks that fit satisfactorily into the parameters of the book. Large parts of Umbria in particular proved especially difficult. Though ravishingly beautiful, the landscape has been poorly served by lax zoning laws that in recent years have allowed development to sprawl unchecked. All around Perugia and Assisi, small ugly houses dot the countryside as though sprinkled from a giant salt-cellar, often as far as the eye can see. It isn't particularly conducive to walking. That said, much still remains unspoiled, not just around Gubbio and the area between Spoleto and the Sibillini mountains in the southeast, where we found most of our Umbrian walks, but also around Todi and Orvieto, and our failure to come up with walks near these stunning towns remains a source of real regret. Perhaps in a future edition. . . .

PRACTICAL MATTERS

Climate and When to Go

In our view it's always good to be in Italy, whatever the time of year. As far as walking goes, it mostly depends on the kind of weather you most enjoy doing it in. The spring and fall are perhaps the best times, as the temperatures are more moderate, but there's no need to limit yourself to those seasons.

Because of the relatively small geographical area we're dealing with, the main variation of climate within the region is less a question of north to south than of high to low.

The lowland hikes that comprise the bulk of the book can be done year-round. You might occasionally encounter snow during the winter, but there is no serious snow under 1000 meters altitude. The higher Apennine trails can be walked from May through October. In either case, you may want to avoid the hottest weeks of summer. The climate during July and August is much like the American Southwest: hot and dry. If you do your walking early in the day, you should be fine. Alternatively, you can choose areas that are cooler: near Florence you have Vallombrosa or, for a longer walk, the routes in the Casentino section of the book. Farther afield, to the south the Sibillini is a possible option for summer walking, and to the north the Garfagnana offers a cool summer respite.

Spring, although it can be rainy, is a gorgeous time of year, warm but not too hot yet. Mid-April until late May (or late May to June for the higher altitude walks, those in the Southeast Umbria and Casentino sections, for example) is best for orchids and wildflowers. September days are just as warm and beautiful as those of spring, and later in autumn you can enjoy an intimate view of the *vendemmia* (grape harvest).

It seldom rains day after day, and you can often wait out a shower. If it looks like you're in for a day of it, there are always the churches and museums; other than the Casentino Excursion and the walks in the Southeast Umbria section, none of our itineraries is so far removed from civilization that you couldn't reach a cultural center, even if only for a day visit.

What to Take and What to Wear

One of the reasons why walking is so easily incorporated into any kind of trip is that you don't need to bring a lot of special equipment. Most of what you'll need for walking you'd probably be bringing with you anyway. All that's really indispensable is a pair of sturdy and comfortable walking shoes (a good choice for city sightseeing as well) and a small backpack for water and other basics.

If you're planning to do just a walk or two, then whatever shoes you've got for traipsing around Florence should do. While ordinary shoes—sneakers or whatever—are fine for most of the walks (certainly the lowland routes), a good lightweight boot is always preferable, if for no other reason than the extra ankle support it provides. That said, when we went back to do the update, we had low-cut shoes. Sometimes referred to as "multipurpose" trail shoes, they look like a sneaker and come in high-top or low-top, just like sneakers, but they have a hiking-type sole that provides more shock absorption and a better grip than the soles on street shoes—without being big, cloddy hiking boots. This is what we bought for the trip and wear as our regular shoes now. If you don't already have comfortable walking shoes, it's probably easiest if you go to a shoe store that has a good line of "sporty" type shoes and a knowledgeable staff; that way you can get advice, and try the shoes on to see what's comfortable. Ask for something for "day hiking." If you can't get to a store, you can always go on-line and look at the catalogs of the sport shoe manufacturers, like Lowa or Merrill, and pick something out of their "day hikes" section.

You could pick a waterproof shoe (which tends to be hotter) or if you're going in the summer, you could pick something recommended for hot weather; but the main thing is that you want to make sure they're comfortable, *before* you leave on your trip.

While you're shopping, you could also pick up a pair or two of hiking socks, the kind that "wick" away the moisture (sweat) from your feet. Ask the salesperson to recommend something, and try the socks on along with your shoes or boots. Don't be surprised if they look thick and hot, even the summer type. They're really comfortable. Try to give them a few trial runs with your "boots" before you leave on your trip.

BACKPACK: If you don't already have a backpack for sight-seeing, you can probably borrow one from someone you know. It's the same thing kids carry their books to school in. They're sold almost everywhere now, at all those types of cavernous stores whose names we don't want to mention but that often contain the syllable "mart"—and, of course, at sporting goods stores. It can be squashed into your suit-case or otherwise makes a very convenient piece of carry-on luggage.

COMFORTABLE CLOTHES: pants that permit a wide range of movement, cotton T-shirts, a light sweater or long-sleeved shirt in case of chill or prolonged exposure to sun, plus a hat, are the essentials.

Many, if not most, of the walks go through farmland, which tends to be unshaded, and the Italian sun is very strong, even when it's not very hot out. You can bring a hat with you, or you can buy one in Italy. Straw hats are inexpensive and have a loose weave that permits a bit of air circulation. They're for sale in the weekly outdoor markets, among other places. You'll need a brim on your hat to keep the sun off your face and neck.

In summer, you may be more comfortable in shorts, even if that means the occasional run-in with scratchy undergrowth. In cold weather, several layers are more effective than one heavy garment. Naturally, you would also want gloves and a hat if it's cold, and perhaps some silk thermal underwear. Common sense is a reliable guide here.

Prudence would urge a lightweight, hooded windbreaker or anorak, especially for high-altitude walking. It doesn't have to be waterproof, although the light Gore-Tex models do have that advantage.

Other miscellaneous items you may want to include in your day pack, along with your water, map and sunscreen, are sunglasses, a lightweight multiuse pocket knife (commonly referred to as a Swiss Army knife, you may want to ensure that your model has a corkscrew; but don't overdo the extras, as they just add unnecessary bulk), a miniature pocket dictionary and a compass (*bussola* in Italian). If you're going in the spring, a small umbrella to carry in your day pack or hang from its side is really all you need to stay comfortable in case you're caught in a shower. The well-prepared walker also carries Band-Aids or moleskin (available at sport stores and most pharmacies) for blisters, a small roll of toilet paper, and depending on his or her level of concern about the matter, a snakebite kit (*succhia veleno,* the Italian name for the antivenin kit for viper bites). We've never carried a snakebite kit (or seen a viper), but perhaps someday we will.

One more reminder: NEVER set out without water.

PACKING SUGGESTIONS FOR OVERNIGHT WALKS

Everything you need for a walk of 2 or 3 days can fit easily into your day pack. If you're going out for longer, you could consider a bigger pack (but you don't need a full-out backpack), or having a little laundry done along the way (or doing it yourself), or just stuffing a few more shirts and pairs of underwear into your day pack. (For more on leaving your main luggage behind, see the How to Use This Book section.)

You'll want to carry the least weight possible; one way to do this is to make clothes serve dual functions when you can. So, for example, the clean T-shirt you change into on your arrival in "town" after your first day's walk becomes your walking T-shirt on the second day. Same with underwear. Your walking pants or shorts remain the same every day (as can your socks), but you'll need something to change into when the day is done, for example, a clean pair of trousers, a skirt or a dress. Silk and linen are two fabrics that are lightweight and respond fairly well to being crumpled up in a day pack, so we found a skirt or trousers of one of these materials served well as evening attire. Remember, it's only for a few days.

Sandals can also be lightweight items. We each shopped for the lightest pair of cheap sandals we could find, knowing we would be wearing them only for the limited walking we would do in the evening (we were much more interested in eating and drinking at night than in walking).

To round out the look: your lightweight windbreaker or sweater.

If it's cold, you may need to augment or otherwise adjust this list, adding a pair of silk thermal underwear, for example.

The only other things you need to pack are your minimum toiletry requirements (for a couple of nights, do you really need any more than a toothbrush, toothpaste, and comb?), maybe a book in case it rains and your passport: you'll be asked for your passport every time you check into a hotel.

Transportation

With a couple of minor exceptions, which are duly noted in the text, all of the walks in this book are accessible without a car. Public transportation in Italy is very good, and you should have little trouble getting around that way. The larger cities have maps and/or brochures in English detailing the railway and bus systems, and their bus stations and tourist offices have self-serve computerized schedule information—also in English—so you can get a schedule to and from any town you choose. The local tourist offices in the smaller towns are also very useful resources; you will nearly always find a person who speaks English there, and he or she will look up schedules, make calls to bus or train stations for you, etc. (Keep in mind that tourist offices, like most other places of commerce, close down from midday to late afternoon.)

Most of the locations at which our walks begin or end are small towns, so it's a good idea to check the bus schedule ahead of time, as you cannot assume there will be a bus ready to go exactly when you are. On Sundays, bus service can be nonexistent. Sometimes we've given time schedules in the Logistics section for a walk: this is meant only to give some idea of frequency. Actual schedules change all the time, so ALWAYS check the current schedule. Once you know when a bus departs, make sure to arrive a little early, because the buses often do—and they don't wait around. Especially in the smallest towns, you may not have another option that day. Always check the return schedule for your trip before you leave, unless you're planning to hitchhike back.

On that subject, if you do miss the bus, you can always hitch. In our case, the times we wanted to hitch were usually after we'd been lost for about five hours in 100-degree weather; invariably at these times we would be on some little gravel road (if not in someone's driveway) in the middle of nowhere. While this certainly tends to limit the potential candidates, it does seem to incline those few candidates more in your favor, and people who pick up hitchhikers seem to be an especially friendly lot. Hitching is not the ideal way to travel, but in a pinch it may be your best bet.

USING THE BUS SYSTEM

The bus system in this part of Italy is very efficient. The buses run on time, the tickets are inexpensive, and the distances you'll be using them for are often short. There are a few particulars to bear in mind, along with the fact that it's very hard to get anywhere on Sundays:

■ Schedule terminology

giornale	every day of the week
feriale	workdays (includes Saturday, unless it says *escluso sabato*); often indicated by a pair of crossed hammers
festivo	Sundays and holidays; usually indicated by a cross
inverno	winter schedule
estivo	summer schedule
scolastico	during the school year (mid-September through mid-June)

■ Bus tickets (*biglietti*) are sold at bus stations and also at the *sale e tabacchi* shops displaying the "T" sign outside. These shops are fairly common, and even small towns have one— a kind of combination cigar/newsstand/stationery store. They can look up a schedule for you if they don't already know it, and they can point you toward the bus stop, if it isn't patently obvious. (Bear in mind that the *sale e tabacchi* shops, like most other businesses, close for the midday break.) Tickets are also sometimes sold at bars, especially those located in or near train stations. If the shops are shut for the midday break, ask in a bar for ticket information.

■ When you get on the bus (and it seems customary to board the bus by the rear door and exit through the front door), you'll find a little machine at the front or back into which you insert your ticket to be stamped. That's it.

■ If you're out of town, you can catch a bus along the road wherever there is a "*fermata*" or "*fermata richiesta*" sign. Sometimes the sign will just say "SITA" or whatever the name of the bus company servicing the route is. Often the schedule for the route is posted at these signs. If you don't have a ticket, you can sometimes purchase your ticket from the bus driver; otherwise, at the end of the ride, just nip into the bar or *tabacchi* where the bus stops, buy your ticket, then return to the bus to have it stamped.

Another useful thing to know is that buses will often stop if you attempt to flag them down. Obviously, this tactic becomes especially useful when you've gotten lost.

■ In the Logistics sections, we've listed the Web site for whatever bus line services the area of the walk. These are very useful and easy to use (sometimes they even have an English version). The word for schedules is *orari* (or *orario*). Tourist offices will also look up schedules for you, and the city bus stations have self-service computerized schedule information in English.

USING THE TRAINS

It's always fun to ride on a train, and there is very good service between most of the hubs in the region. (Generally speaking, the train is better for long-distance routes, the bus for local routes.) The national railway system has an excellent Web site, available in English: **www.fs-on-line.it**.

Buy your ticket before boarding the train (in the larger towns, especially Florence, allow plenty of time for standing in line). For short-distance trips, you can buy tickets from the newsstands or bars located in the train station. Stamp your ticket in one of the yellow machines found in the main part of the station or on the platforms. Once your ticket is stamped, it's good for six hours for trips of under 200 km, or twenty-four hours for trips of distances greater than 200 km. Don't stamp the return portion of your ticket until you're ready to use it.

If you're planning to do lots of travel by train, it may be worth picking up a *Pozzorario,* a thickish orange pamphlet available at newsstands, with all the current schedules. Make sure you get the current one (they come out every May and October), and the one that covers all your itineraries (there are two: a general one for the whole country, and one that covers only the north and central portions of Italy—the *Nord e Centro Italia* version).

TAXIS

When we originally wrote the book, the idea of taking a taxi never occurred to us. Nine years later, we found ourselves viewing things a bit differently. There were a few times when—after a particularly heavy lunch, or on one of the days when the relentless record-breaking heat was particularly extreme—the possibility of returning to town by taxi began to look very desirable indeed.

The presence of many lovely farm-based accommodations along the routes also suggested the idea that if you were staying in one of these, it might be very nice to walk out in the evening to a nearby restaurant for dinner, but perhaps not quite as appealing to walk back again afterward. From that point it was an easy leap to imagine many circumstances in which the use of a taxi in conjunction with walking could prove highly satisfactory.

To that end, we've usually listed a local taxi service in the Logistics section for a walk. We didn't take many taxis, but our rough sense was that a fifteen-minute ride cost about fifteen euros. Ask for a price when you call. The local tourist offices are good sources for current taxi service phone numbers. If it's spur of the moment and you're at a restaurant, you can ask the restaurant to call for you.

DRIVING

If you've got a car, you're also going to have a map, and with a map you should have no trouble getting to any of the starting points for the walks.

If you're doing a walk that begins in one place and ends in another—the case with many of these walks—then you either bus back to your car at the end of your walk or park your car at the end and bus to the beginning. Try to overcome any reluctance you may have about using the bus, especially if it's going to deprive you of the pleasure of any particular walk. For more encouragement, see How to Use This Book, page 27.

Places to Stay

We've listed at least one place to stay in each of our destination towns, but our suggestions are by no means exhaustive, and there are usually several other choices in any area. You can look in a general guidebook or on-line for other recommendations, or ask in the tourist office. If you like to live dangerously, you can wait until you arrive somewhere and then ask around: "*Dov'è l'albergo più vicino?*" ("Where's the nearest hotel?"). This method has all the advantages that attach to spontaneity. The downside is that you may find yourself having to hitchhike to a bigger town.

If possible, it's best to reserve ahead of time, especially during vacation periods. From home, it's easy to do this by e-mail, and we have listed Web addresses for this purpose in the Logistics sections for the walks. If you're making phone reservations, hotel staff will almost always speak some English, though at other types of accommodations, this may not be the case. One nice way to alleviate any shyness you may have about phoning ahead in these instances is to ask the proprietor of whatever lodging you're presently staying in to call ahead for you.

In addition to the usual hotel route, there are other interesting options that may appeal to you. Some towns, Norcia,

for example, have hostels that offer very basic accommodations (and usually meals) at extremely low prices. (You
don't have to be within a certain age range to stay.)

Affittacamere are rooms for rent in private homes. This is
always a less expensive alternative to a hotel, and comes in
handy if you particularly want to stay in town and the single
hotel in town is full. Tourist offices have lists of people renting
rooms on this basis. Or you can ask around: *"C'è qualcuno
che affitta camere?"* ("Is there anyone who rents rooms?").

Monasteries are another source of basic lodging, more
expensive than a hostel but somewhat less expensive than
a hotel, and we have listed several of these.

Another option is *agriturismo,* which warrants its own
heading (see below).

Hotels and *agriturismi* will usually add an additional bed
to a room for a small charge. This can be economical if there
are three of you or if you have kids.

AGRITURISMO

Agriturismo refers to the practice, originally on the part of
family-run farms, of providing lodgings and meals. If
you're interested in slowing the pace of your holiday (which
you'll do anyway by taking walks), overnighting at a farm
will fit right in. Many of our walks have agritourism along
the route. If you have a car, your options are widened considerably. *Agriturismo* can be more economical than hotels,
and is found in some of the best countryside locations that
exist. The accommodation is usually in a renovated old
stone farmhouse or outbuilding, and increasingly there's a
pool available.

The past nine years have seen a tremendous expansion
in this type of lodging. When we wrote the original book,
most of the *agriturismo* was on family farms, and very
basic. This time, *agriturismo* was everywhere, running the
gamut from a room in a farmhouse to luxury apartments
in converted farm buildings on high-end wine estates. It
seems that more often than not these lodgings tend to be

"self-catering," which means they come with a fully eqipped kitchen and you do your own cooking or go out to eat at a restaurant. Having a kitchen is definitely an advantage if you have a car (so you can grocery shop) and are going to be staying awhile (some of them have week-stay minimums). On the other hand, if you're walking and just want to stay overnight, it's definitely an advantage if the *agriturismo* offers meals as well. These dinners—which you eat with the other guests and usually with the host family as well—can be a lot of fun (even if, as is sometimes the case, the owners don't speak much English), and we have found that a lot of the best cooking is done at home. At the very least, it's a departure from the standard restaurant food and ambience: a chance to sample authentic Tuscan cooking, prepared with the farm's fresh produce and olive oil, served in an atmosphere of warm hospitality and almost always accompanied by generous amounts of homemade wine.

You can get more information on *agriturismo* from the Web sites listed below, and view listings that often include photos. (Note that sometimes you have to go further into the site than the opening page to find information in English.) Local tourist offices also have listings of all the *agriturismi* in their area.

> *Terranostra Toscan*
> Tel. 055-3245011; fax 055-3246612
> www.terranostratoscana.it

You can get to Umbrian Terranostra listings by going to:
> www.agrivendolo.it

> *Agriturist*
> Tel. 055-287838; fax 055-2302285
> www.agriturist.it

> *Turismo Verde*
> Tel. 055-20022; fax 055-2345039

(For Umbria, use their main number in Rome.
    Tel: 06-32687430; fax 06-36000294)
    www.turismoverde.it

TOURIST OFFICES

Local tourist offices are great sources of information, including lists of places to stay. Many tourist offices print
glossy brochures listing everything from *affittacamere* to
luxury hotels, including *agriturismo*.

Something useful to know when perusing the lists is
that the abbreviation "Loc." before an address alerts you to
the fact that the establishment in question is located somewhere outside the town center of whatever town it's listed
under. You need to find out *where* the location actually is.
Usually you can find it on an IGM-based map, as the "loc."
(località) is often the name of an old farmhouse or small
hamlet. (See more about this in the Hiking Maps section,
page 31.) Occasionally you can locate it on the map given
you by the tourist office. If you can't find it yourself, just
ask someone. Certainly they'll know in the tourist office,
but usually any local inhabitant will recognize the name.

CAMPING

Camping is another possibility. As we haven't camped in
Italy ourselves, we can't offer much advice on the subject.
There are usually campsites near the larger cities and around
the major tourist areas. During the peak season, in popular places, these campgrounds are generally quite crowded,
and without a reservation you may find it difficult to get a
spot. If you're prepared for it, you can always pitch a tent
in some out-of-the-way spot, as long as it's not in a national or regional park, in which camping is forbidden.
The parks have *rifugi* (mountain huts) for overnighting. They
usually offer meals as well. Local CAI branches will have
complete information.

Miscellaneous

USING THE TOURIST OFFICES

Tourist offices are excellent sources of information, both before you leave home and once you're in Italy.

Almost all the tourist offices have Web sites, which are immensely helpful in planning your trip. They often produce extremely interesting pamphlets, and the information contained in the pamphlets may also be available at their on-line sites. One such pamphlet is Siena province's *Terre di Siena in Bici,* available in English (www.terresienainbici.it). Although it's written for cyclists, the pamphlet's photographs and text provide plenty of fuel for walking fantasies as well.

Once you are in Italy, tourist offices are helpful for answering any questions that come up, such as where you're going to sleep, when a bus runs, current taxi numbers, what interesting events are happening, etc. Many of the local tourist offices sell (and in some cases give away) the 1:25,000 scale maps so useful to walkers.

Note that the main tourist office of a region (e.g., Florence and Siena) has information covering the whole region, even though most of the smaller towns in that region have their own local tourist offices as well.

Towns too small to have their own tourist office often have a *pro loco,* a village association, to which you can also appeal for names of people in town who are renting rooms.

CAI

The Club Alpino Italiano, or CAI, is a large, state-subsidized organization with branches (*sezioni*) in every city and in most towns of any size. Along with public services such as mountain and cave rescue, avalanche forecasts and the training of professional guides, it also administers more than 500 mountain huts (*rifugi*) and marks and maintains thousands of miles of paths all over the country. CAI has been almost everywhere, and its prodigious efforts have made its red and white paint blaze a familiar sight to any walker.

Local tourist offices usually have current CAI information, at the very least the address and telephone number of the local chapter. Everyone we met who was connected with CAI was extremely helpful and friendly. Most sections run hikes on the weekends, which is always an option if you're up for this kind of adventure. While most CAI members don't speak English, if you're doing a lot of walking in a region, a visit to the local headquarters may still prove useful—or at least interesting.

In the eight years since the original edition of this book was published, CAI seems to have undergone a revitalization of sorts, and there are quite a few new hiking maps widely available with newly marked CAI trails. One thing about CAI markings, however, is that they tend to be a bit sporadic. Furthermore, once CAI has placed a marker, someone else might remove it or, if it's a paint blaze, it might become obscured by vegetation. So if you're on a section of CAI trail, use their blazes as an indicator, but don't feel the ship is going down if our directions refer to one and you can't find it.

PHONES AND PHONE NUMBERS

Phones and their attendant systems seem, like all the other technological accoutrements, to be in a more or less constant state of flux. The best way to get the most up-to-date information is to go on-line. For specific questions, you can go to one of the travel-related forums, such as Lonely Planet's "The Thorn Tree" at http://thorntree.lonelyplanet.com. Slow Travel also has very useful information on phoning, at www.slowtrav.com/italy.

Italian Phone Numbers

Italian phone numbers consist of a city code of two to four digits, always beginning with 0, followed by a phone number that itself consists of anywhere from five to eight digits. (Why the anachronistic lack of standardization? Endearingly Italian, it would be sad to see it cleaned up.) The only city codes which do not begin with a zero are cell phone numbers, whose city codes always begin with 3; toll-free numbers, which begin with 8; and Internet service numbers, which begin with 7.

Thus we have Rome at 06, Florence at 055, and Siena at 0577, followed by phone numbers of five digits, six digits or seven digits—examples of all three types appearing within each area code. Beautiful.

The city codes, including the 0, are always dialed, unless you are calling another number within the same city code, in which case you can drop the initial 0 (but you don't have to).

Phoning Italy from the US, Canada or the UK

- First dial the international code for outgoing calls in your country (in the US and Canada 011, and in the UK 00).
- Next dial the country code for Italy (39).
- Dial the city code and phone number you are trying to reach.

   EXAMPLE:

   Centro Agrituristico la Croce:
      0577–849463
   From the US or Canada, you would dial
      011–39–0577–849463.
   From the UK, you would dial
      00–39–0577–849463.

Using Pay Phones in Italy

To use the pay phones in Italy, you generally need a phone card (some pay phones still take coins, but many don't). You can buy these in the *tabacchi* shops or stationery shops, sometimes at bars and in most airports and train stations. They come in preset denominations, and unless you'll be in Italy for a very short time, it's probably easiest to buy the largest denomination card. When you're ready to use it for the first time, snap off the corner (make sure it's not already snapped off when you purchase the card). Insert the card into the slot in the phone. The window on the top of the phone will tell you how much money you have left on the card (which you can see decreasing as you talk).

Calling Home (or Abroad) from Italy

To make an international call from Italy, dial Italy's international access number (00), then the country code (1 for the US and Canada, 44 for the UK), then the area code (dropping the first 0 of the area code, if there is one) and phone number.

But how are you going to pay for the call? At this point in time, international phone cards are probably the cheapest option. Available either in Italy or before you go (from most of the big chain stores, including the ones with "mart" in their name, or on-line from most of the big phone companies or lesser-knowns like IDT: www.idt.net), you buy a card in a preset denomination of minutes, then connect via an access code and PIN. (From a pay phone, you would use your regular Italian phone card to dial that access number.)

Another cheap option, at least in the US and Canada, is to get a calling card from your long-distance provider (good for both domestic and international calls, and there's a good chance you already have one, as they generally come with the service) and sign up for whatever special low-rate international plan they offer on your home phone line. These international plans cost only a few dollars extra per month, and you'll save that on your first call home from Italy. Check with your long-distance carrier to confirm this, but our plan (with one of the big long-distance companies) gave us the same rate when calling home or anywhere else in the US with our calling card as we would get calling Italy from home, which was twelve cents a minute—and no extra connection charges for the call.

You can also use your regular Italian phone card, more expensive than one of the international cards but still cheaper than the remaining options, which entail either operator assistance or using the heavily promoted access numbers to your domestic carrier, who then charges you a hefty connection fee on top of your per-minute charge.

Cell Phones

The absence of any information about these in this section is deliberate. We have had too many beautiful walks up to mountaintops or views of sweeping vistas ruined by the sudden appearance of scenery-busting cell towers to want to aid in the perpetration of this phenomenon in any way.

If you want more information, Slow Travel has good information on its Web site: www.slowtrav.com/italy.

ELECTRICITY

Electricity in Italy runs on 220 volts, so if you're coming from the US or Canada, you'll need to adapt the voltage on any electrical gadgets you bring (like contact lens heaters, electrical shavers, or laptop computer batteries that need to be recharged). From the UK, you need only to adapt the plug.

If you're coming from the US or Canada, you need to buy a voltage converter and an adaptor plug. The voltage converter is to change the 220-volt cycle that comes out of the outlets to the 110-volt cycle that your appliance runs on. The adaptor plug is needed because the plug on your appliance won't fit into the Italian outlets. What actually happens is that you plug your plug into your converter, and the *converter* needs to be able to plug into the wall outlet in Italy, so in fact it's your converter that will need the adaptor plug. Often the converter will come with its own set of plugs to fit the various outlet configurations found around the world, but this is not always the case, so check.

You can buy converters and adaptors at an electronics store like Radio Shack, or you can go on-line for a wide selection of choices. Typing "220 volt travel converter" into your search engine will bring up plenty of offers. Just remember, *it's not just the plug!* Some sites offer the plug using language that suggests that's all you need. You need the voltage converter. You should be able to get the whole setup for around US $20.

Electricity in the UK also runs on 220 volts, so if you're coming from there, you only need an adaptor plug.

Buy this before you leave, because the converters sold in Italy are for adapting *Italian* appliances.

HOLIDAYS AND CLOSINGS

Everything in Italy closes down from around 13:00 until around 16:00. If you're planning to pick up a picnic lunch, make sure you do it before then. Otherwise you'll have to eat in a bar or restaurant: these stay open through lunchtime, but stores don't.

Almost everything is closed on Sunday, and public transport options are severely curtailed. Some shops are open in the morning.

By law, every restaurant has to be closed one day of the week, its *giorno di riposo.* Which of the seven is the "day of rest" will usually be posted in the window of the restaurant, and we have listed them for the restaurants we've recommended. Occasionally we have found restaurants that somehow get around this law, especially during the summer, but they are by far the exception.

Everything will be shut on:

> January 1
> Easter Sunday and Monday
> April 25, Liberation Day
> May 1, Labor Day
> August 15, Assumption Day
> November 1, All Saints' Day
> December 8, Feast of the Immaculate Conception
> December 25 and 26, Christmas

In addition to these specific holidays, it is useful to know that the week around Easter and that between Christmas and New Year's are big travel times for Italians, so book well in advance for these periods.

MAIL AND E-MAIL

To send mail from Italy, stamps are for sale at post offices, stationery stores, and from any of the stores that have the "T" sign outside—the same *sale e tabacchi* shops that sell bus tickets.

To receive mail in Italy, your correspondent should write your name, the name of the town where you'll be picking up your mail, and the words *fermo posta*. You'll need to show your passport when you go to the post office to claim any mail sent to you in this way.

Internet cafes (or in this case, bars) are fairly widespread now, and even the smaller towns usually have one.

EMERGENCIES

In Italy, 113 is analogous to our 911 and dialing it will summon police or ambulance; 112 is used to call the police specifically.

For serious health problems, or if you need an English speaker to assist you, contact your embassy.

LAUNDRY

If the idea of becoming a millionaire appeals to you, you may want to consider opening a chain of Laundromats while you're in Italy—if we haven't already done it. In all of the area covered by this book, we found only *two* Laundromats (up from one in the original edition).

You can always have your laundry done by a hotel or inn, but it's extremely expensive and may take more than one day; so get a price and check on their time frame before parting with your dirty clothes.

Another option in the bigger towns is a *lavanderia,* where you drop off your clothes in the morning and pick them up at the end of the day. Again, this is expensive, but not as expensive as having the hotel do it.

If you're staying at an *agriturismo,* there's usually a washer available for guests' use. In our experience there is more often a clothesline than a dryer. Along with being a good decision environmentally, this system occasioned some very pleasant moments. Time seemed almost to stand still during this unfamiliar (to us) ritual of hanging up clothes, with the sun beating down, the stunning countryside all around, the flowers, the fragrances, and the stillness filled with birdsong, so much richer in this part of the world than in our rural northeastern US home.

PRIVATE PROPERTY

Many of our walks pass through *proprietà privata*. Though you will see signs to this effect posted all over, they seem to be directed more toward cars than walkers. Many CAI routes go through private property, and we had no problems on any of our routes. The French and Italians are not inheritors of the brutish Anglo-Saxon precept of man's-home-is-his-castle-and-all-others-keep-out; in its place is a less selfishly-oriented recognition of balance between individual and community rights. As long as people are respectful (of the property, crops or livestock), why shouldn't they be able to pass through? This civilized attitude is also reflected in their legal systems, which hold the individual (rather than the landowner) responsible for any accidental injury he does himself; obviously a more reasonable position.

Just remember that it *is* someone's property, and be respectful, as you would want other people to be when passing through *your* property. Specifically, leave gates as you found them (whether that be open or shut); don't walk through a cultivated field; don't pick the fruits, vegetables or flowers (including sampling the grapes in a vineyard or picking wildflowers); don't litter; don't make undue noise; don't light fires. In other words, treat the property as you would want your own property treated.

DOGS

The Italian benevolence toward children does not apparently extend to dogs, and the neglected, lonely, forsaken lives most of them lead was a source of repeated despair to at least one of the authors. We heard much hysterical—often frightening—barking, but we never had any actual problems. The usual cause of their hysteria is that they are tied up, fenced in, or even caged: your—perhaps distant—passing is probably the most exciting thing that's happened to them all year. You'd be hysterical too.

If you do meet an aggressive, untethered dog, the best thing to do is walk away. If in doubt, carry a large stick (or steak).

WILDLIFE

A few readers have written to us because they were concerned about snakes. The only kind anyone has reported actually *seeing* are the green snakes, which are not poisonous. The viper is the only poisonous snake in the area, and the only place we've ever seen one is at **www.wilderness-survival.net** (in the "Poisonous Snakes of Europe" section). They are about eighteen inches long and have a zigzag pattern down their backs.

We've been treated very rarely to the sight of a wild boar (*cinghiale*) and heard them in the woods on other occasions. You can often find the beautiful dark brown and ivory striped quills of the local porcupine (*istrice*), but unless you're out at night you're not likely to see one. It's an African-based porcupine, at the northernmost point of its range in Italy.

The birdsong in the region is remarkable, especially in light of the horrifying fact that Italians still hunt thrushes and other songbirds. You'll certainly catch glimpses of the beautiful crested hoopoe (*upupa*), and the rather haunting call of the cuckoo seems almost omnipresent.

GETTING LOST

Almost certainly there will come a time (perhaps many times) when—though you are quite sure you've followed the directions to the letter—the map, the directions and the landmarks around you will cease to corroborate each other. Outlook is everything in these situations.

With perhaps one exception (the Sibillini walk), being lost is unlikely to pose any real danger, so it's pretty much up to you how the experience affects you. Of course, it's easy to be philosophical now, from the comfort of a padded desk chair in a temperate, sunny room, but the fact is that there were many, many times when we cursed not just the writer of any particular guidebook we were using, but *all* guidebook writers. Naturally, we assume that our directions are going to be incalculably superior to any that we ourselves used. But whether we are terribly mistaken in that assumption, or whether directions written by someone else are by nature difficult to interpret, or whether you are waylaid by changing landmarks (dirt roads are paved, new roads appear that weren't there before, signs or other markers may be taken down), it is bound to happen to you. And when it does, you will probably be better off if you encounter the situation with a spirit of adventure and the sense that it's really not such a terrible thing to be lost occasionally; if nothing else, it'll make for a good story later.

Many of our walks are through farmland or other "civilized" areas, and the maps give the names of the old farmhouses, names that have been in place for decades if not centuries. You can look around for someone and ask them the names of the nearby farmhouses, or to show you where a farmhouse you've located on your map is actually situated in the landscape around you. Or you can try showing them your map and asking them to locate your current position on it.

FOOD AND DRINK

While these subjects (especially the former) are covered in much more detail in the text, there are a few general comments we would like to make up front.

■ Notwithstanding the caressing descriptions given to meat dishes throughout the book, the vegetarian half of the team wishes to reconfirm that Tuscany and Umbria are two of the best places on earth to pursue this higher calling.

■ You may already have noticed an inordinate number of references made to "bars." This is due less to our alcoholic tendencies than to the fact that what English speakers generally refer to as "cafes" are called "bars" in Italy. Their main line is in coffee-based drinks, pastries and sandwiches, often with sidelines in *gelato,* e-mail access and bus tickets, though they do serve alcoholic drinks as well. However, despite the name, Italians don't hang around bars getting drunk, the way people do in English-speaking countries.

Whatever you're drinking or eating, it will cost you more to sit down at a table and have it than it will to imbibe it standing up at the bar. There's always a list of prices on the wall. There's usually a cash register, where you take your receipt and pay, sometimes *before* you're served the food or drink. A small tip on the bar is appreciated.

■ Try to make restaurant reservations ahead of time whenever you can, and especially for Sunday lunch, which is an afternoon-long event for Italians. On many of our walks, the place we suggest for stopping en route is the only game in town, and if it's booked up when you get there, you'd better hope you have some chocolate or something in your pack.

■ Tap water and the water at public fountains and spigots is safe to drink.

■ It might have been our timing, but more than once on this trip we had close encounters of a very unpleasant kind, i.e., with the fungicide/pesticide tractors. There we'd be, sometimes with our children in tow, walking along trying to locate the next turnoff, enjoying the views and the heavenly scent of the *ginestre* flowers, when suddenly a much less pleasant scent would overwhelm the first and send us scurrying for cover. To be honest, it was hard to reconcile our clearly over-romanticized feelings about the countryside and the wine with the reality of the heavy artillery out in the vineyards, and one of the results was that we started making a serious effort to procure wine from *biologico* vineyards, that is, vineyards that use methods roughly equivalent to what we call "organic" standards. We were very happy to find out that our favorite Chianti producer, Querciabella, has gone over to this method of production. They produce DOCG Chianti and also some of the best Super-Tuscans. We hope that the adoption of these standards by one of the most important Chianti producers will have something of a domino effect.

The Chianti vineyards seem to be taking the lead in this direction, and as we traveled further south it became increasingly rare to find top vineyards leaning away from the heavy use of chemicals, though there are exceptions (Paolo Bea in Montefalco Umbria springs immediately to mind).

In Italy, as in France, the producers of the very best wine (and by that we are referring to the best *quality* wine, not the top-selling wine) are dedicated to expressing the relationship between the grape, the soil and the climate, and the unique result thus produced (whereas most vineyards are producing for the mass market, and consequently for the mass palate). For some of these growers, this has meant a return to more traditional methods (albeit now transacted with all the cutting-edge technology modern enology has to offer), and the rejection of chemical additives at any point in the process of creating wine is a component of this decision. Because it's merely a component in the larger picture of the winemaker's dedication to producing the finest wine, it's not reported on the label. So you have to either know the background of a particular producer, or ask. If you're interested in getting a better idea of what it is you're drinking besides grapes, yeast and sugar, you can ask in any *enoteca* (wine store) and usually any restaurant who the *biologico* producers are. Nor are the *biologico* or organic producers necessarily the best producers; that's when you really hit the jackpot, when you find the best producers using organic methods.

In the meantime, here is a list of Chianti vineyards that are either *biologico* or organic:

> Querciabella
> Rampolla
> Badia a Coltibuono (in the process of conversion)
> Buondonno
> Casina di Cornia
> Casaloste
> Concadoro
> Conio
> Panzanello

AND FINALLY . . .

Our opinions and recommendations are not colored by bribery. Almost never did any of our hosts even know we were writing a book; thus we expect that any other decent, courteous travelers will receive the same treatment at the establishments listed that we ourselves received.

HOW TO USE THIS BOOK

We have tried to make this book useful to a wide range of travelers—those for whom walking will form a major part of their trip and those who are tentatively considering a single walk; those who have a car and those who don't.

Any of the walks in a chapter can be done within the space of a day, including any travel time, from anywhere else in that chapter or from the nearest city. The Chianti region that leads off the book lies between Florence and Siena, and all the walks in that chapter are accessible by public transport from either of those cities. They are listed roughly in north-to-south order; the further north the walk, the more convenient it is to Florence, and the further south, the more convenient to Siena.

The walks in the chapters "Around Florence" and "The Casentino" are more convenient from Florence, while those in "West of Siena" and "South Tuscany" are more convenient from Siena. However, Florence and Siena are themselves only about an hour's bus ride apart.

None of the walks that assume a Florence or Siena base actually begin inside the city, but require a bus, train or car ride to reach the starting point. The reason for this is that the outskirts of those cities do not offer pleasant walking. The time the bus or train ride takes is listed in the Logistics section for each walk and is usually minimal, so that you can complete an outing in a single day or less.

The Garfagnana ("North of Lucca") is about an hour's drive from Lucca, and while it makes for a good day's outing, it is also a lovely overnight destination. Pitigliano, well off the beaten tourist track in southern Tuscany,

S.L.96

demands at least an overnight commitment, which the town amply repays.

In Umbria, the Gubbio and Assisi walks begin within their respective town borders, while Norcia makes a good base for all the walks in the Southeast Umbria chapter.

See the individual chapters for more detailed transportation information.

Single-Day Walks

With few exceptions (noted in the text), any of the walks in the book can be done as a single day's ring walk, including those listed as part of a sequential (point A to point B) walk, in the latter case by using the local bus. Walks accomplished within the space of a single day require little planning other than checking the bus schedule (if relevant) and perhaps making a lunch reservation or packing a picnic.

Car-free travelers can do a "point A to point B" walk as easily as doing a ring walk, since they will in any case be using public transport at both ends.

If you have a car, either hop the local bus back to your car at the end of the walk, or park your car at the walk's destination and bus back to its starting point. None of these distances are long by bus, usually fifteen to twenty minutes or so. Alternatively, you could use a taxi or, if you're traveling with another couple who also have a car, leave one car at each end.

Try not to let any resistance you may feel to getting on a bus deprive you of the chance to enjoy one of these great walks! If you're apprehensive about taking the bus, try to overcome your initial reluctance and do it once; after that, it's easy. Think of it as part of the day's adventure, and a time to relax while you watch a new scenic route pass by your window.

Bus and taxi information is included in the Logistics sections.

Walks of More Than a Single Day

Any walk you take in the countryside is going to be a departure from the usual tourist routine—the scripted, often harried trajectory from museum to museum, shop to shop, "must-see" to "must-see"—and even if you spend only one day walking, you'll experience a side of the region you never would have otherwise. So many correspondents have told us that their memories of the days they spent walking have stayed with them long after their memories of the other days have blurred into one.

A longer walk only makes it better.

There is something deeply satisfying about walking from one village to the next, across the spectacular countryside lying in between. When you set off without your car (if you have one) and the bulk of your luggage, it's not only your "things" you leave behind, but also a time frame and the determination to control every aspect of your experience. Walking from town to town, you open yourself up a little bit more to what chance sends your way, while at the same time allowing yourself an opportunity to really "get away from it all." The physical pleasure of the walk and the anticipation of the good food and drink awaiting you at your destination (not to mention the cultural perks) are deeply relaxing; not only that, but walking allows you to acquire an appetite, which in Italy can be a surprisingly elusive entity, surrounded as you are by so much temptation.

The sequential walks can be tailored to encompass as many days as you like, since you can join or leave the itinerary at almost any point.

The main thing you need to plan for if you decide to do more than a single day's walk is leaving the bulk of your luggage (and your car, if you have one) behind. (See page 4 for suggestions on what to take on overnights.)

We usually left our luggage wherever we'd been staying before we went out on one of our walks. In our experience, hotel keepers (and this would apply equally to agritourism establishments) were always very accommodating, storing our bags behind the desk or in a closet somewhere, free of charge. At the end of the walk—however many days it was—we'd bus back to the hotel, often staying the night there, in which case the hotel had become the "base" of our itinerary.

A slightly different approach is to bring your suitcases

ahead to the hotel or other lodging at which you plan to end your walk, booking yourself in for that future night and asking them to hold your bags until you arrive.

Another alternative (one we haven't used ourselves) is to leave your suitcases in the "left luggage" room (*deposito bagaglio*) of a train station, where for a small fee your bags can be securely stored. The train stations in larger towns have these, and in smaller stations the *capo di stazione* (stationmaster) may agree to perform the same service.

If you have a car, you can make similar arrangements with your hotel, though depending on their parking situation they may charge a fee. *Agriturismo* establishments may be more willing to let you leave your car free of charge for a few days, insofar as they don't usually have the space constraints of city locations.

Hiking Maps

All the best hiking maps of the region are based on the old 1:25,000 scale of Italian military maps produced—and beautifully drawn—by the Istituto Geografico Militare (IGM). The hiking maps based on the IGM are usually called *carta dei sentieri* (*sentiero* means footpath). The map's scale (1:25,000) is the important thing, and along with the name of the region covered, will be printed somewhere on the front. "Scale" basically refers to how detailed the maps are; the smaller that second number, the more detailed the map. Thus the Kompass series of maps, widely sold and used, at 1:50,000 are not nearly as detailed, and we find the 1:25,000 scale maps infinitely more useful.

When we wrote the original edition of this book, there were many areas for which there was no hiking map (all of the "South Tuscany" chapter, for example), but happily that has all changed now, and there are *carta dei sentieri* for all of the areas in this edition except Pitigliano (see that walk's Logistics section for more information). We strongly recommend purchasing the map covering the region in which you'll be walking. At about 6 euros (for a map covering a large area), they are a real bargain, and may inspire you to take other walks in the region.

Along with all the topographical information (roads, streams, inclines, etc.), the maps show the old farmhouses and their names. Farmhouses are very useful landmarks when walking through the countryside. If you're lost, you can ask someone the name of any nearby farmhouse, then locate it on your map.

Another feature of the maps we found extremely useful is the marking of streambeds (called *fosso* on the maps). In open farm country you can see the streambeds from a mile away because of the concentration of greenery—shrubs and trees—growing along them. They can help you confirm where you are in both open farm country and wooded areas because, since they were created by the flow of water (although they are often dry), they tend to occur at the lowest points in a landscape, and often mark the point at which you've just ended a descent and are beginning to climb. Along with the farmhouses, they were probably our most frequently used landmarks.

Maps are widely available at newsstands, bookstores, local tourist offices, and in various other stores, restaurants and hotels you come across when you're walking. The Chianti region has produced a new set of its own walking maps, based on the IGM, which are available at the local tourist offices of that region.

If you're eager to get your hands on them before you go, you can order all the Tuscany maps on-line from Libreria Stella Alpina at www.stella-alpina.com. On the home page, click on *Entra,* then click on *Cartografia,* and from there click on *Edizioni Multigraphic.* When that opens, scroll down to the section headed *Appennino Centrale . . . Toscana Interna,* and you'll find all the Tuscany maps we list in the Logistics sections.

Libreria Stella Alpina
Via F. Corridoni, 14 B/r
Tel. 055-411688; fax 055-4360877

Distances

We chose to use metric distances in the book because all the Italian maps are based on the kilometer, and the grid lines drawn on the maps show kilometers.

1 kilometer = .621 miles
1 mile = 1.609 kilometers

An easy way to think of it is that a kilometer is about ⅝ of a mile, and a mile is about 1½ kilometers.

1 meter = 39.37 inches

Conveniently, 39.39 inches is pretty close to a yard, and we estimated everything in yards, so when we say "walk 4 meters," you can rest assured that we mean "walk 4 yards."

But what about when a distance given is 200 meters (yards)? That's not as easy to visualize as 4 meters (yards). And how long does it take to walk 200 meters (yards)?

On flat ground, it takes us about ten minutes to walk a kilometer. We're fairly brisk walkers. On the other hand, we've noticed a meandering, leisurely pace common with our friends who aren't big walkers. A kilometer takes them about fifteen minutes. When we've given the time it takes to walk a certain distance, we've tried to base it on a walking speed somewhere in between these two types of walkers. These estimated times are only rough guides; adjust them for your own pace. We've tried to take account of the type of terrain as well: is it flat or is it steep? Remember, too, that these estimated times are the time it takes *without stopping*. That means that if you stop—to look at a flower, or your map, or the book—it's going to add on to the time it takes to complete that particular stretch.

So, how long does it take to walk 200 meters? There are 1000 meters in a kilometer. Therefore, 200 meters = ⅕ kilometer. If it takes you ten minutes to walk a kilometer, it will take you one-fifth that amount of time to walk 200 meters, i.e., two minutes. (That's why the rest of the world uses the metric system: it's so much easier!) If it takes you fifteen minutes to walk a kilometer, then it will take you three minutes to walk one-fifth of a kilometer, or 200 meters.

Once you get an idea of how fast you walk, you can use this handy "cheat sheet" for quick reference until you get the hang of it.

> @ *10 minutes per kilometer*
> 100 meters = 1 minute
> 300 meters = 3 minutes
> ½ km = 5 minutes
> 800 meters = 8 minutes
>
> @ *12 minutes per kilometer*
> 100 meters = just over a minute
> 300 meters = 3½ minutes
> ½ km = 6 minutes
> 800 meters = 9½ minutes
>
> @ *15 minutes per kilometer*
> 100 meters = 1½ minutes
> 300 meters = 4½ minutes
> ½ km = 7½ minutes
> 800 meters = 12 minutes

One last note on distances. Please use our estimates suggestively, rather than as statements of fact. We weren't measuring with anything more than our best guess.

Notes on Our Maps and Directions

1. Our maps are intended as a secondary reference to the primary reference of the written directions. In other

words, if in doubt, we'd take our chances with the written instructions over the maps.

2. When you're out on the trail and see another track branching off the one you've been following, if we haven't mentioned it specifically, assume that you don't take it. Usually we haven't mentioned these deviations individually in the text, though occasionally we have given the general advice "ignore deviations." On the maps, these other tracks branching off the main route are marked as little "tabs" leading off the main route. We haven't marked every single one, by any means. Therefore, use them only as a general guide, one piece of information among others.

3. When the directions say "T-junction," this junction will not necessarily be an exact T, and in some cases could even be interpreted as loosely as "meeting another path where you have to turn left or right."

Logistics Sections

The Logistics section for each walk lists various bits of practical information. Hotel and restaurant recommendations in the Logistics sections will generally apply to the destination of the walk. Thus, in the sequential walks, the information pertaining to the town from which any day's walk begins will be found in the Logistics section of the previous day's walk.

Difficulty Level

We haven't rated the walks for difficulty, because other than the Sibillini walk, none of them is particularly difficult. The difference in difficulty is essentially one of length: a 3-hour walk is "easier" than a 6-hour walk.

Doing the Walks in Reverse

Unless you are very well practiced in reading detailed maps (and have the IGM map for your walk) and have a lot of extra time for getting lost, we urge you to follow the walks in the direction they're written. In many cases it would be very difficult to do the walks in reverse (because footpaths and turnoffs noticeable going in one direction are not necessarily easy to spot going in the other direction), and attempting to do so could be an exercise in frustration.

Abbreviations

ATW: at time of writing (i.e., be aware that things may have changed since then)

CAI: Club Alpino Italiano

GEA: Graude Escursione Appenninica

IGM: Istituto Geografico Militare; used in the text to denote maps of 1:25,000 scale.

km: kilometer

m: meter(s)

UPDATING AND
THE WEB SITE

We have done our best to make this guide as accurate as possible, but it is in the nature of the places described in a book like this to be in a constant state of flux. Dirt tracks become paved roads, meadows find gainful employment as vineyards, CAI marks a new route, restaurants slide downhill or go out of business.

During the course of the past eight years many people have written to us about things that have changed, or to ask before they go whether we've had any updates to the walks they're hoping to do. In the latter case, we've passed on whatever information we've received from other readers. It occurred to us—and to some readers—that this transmission of information might be done more effectively by setting up a Web site. We hope it will prove a helpful (if rudimentary) companion to the book. We still welcome letters as well, and will post information received in them on the site.

While updates on the walk directions are the most important pieces of information, we would also greatly appreciate any reports on our restaurant or lodging recommendations, discoveries of your own, or just anecdotes about your experiences. . . .

www.walkingandeating.com

THE WALKS

TUSCANY

CHIANTI

This is the heart of Tuscany, bounded north and south by Florence and Siena; east and west by the rivers Staggia and Elsa. With its dense concentration of vineyards, olive groves, old farmhouses, kitchen gardens, orchards, hilltop cypresses, terraced slopes and wooded valleys, it remains the definitive embodiment of the idea of the "Tuscan landscape."

Partly because of its popularity with wealthy ex-patriots (especially British ones), recent travel books have tended to take a somewhat catty tone in describing the region, dwelling on its gentrification, its adoption as the honorary British county of "Chiantishire," rather than its spectacular beauty: a peculiarly harmonious blend of the natural and the man-made that Fernand Braudel justifiably described as "the most moving countryside that exists."

Recent developments have certainly had an impact, but the fact is this has never been a static landscape; indeed its charm lies precisely in its continuous adaption to and absorption of human history. Every age has left its mark. Castles and fortified hamlets survive from the medieval period when much of the area was essentially a theater of war between Florence and Siena. With the discovery of the Americas a profusion of new crops (tomatoes, green beans, peppers, corn, numerous fruits and squashes) made their way across the Atlantic, radically altering European agricultural practices. In a warm, fertile, but hilly region such as Chianti, with its scrupulous cultivation of every nook and cranny of land with whatever crop its microclimate best suits, this is still reflected in a pleasantly rich irregularity in the textures of the landscape. In the eighteenth century, the *mezzadrile* or sharecropping system was consolidated, whereby the *contadini* (peasants) were given some rights over the land they cultivated, in return for a fixed share of the fruits of their labor. One of the conditions for leasing a farm was that the *contadini* family would build a new terrace every year. Matthew Spender describes the process in his fascinating account of Tuscan life, *Within Tuscany*:

> "The terraces would be made parallel to the horizon, following the contours of the hills, starting at the bottom of a hillside, removing the forest and scrub oaks and pulling the earth down to the side of the new wall, which was made from the stones found right there in the ground. Vertical gullies at regular intervals ensured that the run-off would not cause erosion of the precious earth. It could take a decade to rebuild a hillside from the bottom to the top."

A great many of these dry stone terraces still stand today, adding to the overall hand-hewn, sculptural quality of the landscape.

It was in the mid-nineteenth century, with the pioneering viticultural work of Baron Bettino Ricasoli (who had succeeded Cavour as leader of a newly united Italy), that Chianti acquired its modern identity as a wine region. At the family castle of Brolio, Ricasoli developed the process of double fermentation—the second time with dried grapes—known as *governo* and still used today. The baron also established the proportions of Sangiovese, Canaiolo Nero, and Malvasia grapes that came to be adopted (with minor variations) by the whole Chianti region. Naturally enough the immense popularity of these wines persuaded landowners to turn increasing amounts of their property into vineyards. This certainly hasn't helped protect the region from the general drift toward monoculture afflicting all farming regions today, but it's worth remembering that of the 70,000 hectares of Chianti Classico territory, only 6,500 are dedicated to the exclusive cultivation of vines.

The sharecropping system survived until the 1960s, when it was dismantled by a series of new statutes, socialist in intent if not altogether in their effect. The *contadini,* whose labor had supplied the landlords' *fattorie* (farms) with produce to sell as well as feeding their own families, became salaried agricultural workers. Wages couldn't compete with those of factories in the nearby towns, and the result was a rapid, large-scale exodus from the countryside. On almost all of the walks in this book you'll see the results of this, in the form of abandoned farmhouses—picturesque, forlorn; some of them still more or less intact, with the ground floor where the animals were kept (a kind of live heating system for the rest of the house) still bedded with straw from their last occupants; others in ruins, overrun with the blackberry brambles that mark the first stage in the forest's repossession of its original domain.

Gentrification more often than not has simply meant converting these otherwise doomed buildings into private homes: obviously a less appealing option than having them continue as working farms, but better than complete annihilation. More to the point, an emerging generation of younger wine growers has already begun reviving traditional methods of organic cultivation and low-tech production, with encouraging results. Depending on their success it may be that the industrial-scale agriculture of big landowning consortiums will one day become a thing of the past.

"It is queer that a country so perfectly cultivated as Tuscany, where half the produce of five acres of land will have to support ten human mouths, still has so much room for the wildflowers. . . ." D. H. Lawrence's observation from the 1920s still holds true for much of Chianti today. For all the indelicacy of mechanized farming, the quantity and variety of wildflowers blooming along the margins and ditches, among the crops themselves, in woods and orchards, down the verges of roads and old mule-tracks, is fantastic, and forms one of the many great delights of walking in this area. The iris, once the symbol of Florentine freedom, no longer grows wild, but there are poppies, asphodels, cyclamens, orchids, campanulae, wild herbs and dog-roses in abundance. Giant thistles—more artichoke than thistle—open up great purple brushes in summer, and the prolific yellow *ginestre* (broom) flowers brilliantly all over the land-scape from May to August, filling the air with a pleasant soapy fragrance. The naturalist Gary Paul Nabhan lists fila-ree, gypsywort, comfrey, timothy, chicory, butter-and-eggs, cheeseweed, hawkbit, foxtail, sow thistle, lambs' quarters, hogweed, mustards, false basils, borages and sages, among the commoner roadside weeds and flowering herbs. On almost any of these walks you're likely to find your socks covered with a mass of burrs, seeds and pollen from these tenacious plants.

Mixed oaks, hornbeam and dwarf maples (survivors of the old *vita marittita* system, in which they were used to prop up the vines) make up most of the woods and cop-pices. Higher up on the northern slopes grow chestnut groves and white firs (brought into the region by the Val-lombrosan monks when they established their abbey at Badia Coltibuono in the twelfth century). A more mediter-ranean mixture—cypress, juniper, arbutus—prevails on the southern slopes.

As for the birds and beasts, watch for the splendidly crested hoopoe, fairly common around here, as are the *istrice* (porcupine) and the *cinghiale* (wild boar). The porcupine is mainly nocturnal, so you're unlikely to see the creature it-self, but it has a habit of shedding its needle-sharp black and white spines along woodland paths, providing one of the more elegant souvenirs of these walks. Boars too, while numerous, are elusive, though you may well spot their hoof prints, or the mud-slides they revel in, or if you're lucky the occasional dropped tusk. The indigenous Tuscan variety has been all but ousted by a larger, more fertile breed imported from Hungary after World War II. Given that it enjoys nothing better than uprooting a vineyard, its ubiquitousness tends to be appreciated more by restaurateurs than local farmers.

The Walks

These are some of the most enjoyable and easily managed of the walks in this book. Almost all of them combine stunning landscape with historical, cultural, oenological and gastronomical points of interest. Most of them are rugged without being excessively strenuous, and all of them score high in terms of *ambiente:* the general feel and atmosphere.

While you can effectively make a single-day ring walk from any of the walks by using the bus to return to your starting point, there are also six actual rings, one of which uses part of the Chianti Excursion. All but two are completely accessible by public transport, and even the two exceptions (Badia a Passignano and San Michele/Volpaia) can be reached by a short taxi ride. Most of the itineraries have easy bus connections back to Siena and/or Florence.

Single-day walks are good if you're based in Florence or Siena and want to spend just a day (or two) in the countryside as a change of pace. They're also great if you want to base yourself in one place—a house, or one of the wonderful *agriturismi* in the area—and take day walks from your base.

There are also several possibilities for making two-day rings, or walks of three, four, five or more days. The three-day Chianti Excursion takes in some of the most interesting country in Chianti, including the wine towns of Greve and Radda, the park of San Michele (the highest point in Chianti), the ancient castle of Volpaia, and the lovely little hamlets of Badia Montemuro and San Sano. You can follow this itinerary as it's laid out, or tailor it in any number of ways (see the Chianti Excursion for more details), an unsurpassable way of seeing the region if you have the time.

Food

There's no Chianti cuisine as such, or at least none as distinct as the wine. Simple, generally well-prepared Tuscan food with Florentine and (such as they are) Sienese accents is the basic fare. Its roots are in peasant cooking—*cucina povera*—where leftovers are assiduously recycled. Bread in particular is never allowed to go to waste: reheated, garlicked and flavored with oil, it becomes the basis for *bruschetta* or *fettunte,* or *crostini*—toasted slices spread variously with chopped tomatoes, white beans, a paste of chicken livers and spleen, anchovies and capers, and so on. Soaked in water, squeezed out and crumbled, it is mixed with tomato, onion, basil and cucumber, to form the delicious summer salad called *panzanella*. Simmered with tomatoes and olive oil it becomes the substantial soup known as *pappa al pomodoro,* and cooked up with leftover vegetables (generally cabbage, beans, potatoes and carrots) it provides the comforting, porridge-like texture for the famous *ribollita*.

In country restaurants, almost always congenial places to spend an evening, the "kitchen" often consists of little more than a large wood-burning grill where veal chops and steaks, or pork studded with garlic and rosemary sizzle over the embers. Considering the superb produce available in the markets, vegetable side dishes can be disappointingly meager in range and quality. The white cannellini beans are an exception: often available, generally cooked in an earthenware terrine with oil, salt and pepper; almost always delicious.

There are a number of flossy restaurants catering to rich tourists. On the whole these are places to avoid: Tuscan food as a rule is best when it's at its most straightforward. It doesn't respond well to the complicating and fussy touches by which these establishments justify their inflated prices.

The region abounds in *fattorie,* the old estate houses, where you can taste and buy wine as well as olive oil, honey and other local products.

1 ■ CHIANTI EXCURSION

This series of walks, any single one of which is highly recommended, is particularly versatile, especially if you incorporate the Lamole Ring Walk into the mix. Options abound for two-day rings or for walks extending to as many days as you care to spend in the area.

To begin with, you could follow the Chianti Excursion just as presented, or you could begin from Lamole rather than Greve. Lamole is closer to San Michele than Greve is, and has an exceptional restaurant. It is a tiny hamlet rather than a full-fledged town such as Greve is, another consideration to take into account. You might decide to have lunch at Lamole, then take a leisurely stroll later in the afternoon to San Michele for dinner and overnight, carrying on to Radda the next day. Alternatively you might decide to stay overnight in Lamole; the pool at Le Volpaie (if you're staying there) makes a nice place to spend an afternoon, especially with the prospect of a sunset dinner on the terrace of Ristoro di Lamole ahead of you. The next day you could walk from Lamole, stopping for lunch at San Michele, Badia Montemuro, or Volpaia, and from there carry on into Radda. Or *not;* between Volpaia and Radda lies the attraction of Il Terreno, an agriturismo where (whether you are staying overnight or not) you could enjoy an altogether different dining experience, seated at a large table (outdoors in good weather) with the

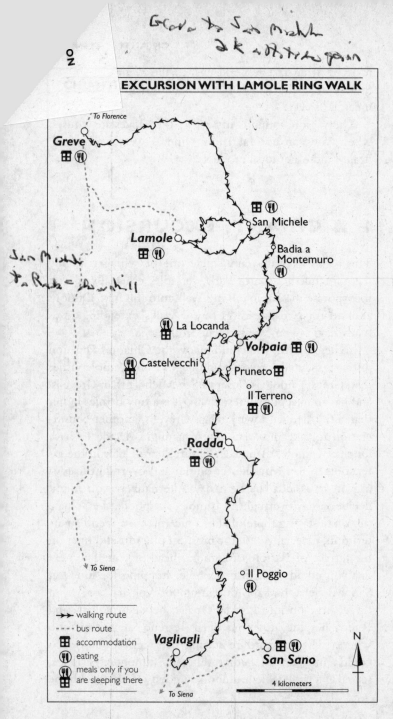

EXCURSION WITH LAMOLE RING WALK

Greve to San Michele
2 k with little gain

San Michele
to Radda = downhill

To Florence

Greve

Lamole

San Michele

Badia a
Montemuro

La Locanda

Volpaia

Castelvecchi

Pruneto

Il Terreno

Radda

To Siena

Il Poggio

→→ walking route
---- bus route
accommodation
eating
meals only if you
are sleeping there

Vagliagli

San Sano

To Siena

4 kilometers

N

other guests, eating a great home-cooked meal accompanied by plenty of wine from their estate.

Or you might start from Greve and add a day by dropping down to Lamole from San Michele.

Once you get to Radda, you could continue on to San Sano or Vagliagli, or you could opt to head back to San Michele (or Lamole, or Greve) by taking the Radda Ring Walk to Volpaia, and then the Volpaia to San Michele portion of the San Michele and Volpaia Ring Walk.

Two-day ring options might include Lamole to Volpaia, or Radda to San Michele (which would also make a nice three-day ring), or Greve–San Michele–Lamole, with a bus back to Greve after lunch in Lamole. Or you could walk from Greve to Radda and bus back to Florence or Siena from there.

There are many pleasing permutations of the excursion, and by taking a look at the diagram (for bus routes and approximate walking times) you can map out any version of the itinerary that appeals. Check the Logistics section of each stage of the walk for dining and lodging options, and be sure to book ahead, as these options are very limited in some locations.

GREVE (OR LAMOLE) TO PARCO SAN MICHELE

TWO NOTES: While we don't give directions for doing the walk in reverse, it is quite easy to do so.

As mentioned in the chapter introduction, you may prefer to use Lamole as the starting point for the excursion, in which case please refer to Lamole Ring Walk, p. 99, and use the Lamole–San Michele portion.

This is a steady climb connecting Chianti's unofficial capital, Greve (home of an annual wine festival), with the old chapel and converted villa of San Michele in the wooded ridge of the highest part of the Chianti hills. The itinerary follows a little-used dirt road all the way, so it's difficult to get lost. As you climb from the cultivated valley, past the villas and *fattorie,* the views over East Chianti's vineyards and olive groves widen impressively. High on the ridge you'll see the cross marking Mt. Domini, from which you can see spectacular views over the Chianti and Valdarno regions.

Greve is a pleasant little market town, famous for its funnel-shaped, arcaded Piazza Mercatale, with a statue of the sixteenth-century explorer Verrazano in its center. The old stone buildings of San Michele are now a restaurant and hotel with rooms varying from very cheap to moderate. It's a friendly, clean, somewhat ramshackle place, popular with hikers as well as local wine growers, who occasionally organize sumptuous (and surprisingly inexpensive) wine-tasting banquets. A wonderfully peaceful place to spend a night or two.

Food

GREVE

There seem to be more restaurants than diners in Greve, especially in the main piazza, where several look in danger of folding for want of customers. The best place to eat is a short walk from here, at La Cantina, a warm, cheerful, extremely popular pizzeria/trattoria. The excellent pizzas are a far cry from the cheese-slathered oil-sponges you bite into in the US. They are thin-crusted to the point of austerity, their toppings—rippling slices of prosciutto, or entire salads—mostly put on *after* cooking, though perhaps the best is the *boscaiola*, whose sauce of mushrooms, tomatoes and truffle oil comes steaming from the oven. There are also some wild-sounding pastas, including one with quail and prune sauce. Service can be slow, and it's a good idea to make a reservation.

La Torre delle Civette is another friendly eatery, serving pizza, focaccia and other basics. It's very inexpensive (an excellent half bottle of Lamole di Lamole Chianti Classico for 6 euros), and despite some dishes being served with sachets of ketchup and mayo, the food is good.

For something a little different, you might try the Enoteca Fuoripiazza, a wine bar with an adventurous snack menu that includes a crab-stock-infused gnocchi with carrots, delicious crepes with ham and taleggio, and a souffle with pine nuts, pecorino and spinach. The portions are small, so order several dishes if you want a big feed.

On Saturdays the square becomes a busy market with stalls selling *porchetta* as well as some of the best cheeses and salamis of the region.

PARCO SAN MICHELE

Despite the ugly cell phone tower (which seems to have doubled in size since we were last here), this restaurant/hotel/hostel/parco in the high hills of Chianti remains a lovely spot to relax for an hour or two over a good meal. Food, service and prices are all thoroughly agreeable. The new menu includes a very hearty mixed *crostini* of tomato and liberally spread chicken liver pate; good ravioli with butter and sage (interestingly, sprinkled with cinnamon); an indifferent *papardelle* with *ragu;* creamy gnocchi with fresh tomato and mascarpone; excellent sliced beef with arugula and balsamic vinegar; and good vegetables, particularly the fresh and plentiful spinach and garlic. The *tiramisu,* which in our last edition we claimed was one of the best in Tuscany, wasn't available when we went this time. No doubt if it reappears it will be well worth ordering. The attractive gardens have a small slide and swing set for kids.

LOGISTICS

CHIANTI EXCURSION: GREVE–PARCO SAN MICHELE, 3–4 hours

ⓘ   Miscellaneous info

🚐   Transport

Ⓜ   Maps, guidebooks and trail info

🍴   Eating

⊞   Accommodation

ⓘ
Viale G. Da Verrazzano, 59
Tel. 055-8546287
fax 055-8544149
e-mail: info@chiantiechianti.it

Hours:
Mon.–Fri. 10:00–13:00 and
14:30–19:00; Sat. 10:00–13:00
and 14:30–19:00
Closing day: Sunday

The tourist office is a wealth of information, and carries the IGM maps (1:25,000) Chianti Progetto Integrato Escursionismo. If they are out of these, they also usually stock other 1:25,000 scale maps. (Also available at the newsstand-type shops in Piazza Matteotti.) Their agency, Chianti Slow Travel, books Wine Educationals in Chianti and professional cooking classes either in famous restaurants of the region or in farmhouses.
Tel. 055-8546299
fax 055-8544240
e-mail: info@chiantiechianti.it

🚐
SITA
Tel. 055-47821 (or toll-free from inside Italy: 800-373760)
www.sita-on-line.it
To/from Florence:
Route 345 (Firenze–Greve–Radda–Castellina–Gaiole)
Buses between Florence and Greve are fairly frequent.
Length of journey: About an hour

TAXIS

Sirabella, tel. 055-8546309
cell 347-6949496
Gemini, tel. 055-852025
   Rates between Greve and San Michele should range between 20 and 30 euros.

If you opt to start the walk from Lamole, there are about three buses a day from Greve to Lamole. From Florence there's a 10-minute layover in Greve; from Greve to Lamole is another 20 minutes.

Ⓜ
Maps are widely available in the newsstand-type shops in Piazza Matteotti. Do yourself a favor and get one that has a scale of 1:25,000. Multigraphic puts these out (Carta Turistica e dei Sentieri).
   Also available for free from the tourist office are the Chianti Progetto Integrato Escursionismo maps, also 1:25,000. There

are four of these, covering the various areas of Chianti. You'll need the one called Tavola 2 & 3 to get you as far as Volpaia, and Tavola 4 to get to Radda and beyond.

(🍴)

GREVE

Pizzeria La Cantina
Piazza Trento, 3 (across from the bus stop)
Tel. 055-854097
Price: Inexpensive
Closing day: Friday

Pizzeria La Torre delle Civette
Via L. Cini, 5
Tel. 055-853480
Price: Inexpensive
Closing day: Tuesday

Enoteca Fuoripiazza
Via 1 Maggio, 2 (next to the bus stop)
Tel. 055-8546313
fax 055-853555
Price: Moderate
Closing day: Monday

PICNICS

The Saturday market has good *porchetta*, roast meats and game, among other things. There are also several *salumeria* (delis) in Greve.

SAN MICHELE

Villa San Michele
Parco Naturale di San Michele

Tel. 055-851034
Price: Inexpensive
Closing day: April 1–November 3, open every day; December 23–January 3, open every day; March, open Sat. and Sun. only

🎴

GREVE

Del Chianti
Piazza Matteotti, 86
Tel. 055-853763; fax 055-853764
Price: Double room, with breakfast, 95 euros; single room, with breakfast, 75 euros

Da Verrazzano
Piazza Matteotti, 28
Tel. 055-853189; fax 055-853648
Price: Double room, 89 euros; single room, 77 euros

SAN MICHELE

Villa San Michele
Parco Naturale di San Michele
Tel. 055-851034
Price: Double room with breakfast, 52–68 euros; with extra bed, add 11 euros; apartments for two people, 78 euros (or 516 euros per week); for four people, 103 euros (or 670 euros per week); room in the hostel, with breakfast, 15 euros. Meals can be added at 16 euros for the first one and 10 euros each additional.

This is really a very lovely, relaxed spot. In addition to the front building with the hotel rooms, which are themselves quite simple (one exceptionally nice room in the front—slightly more expensive—has its own terrace with table and chairs, others have access to communal terrace), there is a large building in the back that serves as a hostel. It, too, is perfectly nice, and a great option if you're on a tight budget.

AGRITURISMO

There are several *agriturismi* on the road up to San Michele from Greve, but they are all of the self-catering type, i.e., they're apartments with kitchens, and don't serve meals. We list them below, nonetheless, for those with a car who want to base themselves somewhere. Most have pools. There are plenty of nice *agriturismo* options in the area. Get in touch with the tourist agency (details above) for a list.

Le Cetinelle, toward the top of the Greve–San Michele road, about 5 km out of town, is a particularly friendly place, and serves breakfast (although again, there are kitchens, not dinners).

There is a small vineyard called Belvedere that has two double rooms for rent. It's about a 15-minute walk from town, and could be a nice alternative to the town hotels. They don't serve dinner either, but are close enough to town that you can

walk home after dinner in town. Rooms are 60 euros for two people, and we mention it particularly because they are a *biologico* (organic) vineyard.

Le Cetinelle
Via Canonica, 13
Tel. 055-8544745
**www.greve-in-chianti.com/
cetinelle.htm**
e-mail: lecetinelle@libero.it
Price: Double room, with breakfast, 68 euros

Belvedere
Via Mantegazza, 68
Tel./fax 055-853070
Price: Double room, 60 euros

Il Santo
Via Melazzano, 3
Tel. 055-853733
**www.greve-in-chianti.com/
ilsanto.htm**
Price: Double room, 62 euros

Patrizia Falciani
Via Melazzano, 5
Tel. 055-8544505
www.patriziafalciani.it
Price: Double room, 62–68 euros
A path leads from this farm into town, probably about a 10-minute walk. Reputed to fill up early, so book well ahead.

Terre di Melazzano
Via Melazzano, 10
Tel. 055-85319
info@terredimelazzano.it
Price: Double room, 77 euros

Fattoria Poggiarelli
Via di Petriolo 55-56
Tel. 055-853414
fax 055-289356
www.poggiarelli.it
Price: Double room, 76 euros,
includes breakfast. No minimum
stay. Apartments, which have a
three-night minimum stay,
available from 85 euros (for two
people) up to 110 euros (sleeps
six people).

This *agriturismo* is on the way
up to Lamole, rather than the
way up to San Michele; you
would need a car.

Fattoria di Rignana; Loc. Rignana
If you have a car, a nice place to
stay is the *agriturismo* at Rignana. Located down a country
track (signposted) about 6 km
SW of Greve (and about 3 km
SE of Badia a Passignano), out
the Montefioralle road. Five
apartments; also nice big rooms
furnished with country antiques
in the old farmhouse. Forty
beds total. Pool. Restaurant on
the premises, Cantinetta di
Rignana.
Tel. 055-852065
www.rignana.it

Directions

Leave Greve from the narrow end of the funnel-shaped
main square, Piazza Matteotti. This leads into Piazzetta
Santa Croce and its church, where you turn left. Cross the
main road there, and continue to the end of the road
you're on. At the end of the road, turn right **A**, following
signs for the cemetery and Villa San Michele.

Follow this road as it climbs up to the cemetery **B**,
winding to the right of it.

This itinerary is a fairly steady climb all the way, but the
steepest part is at the beginning. The asphalt ends just after the Melezzano villa (not to be confused with the Terre
di Melezzano). Carry on straight ahead.

About an hour out of Greve you'll reach the turnoff
for Canonica on the left **C**, ATW marked by a small hand-
written sign. This is a tiny old village of seven houses and
an old church (the detour is a little less than ½ km).

Beyond the turnoff, the road passes through the Pian
della Cononica area, a high, fairly level ridge.

Just over 2 km from Canonica, you'll reach Monte Domini, marked by a cross on a hill to the left of the road. For

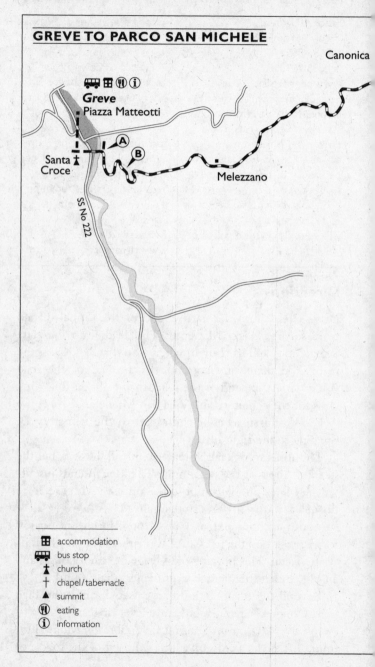

GREVE TO PARCO SAN MICHELE

Canonica

Greve
Piazza Matteotti

Ⓐ

Ⓑ

Santa
Croce

SS No 222

Melezzano

	accommodation
	bus stop
	church
	chapel/tabernacle
	summit
	eating
	information

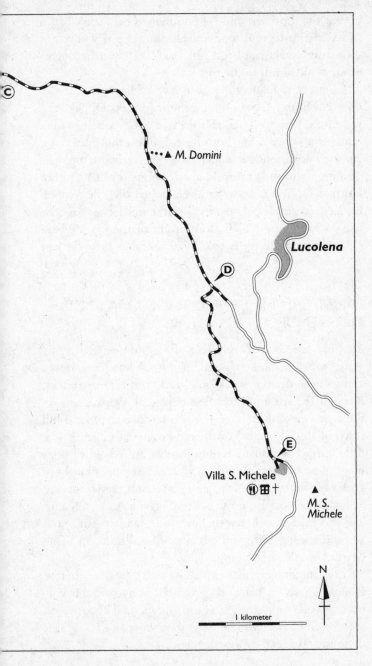

C

▲ M. Domini

Lucolena

D

E

Villa S. Michele

▲ M. S. Michele

N

1 kilometer

one of the most vast and beautiful views over the Chianti and Valdarno regions (and a great photo op if you've got someone to take a picture of), take the short detour to reach it and climb to the top.

Continue to follow the road as it winds its way to the top. One km from Monte Domini the road forks **D**. Take the right fork, very well signed, for Parco San Michele, which is about another 2 km from here. Stay on the main road, ignoring deviations, including a large gravel fork to the right (leading up to the unfortunate cell phone towers) another km past **D**. You'll know you've reached the villa (which has a charming chapel next to it) by the small stone pagoda-like gateway set a bit off to the right of the road (where CAI 00 and 28 diverge **E**) as CAI 00 continues on to the left.

PARCO SAN MICHELE TO RADDA, VIA BADIA MONTEMURO AND VOLPAIA

This is a long but exceptionally pretty and generally easy walk from the highest point in the Chianti hills, down along meandering woodland paths and farm tracks, through the stunning fortified village of Volpaia and on through vineyards to a steep but brief ascent into the hill town of Radda, capital of the old League of Chianti. The little village of Badia Montemuro has an old abbey built by the Camaldolesi monks (to visit, see Signora Finaghi in Badia a Montemuro). Volpaia, with its cool, stone-covered alleys, is one of the most interesting villages in Chianti, and the landscape between here and Radda, with views across the valley to the little Romanesque church of Santa Maria Novella, is stunning.

You might consider breaking the journey before Radda. There are places to overnight in and around Volpaia, or you could stop off at the *agriturismo* Il Terreno, either for dinner (in which case you might want to taxi from there into Radda), or for overnight.

Food

BADIA MONTEMURO
L'OSTERIA — Not open anymore

This small eatery, with its erratically synchronized service, Breughelesque clientele, and ramshackle room half open to the fields below and the abbey above, may not be everyone's idea of elegant dining, but we liked it even more this time around than last time, when we commended it for being unspoiled by tourism and quietly dedicated to excellent cooking. It has grown a little larger and considerably broadened its menu, but it remains the living definition of an old-fashioned rustic restaurant. Faddists of the lard cult currently popular in New York will enjoy the truly amazing *bruschetta del contadino,* made of pork fat, anchovy and onion. There's a cheese sampler menu, featuring cheeses in oil and honey, and a wonderful grilled whole tomino cheese on toast. The robust pasta dishes include a farfalle with zucchini and cream, and an excellent penne with gorgonzola, mascarpone and nuts. They do a very good grilled vegetable dish that includes radicchio—one of the least used but best vegetable candidates for the grill. Meat dishes are simple but good, substantial and inexpensive: 7.50 euros gets you three succulent grilled lamb cutlets. Be sure to ask for daily specials (always worth doing, especially in smaller restaurants). You might also want to ask them to go easy on the salt, as they tend to overdo it a bit. For dessert there's a good *tiramisu* and *panna cotta*. The local, unmarked bottles of wine and *vin santo* are cheap and very drinkable. All in all, if you can time it right, this is the place to eat lunch—then have your coffee in Volpaia.

There's a playground outside, though our kids mainly amused themselves feeding pasta to the two kittens begging in the doorway. You can also buy picnic food from the small store attached to the restaurant.

VOLPAIA

The three restaurants in the gorgeous little piazza here cover the full range. The Castello di Volpaia is an upscale operation with a fancy restaurant featuring one of those multilingual, expensive menus that tend to fill us with gloom—so much so that in this case we couldn't bring ourselves to eat there. But if you're in the mood to lay out a lot of bucks for some stuffed guinea fowl breast in *vin santo* sauce, it's certainly an attractive place to sit.

We chose to enjoy the amazing arch of white roses over its doorway from the restaurant opposite, La Bottega. The food here is uneven (it seems to have picked up some affectations from its proximity to the Castello) but it's reasonably priced and the service is friendly. Avoid the very silly *fantasia di crostini* unless you like mayonnaise on toast. A pasta with asparagus, gorgonzola and nuts that floated past us looked unappetizingly gray (but perhaps it tasted better than it looked). On the other hand, they make a good pecorino and radicchio salad, a simple and tasty ravioli with butter and sage, a very hearty wild boar stew with olives and spinach, and for dessert a delicious *panna cotta* with wild berries.

In the end, however, we liked the little Bar Ucci best

of all. This unpretentious, modestly priced establishment serves excellent salads, appetizers and pasta dishes. We had wonderful mixed *bruschetta* with salsa verde as well as both raw and cooked tomato sauces. There was a delicious *farro* (spelt) salad, an equally good, oniony *panzanella,* and some exquisitely minty grilled eggplant. The perfect place for a simple lunch on a hot day.

For more on the dining option at the *agriturismo* Il Terreno, see the Web link listed in their entry in the Eating section below.

RADDA

For Radda food review, see the Radda Ring Walk, p. 90.

LOGISTICS

CHIANTI EXCURSION: PARCO SAN MICHELE–RADDA, VIA BADIA MONTEMURO AND VOLPAIA:

San Michele–Badia Montemuro, about 45 minutes;
Badia Montemuro–Volpaia, about 2 hours;
Volpaia–Radda: about 2½ hours

ⓘ   Miscellaneous info

🚌   Transport

Ⓜ   Maps, guidebooks and trail info

🍴   Eating

🏨   Accommodation

ⓘ
RADDA

Piazza Castello, 6
Tel. 0577-738494
e-mail: proradda@chiantinet.it

🚌

NOTE: There are no buses to San Michele. You have to walk up from Greve or Lamole, as per the preceding itinerary. Alternatives are trying to hitch up from Greve (there are very few cars, but those that do go by are quite likely to stop) or getting a taxi. Neither is Volpaia served by buses. Again, hitching and taxis are good alternatives should the desire arise.

SITA
Tel. 055-47821 (or toll-free from inside Italy: 800-373760)
www.sita-on-line.it
Florence
Route 345
ATW three per day from Radda to Florence (none on Sun.):
7:10, 8:45 (neither Sat. nor Sun.), 18:15.

CHIANTI

Length of journey: 1½ hours
Buses stop in Greve on the way
to Florence.

TRA-IN

Tel. 0577-204111 or 204245 or 6
www.trainspa.it
Siena: Note that intercity buses
usually leave from and return to
the Siena railway station, just
outside town. The inner-city buses
make regular trips between town
and the railway station.

Route 125
Five or six buses per day (except
Sun.) in each direction, beginning
around 7:00, ending around
18:00 or so (ATW there's a bus
from Siena at 19:20.)
Length of journey: About an hour

TAXIS

Signore Colella: 335-5647475
Signore Ansalone: 335-5237021.
 His is actually a limosine
service for airport transfers, day
tours around Chianti, etc. But he
might take you if he's available.
 You can also ask at the tourist
office.

Ⓜ
See Logistics section of Greve–
Parco San Michele portion. Also,
the tourist office in Radda has
the Chianti Progetto Integrato
Turismo maps, and other
1:25,000 maps. Radda's news-
stand/stationery stores also
usually carry 1:25,000 maps.

Ⓧ
BADIA MONTEMURO

L'Osteria
Loc. Badia Montemuro
Tel. 0577-738036
Price: Inexpensive
Closing day: Tuesday

VOLPAIA

Bar Ucci
Piazza della Torre (Volpaia's main
piazza)
Tel. 0577-738042
Price: Inexpensive
Closing day: Monday.
Open for lunch, and usually for
dinner until at least 20:00 or
20:30. It's best to call ahead to
be sure of dinner. Also, if you
have a group, they'll stay open,
but in that case you need to
reserve ahead of time.

La Bottega
Piazza della Torre, 2
Tel. 0577-738001
e-mail: labottega@chiantinet.it
Price: Moderate
Closing day: Tuesday
Open for lunch and dinner.

BETWEEN VOLPAIA
AND RADDA

Il Terreno
See IGM map.
Tel. 0577-738312
fax 0577-738400
www.podereterreno.it
Price: 35 euros per person,
includes their wine

Closing day: None

This is an *agriturismo,* at which you can have dinner (even if you're not staying there) if you book ahead—certainly no later than early morning of the day you wish to eat there. An article written in 1998 by the *San Francisco Chronicle*'s travel editor, John Flinn, about the Chianti Excursion describes Il Terreno. If you're interested, here's the Web address: **http://www. sfgate.com/cgi-bin/ article.cgi?file=/examiner/ archive/1998/08/23/ TRAVEL15290.dtl**

RADDA

See Radda Ring Walk for Radda restaurants, p. 90.

⊞
VOLPAIA

Podere Vergelli
Just on the edge of town
Tel. 0577-738382
Price: There are two apartments, both have kitchens, and you can eat in her small garden. (You can also eat in Volpaia, a few steps away.) We saw the apartment for two persons, and it was nice.

Apartment for two persons, 65 euros.

Apartment for four persons, 100 euros.

Loriana and Lina Carusi (*affitta-camere*)
Volpaia. To find her: Facing the

enoteca di Castello di Volpaia, turn right and walk about 20 m, then make another right. Watch (in less than 100 m) for a door with lots of flowers and a sign, *Casa Selvolini.* If you have any problems, you can ask someone at the *enoteca* or at one of the restaurants.
Tel. 0577-738626
fax 0577-738329
Price: Apartment for two persons, with kitchen and bath, 60 euros per night. Apartment for four persons, with kitchen and two baths, 100 euros.

BETWEEN VOLPAIA AND RADDA

Il Terreno (*agriturismo*)
See IGM map.
Tel. 0577-738312
fax 0577-738400
www.podereterreno.it
Price: 90 euros per person per day, includes dinner

Il Terreno is transitioning to organic, and say they'll be completely organic by the time this book is published. They produce several wines. Dinner there is an experience. See their listing in the Eating section above for more information.

Il Pruneto
See map.
Tel. 0577-738013
e-mail: pruneto@chiantinet.it
Price: Studio apartment for 70 euros per night (or 400 per

week) sleeps a maximum of two or three people. A larger apartment, two bedrooms, two baths, kitchen, is 150 euros per night (1000 per week). During May and June they will probably only book weeklong rentals, but if they're empty they'll accept an overnight.

Farmhouse in a beautiful location. They don't serve dinner, but you can walk to Il Terreno for dinner, about a 15-minute walk (they'll give you a map).

Castelvecchi
See IGM map.

Tel. 0577-738050
fax 0577-738608
www.castelvecchi.com
Price: From 83 euros per night for a double room with breakfast, and upward from there

This is a big operation in beautiful old buildings, with a restaurant for guests, cooking classes, horseback riding, a pool or two, tennis courts, and all manner of accommodation arrangements.

RADDA

See Radda Ring Walk for Radda accommodations.

Directions

Walk out the driveway of Villa San Michele, and on reaching the pagoda–style gate **A** on your left, turn right onto CAI 00 (ATW there's a wooden sign for "Lamole").

In a minute or two you'll reach a fork, with CAI signs on a pole in the middle for "Panzano 32" and "Volpaia 52" as well as "00." Take 52/32 to the right. Follow the path along here for another 5 minutes, until you meet an intersection of several paths **B**. The path that bends sharply back to your left and uphill is also CAI 00; you *don't* want that, you want the next one to the left (at about 90°). ATW there's a little wooden shelter you'll pass on your right.

Keep following this path, ignoring deviations.

When you meet the (quiet) asphalt road **C** in another 25 minutes or so, turn right.

In another 5 minutes you'll come to a turnoff on the right for Badia Montemuro; take this into the hamlet. To visit the abbey (if you haven't happened to arrive during a Mass) you can ask in the *osteria*.

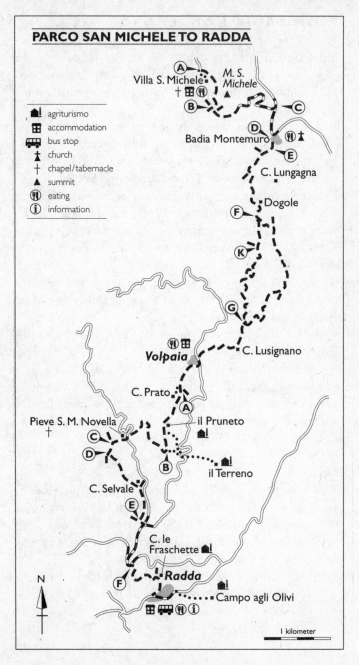

PARCO SAN MICHELE TO RADDA

Villa S. Michele — M. S. Michele — Badia Montemuro — C. Lungagna — Dogole — C. Lusignano — Volpaia — C. Prato — Pieve S. M. Novella — il Pruneto — il Terreno — C. Selvale — C. le Fraschette — Radda — Campo agli Olivi

Legend:
- 🏠 agriturismo
- ⊞ accommodation
- 🚌 bus stop
- ⛪ church
- † chapel/tabernacle
- ▲ summit
- 🍴 eating
- ⓘ information

N

1 kilometer

FROM BADIA MONTEMURO

Passing the *osteria* **D** on the right, follow the road down-hill and make the first right, then immediately turn right again, wrapping back underneath the *osteria*. Passing two old buildings on the left, the asphalt gives way to a small gravel road.

A minute later watch on the right for two tracks: a gravel driveway leading up to an iron gate, and immediately beyond it a slightly smaller dirt track. Take the dirt track **E**. (ATW signed "51/55 Dogole and Volpaia.")

Keep to the main path, ignoring deviations including a lesser track off to the right about ten minutes past **E**. Just past this lesser track, at a more serious fork, bear down-hill left (ATW a CAI red and white paint blaze on a boul-der here).

This is a shady woodland path, very pretty and tranquil; could be muddy at wet times of the year, as there are some small stream-crossings.

About 30–40 minutes out of Badia Montemuro you'll pass the large abandoned farmstead of Dogole on your left. A few minutes later you'll come to a serious fork **F**.

Here you have the option of making a loop. If you're going only one way, we recommend option A as it's shorter and avoids a somewhat arduous climb at the end. Use op-tion B if you want to do a ring.

Option A

Bear right at this fork **F**, then follow this pleasant, shaded, peaceful woodland path for about 2 km, always staying to the main path. (Note that you'll pass a fork **K** noted on the map, but this fork is relevant only when you're traveling *toward* Badia Montemuro.)

About 30–40 minutes past **F** the path comes out at a junction **G** with a path coming uphill from the left. Con-tinue forward, bearing to the right.

Option B

Bear left downhill at this fork **F**. About 5 minutes later the path crosses a stream and comes out of the woods at a junction. Ignore the uphill left track, and continue straight on, downhill.

About 20 minutes later, coming to another fork (both prongs of which are leading almost straight ahead), take the right downhill, rather than the left uphill. (ATW there are metal trail signs here.)

In 20–30 minutes, a rather arduous climb leads to a left bend in the road, where you are joined by another track coming in from the right **G**.

From **G**, follow this dirt road, in 5 minutes or so passing Casa Lusignana on the left, where there's a nice panorama over the Val di Pesa.

Follow the main track (passing a pond and an old chapel on the left after a minute or two) out to a T-junction with a small asphalt road; turn right, following this road into Volpaia.

FROM VOLPAIA

Facing the Ristorante La Bottega, and with your back to the Castello di Volpaia, take the steps leading down to the right of the restaurant. Bear right, passing under an arch (ATW signed to the cemetery).

A dirt road takes you down through a beautiful row of cypresses. At the end of this elegant avenue, you'll pass a large stone tabernacle on the right. Cypresses (a bit scruffier here) again line the track, and you want to stay between them: ignore deviations to the right, including one marked to "Prato" about 100 m past the tabernacle.

In another minute or two you'll reach a T-junction (ATW marked on a boulder to "Cassetto" right, and "Coltassala" left). Turn right here **A**. (The cypresses end.)

Across the valley on a hilltop ahead and to the left sits Radda. In a minute or two, as you approach a house on your left (Cassetto), there's a view across the valley to the right of Santa Maria Novella.

Keep to this main track, passing Cassetto and another house (Pruneto) visible beyond that, also on the left.

Soon after passing one more house on the left, the track begins to descend and enters a small wood. Ignore a small deviation on the left about 3 minutes past that last house. But 50 m later *do* take the right turnoff where the main path bends to the left **B**. ATW signed to "Santa Maria Novella" on a boulder.

(NOTE: If you're going to Il Terreno, this is where you'd turn off, to the left.)

Stay to this path now (ignoring a farm track crossing it in a minute or two, and another smaller deviation to the right about 5 minutes later). This shaded woodland path is easy to follow.

After crossing a stream the path climbs for a few minutes, then comes out at a small asphalt road, across from Santa Maria Novella.

(NOTE: To see Santa Maria Novella, go in the front drive—ATW where the metal chain is—just across the road, take a hairpin right turn, then continue up the driveway to a small house and ask.)

Still standing across from Santa Maria Novella (i.e., ignoring the note about visiting it) where you've come out onto the asphalt, you'll be facing its main entrance. Bypassing this main entrance just across the road, turn left on the asphalt road and walk until you reach a break in the stone wall on the right. There's a gravel drive here that will lead behind Santa Maria Novella. Take this.

The track climbs up through an olive grove and comes to a T-junction at a vineyard **C**. Turn left.

In a minute or two you'll pass a tabernacle on the right **D**. Bear left here.

The path descends, with vineyards on the right, hedge on the left. At the bottom of the vineyard the path turns left through an opening in a fence, then immediately turns right, entering between two more vineyards with wide views left and right.

Bear to the right of the stone wall of Casa Selvale, continuing downhill with the vineyard on your right.

Near the bottom of the vineyard, watch for the path to fork off to the left and enter a small wood, about 150 m below Casa Selvale. Take this fork.

In 5–10 minutes this path ends at a T-junction with another dirt road **E**. Turn left, immediately coming to a small asphalt road. Turn right onto this.

Follow this road for 600 m (about 10 minutes). When you reach the T-junction with the main asphalt road, cross over the road and turn left, over a bridge with brick guardrails. (Ignore a trail up to the right just before the guardrail, CAI 52, which is longer and involves a lot of time on busy roads.)

Standing just at the far end of the guardrail, face the embankment and you'll notice a narrow single track slanting leftward up the embankment **F**. Climb up this to the top of the embankment. Here you'll see two fields in front of you, a terraced one to the left, and a grassy meadow (which could conceivably be a vineyard in the future) with the tower of Radda rising behind it. Bear right into this grassy field (avoiding a negligible track to the right, just before the field) and turn right, skirting the bottom of the field, with the lush vegetation of the streambed to your right.

Cross along this edge of the field, heading for the stand of tall cypresses at the other end.

When you reach the corner of the field there is a very large gap in the vegetation on the right, with a farm track going through (sometimes muddy). Take this track, leaving the field and immediately bending left uphill.

Follow this steeply uphill, bending to the right at which point you'll see the tops of two stone houses above you (with the aforementioned cypresses now a few meters to your right).

Just before the path bends right, into the cypresses and

pines (about 30 m below the house), leave the track and turn left and downhill, toward the vineyard (beyond which you see Radda). In 20 m, reach the vineyard and turn left along the farm track there.

Follow this as it skirts the vineyard and climbs up to a gravel road (with a new house about 100 m to the left). Turn right on the gravel road.

In 50 m, leave this gravel road as it bends right, in favor of the dirt track on the left, again climbing, with vines to your left, and a bit further on, olive groves to your right.

Stay on the main track as it skirts the top of the vineyard and then climbs up to a house, Casa Freschette, ahead of you (ignore a farm track downhill to the left).

At the entrance gate to Freschette, bear right and continue climbing another 300 m, where you'll meet the main road to Radda. Turn left, reaching Radda center in about 200 m.

RADDA TO VAGLIAGLI OR SAN SANO

A beautiful, meandering walk through woods and farmland, and down along a peaceful forgotten valley. The San Sano ending is the prettier: you don't have to walk along a busy road, and the village itself has more charm than Vagliagli. Use the Vagliagli ending if your main concern is frequency of buses (see the Logistics section for details). The Vagliagli ending takes you past the Villa Dievole, to which legend attributes a former diabolical inhabitant, though its new incarnation is as a resort complex with a leaning toward healthy living and la dolce vita. Both routes take you past the Romanesque church of San Giusto and the delightful little castle of San Polo in Rosso, now used by the vineyard of the same name as its business office.

You can also get a bus into Siena from both places, though you should check timetables in advance. ATW, there are three buses a day from San Sano and seven from

Vagliagli. There are also three buses a day from San Sano to Gaiole, about a 15-minute ride.

Food

Without a doubt the best food on this walk is to be had at Il Poggio. Why then, one might ask, did we arrive there for Sunday lunch without a reservation? We hope our trauma over this event has made us more responsible in this edition when it comes to urging you to make reservations (whenever possible), and especially for Sunday lunch (or when you're walking three hours with the express hope of eating at a certain restaurant).

The upshot is that this is the one restaurant in the entire "Chianti" chapter for which we are using our original review. The details may no longer hold true, but the general tenor does:

Il Poggio, near San Polo, is a very good place to eat: imaginative but unpretentious cooking, a lively atmosphere, and gorgeous views from the outside tables. Vegetables are treated with unusual care here. The *zuppa di verdura* (vegetable soup) is fresh and tasty, and you should also sample the spicy marinated eggplant and the pan-cooked onions. The pasta specialty, *al Gianneto,* is a delicious piccante meat sauce with parsley, served over tortellini or spaghetti.

Vagliagli now has a dubious-looking luxury agritourism establishment, Dievole, which is conveniently on your way, and where you can join coach parties for an expensive lunch if the spirit moves you. We would be interested in hearing reports about this place for our Web site. In San Sano, the Trattoria della Rana is as popular, charming, bustling and inexpensive as ever, and both the food and service have improved. The wider range of pastas includes a heavy but tasty *pici* with garlic and parsley, excellent *papardelle* with sauces of rabbit or wild boar, and there are many vegetable dishes: stuffed tomatoes, baked artichokes, and a nice *sformato* (like a puddingy cauliflower cheese). The grilled meats were a little dry, with a slight propane flavor, but if you feel like gorging lion-style on a week's worth of protein, the astounding slabs of *fiorentina* steaks that several people around us were ordering certainly looked very good.

LOGISTICS

CHIANTI EXCURSION: RADDA–VAGLIAGLI OR SAN SANO:

Radda–San Sano, about 4 hours; Radda–Vagliagli, about 4½ hours

---

ⓘ   Miscellaneous info

🚌   Transport

Ⓜ   Maps, guidebooks and trail info

🍴   Eating

ⓘ
RADDA

Piazza Castello, 6
Tel. 0577-738494

SIENA

Il Campo, 56
Tel. 0577-280551
www.terresiena.it
This Web site is extremely good. It lists all the local tourist offices in Siena province. There is also a link to ask them to send you information. One excellent pamphlet they put out (available in English) is "Terre di Siena in bici: Biking Through Siena's Countryside." This 44-page pamphlet makes very exciting reading.

🚌
TRA-IN

Tel. 0577-204111 or 204245 or 6
www.trainspa.it
Siena: Note that intercity buses usually leave from and return to the Siena railway station, just outside town. The inner-city buses make regular trips between town and the railway station. All but one of the buses from Siena to Radda leave from the railway station.

SAN SANO

All the buses from San Sano to Siena (route 127) go to the railway station. ATW there are three buses per day. The 7:58 bus goes directly to Siena (about a 35-minute ride), but for the afternoon buses you must go in the opposite direction, to Lecchi

(4 minutes away) and change in Lecchi for the Siena bus. ATW, San Sano 13:30 bus arrives Lecchi 13:34; change at Lecchi for the 14:06 to Siena, arriving at the railway station at 14:40. The last bus from San Sano is at 14:48; change at Lecchi for the 15:11 to Siena. Bear in mind that you can check the current schedule on-line before you go. There are also three buses a day from San Sano to Gaiole, at 13:30, 14:48 and 19:55 (this last runs Mon.–Fri. only).

VAGLIAGLI

There are seven buses a day from Vagliagli to Siena, and they all stop at the intersection with the road you'll come to from Villa Dievole—map point **N**— so if you can time your walk to bring you to that point around the time of a bus arrival, you won't need to walk along this main road all the way into Vagliagli. (If you miss the bus, you could always hitch on that main road stretch into Vagliagli.) Coming from Dievole, when you meet the main road—map point **N**—cross over and look for the bus stop (*fermata*) sign. (If all else fails, wave the bus down.)

All the buses from Vagliagli go to Piazza Gramsci in Siena, except the early morning one (ATW 7:30, at which time there is also another bus that does go

to Gramsci) which goes to Piazza Domenico. ATW bus times from Vagliagli are 7:30, 9:40, 13:50, 14:25, 16:10 and 19:15. *Length of journey:* 30–40 minutes

Ⓜ

See Logistics section of Greve–Parco San Michele portion. Also, the tourist office in Radda has the Chianti Progetto Integrato Turismo maps, and other 1:25,000 maps. Radda's newsstand/stationery stores also usually carry 1:25,000 maps. In Siena, bookstores carry a good selection of maps and guidebooks.

🍽

Ristorante Il Poggio
Loc. Poggio San Polo
Tel. 0577-746135 or 0577-746176
Price: Moderate
Closing day: Monday

This restaurant is located on the wide dirt road that leads to Castel San Polo in Rosso, and is indicated in the walk directions. We also give alternative directions (see next page) that lead more directly to the restaurant, for those who are going to stop there.

Trattoria Grotta della Rana
San Sano
Tel. 0577-746020
Price: Moderate
Closing day: Wednesday

Il Tavolo dei Maestri di Vigna (at
Villa Dievole)
Dievole
Tel. 0577-321891
www.dievole.it
Price: Expensive
Closing day: Sunday
They also have wine tours
every day except Sunday.

Hotel Residence San Sano
Loc. San Sano 21
Tel. 0577-746130
fax 0577-746156
www.sansanohotel.it
Price: From 115 to 135 euros
per night for two, including
breakfast
Building was renovated from
a thirteenth-century fortress.
Eleven rooms. Restaurant. Pool.
German owner speaks English
and knows a lot about walks
in the area. Three-night minimum, but if room, they will take
a one-night reservation. Dinner
for guests only (except Mon-
days), on request, 25 euros.

Villa Dievole
Dievole
Tel. 0577-322632
www.dievole.it
Price: Prices begin at 125 euros
per night for two, in Casa Olivo,
and include buffet breakfast

ⓘ
**SHORTCUT TO IL
POGGIO RESTAURANT**

Because the restaurant Il Poggio
is a rather long slog down the

gravel road from map point **X**,
here are alternate directions,
from Galenda to Poggio San
Polo (where Il Poggio is located), which accomplishes
this stretch in one third of the
distance of our directions
and obviates the stretch on
the gravel road (until you continue on your way from Il
Poggio). We have not actually
walked this route ourselves; we
found these directions in an
Italian guidebook and have
merely translated them. We
hope that some brave soul will
try this route and be so kind as
to post the results on the Web
site.

FROM GALENDA

Reaching Galenda, which you
cross, passing through a series
of twistings and turnings, you'll
come to a fountain (of drinking
water) on the left. Straight
ahead the path resumes its
grassy character, and is flanked
on the right by a wall with a
hedge of silvery cypresses and
on the left by a fenced olive
grove. The path comes to a
tabernacle and offers a lovely
glance on the hamlet of Poggio
San Polo. From there you enter
a wood of oaks and Mediter-
ranean shrubs, and reaching the
bottom of the valley at a big
crossroads, you follow straight
ahead, crossing a little stream.
Climbing again, you find on the

left an abandoned terraced olive grove, while on the right the countryside is well-tended, cultivated with beautiful terraces.

Reaching a gate, you turn right, descending gently, first between *ginestre* (broom shrubs) and then in an abandoned vineyard. Reaching the bottom of the vineyard, you turn left round a hedge and continue following the evident path that ascends between terraces of olive trees and grapevines on the right and a newly planted vineyard on the left. At the crest, take the little road to the left with a pond and farm walls on the side that brings you to the hamlet of Poggio San Polo (map pt 527 m). (You'd turn right on the main gravel road here to go to San Polo in Rosso, reached in 1.2 km).

Directions

Leaving Radda by the long flight of steps that go down behind the stone wall on the main street by the bus stop (ATW they lead down to the Da Michele Pizzeria/Ristorante), turn right at the bottom of the steps and follow the gravel path sloping downhill. Where it meets an asphalt road, turn sharply to the left.

Reaching the Convento di Santa Maria, turn right, downhill, by the stone wall near the stone well **A**. Bear left past the wall onto a stone road.

Follow this track as it leads downhill between a stone wall (behind the convent) and a very long building lined with evergreens. At the end of the wall and of the building, take the first right-hand path, downhill **B**.

Follow this path downhill to the bottom of the valley where it crosses an old streambed on a small bridge. After crossing the bridge, turn left for a few meters, then immediately right, following the path uphill along the periphery of the field (there's a drop to the next field on the right).

Keep climbing as you bend left under woods. Keep walking along the edge of the field, with the woods immediately to your right, and in 50 m an olive grove to your left.

RADDA TO VAGLIAGLI OR SAN SANO

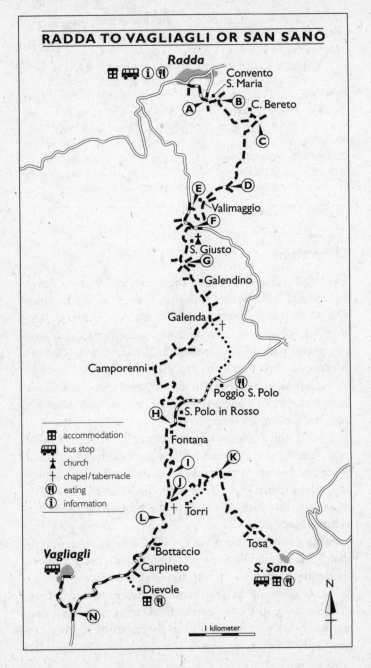

Radda

♦ accommodation ♦ bus stop ♦ information ♦ eating

Convento S. Maria

(A) (B) C. Bereto

(C)

(D)

(E)

Valimaggio

(F)

✝

S. Giusto

(G)

• Galendino

Galenda ✝

Camporenni •

♦ Poggio S. Polo

(H) • S. Polo in Rosso

Fontana

(I) (K)

(J)

Torri ✝

(L)

Tosa

Vagliagli 🚌

• Bottaccio

Carpineto

S. Sano 🚌♦♦

• Dievole

(N)

accommodation
bus stop
church
chapel/tabernacle
eating
information

I kilometer

N

Follow the woods as they bend up to the right in another 100 m or so. Ten meters from where they bend, turn left along the lower side of a hedged terrace. In another 50 m, pass below an old shed and bear up to the right on the steep path that passes to the right of a thick hedge, and has an olive grove on its left. (Going left here would take you to a house, Casa Bereto.)

After 2–3 minutes you'll come out at a wider path opposite a little wayside cross surrounded by four cypress trees. (This is about 15 minutes from the little bridge.) Turn right here **C**.

Stay on this path, ignoring deviations. A very pleasant ridge walk along here, with views of the Chianti hills on both sides. After about 20 minutes, the path merges with another similar-sized path coming from the left **D**. Continue on here, bearing right.

About 150 m later, when the path forks, bear right past the farm of Valimaggio.

In a few minutes the path joins with another, slightly larger gravel road; continue downhill.

This road comes out on a quiet asphalt road. Turn left **E**. Walk down to the fork and bear left, toward San Sano.

Ignoring a track to the right in 70 m (just after the bridge), take the next right-hand turn **F**, signed to "San Giusto in Salcio." The asphalt ends just after the turn, giving way to gravel again.

In 300 m you'll come to a very pretty Romanesque church, San Giusto, with a handsome bell tower and parish buildings still intact. (This is about an hour to an hour and a half from Radda.)

Continue along the road past the church, beginning to climb more steeply. Stay on this road, passing a big wooden cross on the left after 200 m. After another 250 m, a more minor path branches off to the left, uphill: take this path. (If you reach a sign for Le Selve along here, you've gone too far, by about 100 m.) This path leads to a vineyard on the right, and then almost immediately you fork again (this fork is almost a four-way fork, if you count the smaller track all the way up on the left): take the second to right fork **G**, i.e., the one that passes just left of the hedge—and then the wall—of the vineyard on your right (the first right being the perimeter track of the vineyard itself).

After about 200 m you'll reach a T-junction; turn left. In 50 m, below a house up on the left (Galendino—not to be confused with Galenda), take the right fork forward (not the sharp right that doubles back).

In another 70 m, fork right again, downhill. The path continues straight across the bottom of this valley and begins to climb (ignore the turnoff to the left at the bottom of the valley).

At the top of the hill (after 5–10 minutes of climbing) the path passes above a swimming pool on the right and comes out to a T-junction at a large, rambling stone farmhouse, Galenda. (Note that if you want to try the shortcut to the restaurant Il Poggio, you should pick up those directions here, from the Logistics section above.) As you reach the main building, turn right on the dirt road, rather than carrying on through the arch.

Keep to the main path, which passes another pool and another building, climbs up and then turns left (ignore the right fork) along the ridge of a hill with good views on either side (including the little tower of Castel San Polo in Rosso).

Stay on the main ridge path, ignoring deviations on either side. After 10–15 minutes the path begins descending, until it reaches the abandoned farmhouse of Camporenni. Here, before passing the house, turn left; stay on the main track as it winds to the bottom of the valley and crosses a stream, after which it climbs for about 15 minutes, coming out at a wide gravel road, which is the car road from Poggio San Polo.

For Ristorante Il Poggio (if you haven't taken the shortcut), turn left here and follow the road to the end of the little village reached in another 10 minutes' walk from here.

Otherwise, turn right here, coming after about 200 m to the charming Romanesque Castel San Polo in Rosso (about 3 hours from Radda).

Passing the castle, the road forks again in about 200 m; bear right on a dirt track **H**.

In a moment you'll pass a group of houses on the left (Fontana). Continue on the main road as it descends below the houses. In another 2 minutes you'll come to a fork; the left fork leads back up to the houses; take the right fork.

From here a rugged stone track winds down through a nicely wooded valley. There are occasional CAI red and white trail marks, and the path is easy to follow, very pleasant, and often shaded.

After about 15 minutes the path crosses a little stream **I** amid very lush vegetation. If you're going to Vagliagli, skip ahead now to the directions below for Vagliagli Route.

SAN SANO ROUTE

From **I**: If you're doing the San Sano ending, be alert here: In 5–7 minutes you'll come to a little tabernacle partly hidden by the vegetation on the left, with a delightful painted Madonna in it. Retrace your steps a few paces, and you'll see a path going off to the right (to the right now that you've turned around; i.e., it would have been on your left originally) **J**. Take it.

In 8–10 minutes, after some minor twists and turns, the path swings around sharply to the right and then bends left. In another 2–3 minutes a minor spur goes off to the right: ignore this (it leads to the abandoned house Torri in about 200 m).

Continue on around to the left, and in a minute or two you'll come to a T-junction with another path. Go right **K**.

Continue following the main path until you reach a T-junction with a gravel road. Go left, passing between the chapel and house of the farmstead Tosa.

After a couple of minutes the gravel gives way to asphalt, soon winding into San Sano. Bear right as you enter the village, and you'll find a store and restaurant (Grotto delle Rana) on the right in 30 m.

VAGLIAGLI ROUTE

From **I**: About 10 minutes after crossing the little stream **I**, the path emerges from the woods, bends right and re-enters woods on a narrow, single track, where it crosses over the stream again **L**.

After another 15 minutes or so of climbing along this stony path, you'll come out of the woods at a T-junction with a bigger track at an old stone building, Bottaccio. Turn right, passing Bottaccio on your left. In another 5 minutes, stay on the main path past Carpineta. Less than a minute later, bear right at another junction.

In 200 m you'll pass Dievole on your left, now a huge vacation/health resort.

Continue on along the main road until it comes out on the main asphalt road **N**, another kilometer.

Go right on the main asphalt road and on into Vagliagli, where you can get a bus to Siena. Alternatively, you can get the bus at this intersection with the main asphalt road.

2 ■ SAN MICHELE AND VOLPAIA RING WALK, via Badia Montemuro

In response to readers' requests for more ring walks, we offer this circuit linking three small places of large charm—the high-altitude (for Chianti) restaurant/hostel of San Michele, the pretty village of Badia Montemuro (which has one of our favorite restaurants) and Volpaia, which is by any estimate one of the loveliest spots in Tuscany.

Notwithstanding one short stretch on a little-used tarmac road, this walk is extremely pleasant, passing through quiet farmland and deep woods, and maintaining for most of its length that feeling of miraculous remoteness that walkers (or at any rate the authors of this book) value so highly.

On the Volpaia to San Michele section, there's an alternate, via Casa Lungagna, which we have included only as an alternate route because it passes at such a close distance an old house we anticipate will be "done up" in the future. Try it if you like.

Neither San Michele nor Volpaia are served by buses, so if you don't have a car we'd recommend you do this as a two-day walk between Greve and Radda (which are both well served by buses), beginning at either of those locations. If you just want to do this as a one-day walk, you can try hitching from Greve or Radda to San Michele or Volpaia respectively, or take a taxi to the starting point.

Food

See the Food sections of the Chianti Excursion, p. 53 (Parco San Michele), p. 59 (Badia Montemuro) and p. 62 (Volpaia).

LOGISTICS

SAN MICHELE AND VOLPAIA RING WALK, VIA BADIA MONTEMURO,
4–5 hours

(i) Miscellaneous info

🚌 Transport

(M) Maps, guidebooks and trail info

(🍴) Eating

▦ Accommodation

(i)
GREVE

Viale G. Da Verrazzano, 59
Tel. 055-8546287
fax 055-8544149
e-mail: info@chiantiechianti.it

RADDA

Piazza Castello, 6
Tel./fax 0577-738494

🚌
See Greve or Radda listings.

CHIANTI

(M)

See Greve or Radda listings.

(⊗)

SAN MICHELE

Villa San Michele
Parco Naturale di San Michele
Tel. 055-851034
Price: Inexpensive
Closing day: April 1–November
3, open every day; December
23–January 3 open every day;
March, open Sat. and Sun. only

BADIA MONTEMURO

L'Osteria
Loc. Badia Montemuro
Tel. 0577-738036
Price: Inexpensive
Closing day: Tuesday

VOLPAIA

Bar Ucci
Piazza della Torre (Volpaia's
main piazza)
Tel. 0577-738042
Price: Inexpensive
Closing day: Monday

Open for lunch, and usually
for dinner until at least 20:00 or
20:30. It's best to call ahead to
be sure of dinner. Also, if you
have a group, they'll stay open,
but in that case you need to
reserve ahead of time.

La Bottega
Piazza della Torre, 2
Tel. 0577-738001
e-mail: labottega@chiantinet.it

Price: Moderate
Closing day: Tuesday
Open for lunch and dinner.

(⊞)

SAN MICHELE

Villa San Michele
Parco Naturale di San Michele
Tel. 055-851034
Price: Double rooms, with
breakfast, 52–68 euros; with
extra bed, add 11 euros. Apartments for two people, 78 euros
(or 516 euros per week); for
four people, 103 euros (or 670
euros per week).

Room in the hostel, with
breakfast, 15 euros.

Meals can be added at
16 euros for the first one and
10 euros each additional.

This is really a very lovely,
relaxed spot. In addition to the
front building with the hotel
rooms, which are themselves
quite simple (one exceptionally
nice room in the front—slightly
more expensive—has its own
terrace with table and chairs,
others have access to communal terrace) there is a large
building in the back that
serves as a hostel. It, too, is
perfectly nice, and a great
option if you're on a tight
budget.

VOLPAIA

Podere Vergelli
Just on the edge of town
Tel. 0577-738382

Price: There are two apartments, both have kitchens, and you can eat in her small garden. (You can also eat in Volpaia, a few steps away.) We saw the apartment for two persons, and it was nice.

Apartment for two persons, 65 euros.

Apartment for four persons, 100 euros.

Loriana and Lina Carusi (*affittacamere*)
Volpaia. To find her: Facing the *enoteca* di Castello di Volpaia, turn right and walk about 20 m, then make another right. Watch (in less than 100 m) for a door with lots of flowers and a sign, "Casa Selvolini." If you have any problems, you can ask someone at the *enoteca* or at one of the restaurants.
Tel. 0577-738626
fax 0577-738329
Price: Apartment for two persons, with kitchen and bath, 60 euros per night.

Apartment for four persons, with kitchen and two baths, 100 euros.

Directions

SAN MICHELE TO VOLPAIA

For the San Michele to Volpaia portion, use the directions given in the Chianti Excursion section, p. 66

VOLPAIA TO SAN MICHELE

With your back to Castello di Volpaia, drop down to the left of the La Bottega restaurant, passing a church on the right.

Follow the asphalt road, which bends left; then as it bends sharply right, there's a gravel road to the left, flanked by a high stone wall: take that road.

Follow this road for 10–15 minutes, passing a small chapel and a pond on the right, and a couple of minutes later a house, Casa Lusignano. Bear left just beyond the house.

About 5 minutes past the house there's a stony fork up to the left **G**, as the main path bends downhill to the right. Take this left-hand path.

Stay on the main path, which crosses the stream four times. About a half hour from the beginning of this path you'll reach a serious fork **K**, at a place where you are basically standing on a ridge; the land slopes down both to the left and to the right of you. A very slightly smaller, slightly uphill fork goes off to the left. Take the other, right-hand, more-or-less descending path.

Passing **F** (the junction with the other side of the loop), a few minutes later you'll pass the ruined farmstead of Dogole on your right.

(NOTE: An alternative walk via Casa Lungagna would branch off here. If you want to go that way, see the directions below.)

Stay on the main path (which is now the "official" route marked by the province) past Dogole. After 15–20 minutes the path bends to the right and is joined by another path coming in from the left (ATW there are red and white paint blazes on a boulder here). Bend right.

After another 10 minutes or so the path ends at a gravel road **E**; turn left.

This road winds up to Badia Montemuro in another few minutes.

FROM BADIA MONTEMURO

With the *osteria* **D** on your left, walk out to the big asphalt intersection and bear left up the asphalt road.

Pass the big blue and white "Greve in Chianti" road sign on the right side of the road. The road rises straight up from here; at the top, where it bends left, take the wide gravel road on your left **C**.

About 25 minutes later you'll come to a junction **B**. (ATW there's a wooden shelter on the left here.) There are three paths to your right: take the middle one (which is at about a 90-degree angle to you).

Bear left where another path (CAI 00) joins your path about 5 minutes later. In another minute you'll arrive at the pagoda-style gate **A** of San Michele.

SAN MICHELE AND VOLPAIA RING WALK

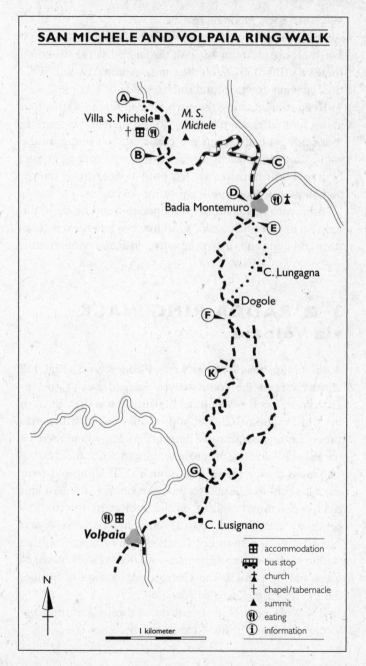

Villa S. Michele

M. S. Michele

Badia Montemuro

C. Lungagna

Dogole

C. Lusignano

Volpaia

N

accommodation
bus stop
church
chapel/tabernacle
summit
eating
information

1 kilometer

Volpaia to Badia Montemuro:
Alternate Route from Dogole via Casa Lungagna
FROM DOGOLE: About 1 m past the far end of the structure,
there's a small footpath on the right, leading downhill. Take
this, curving down around the back side of Dogole.

Keep straight along this path, descending to a stream in
about 5 minutes, then bending to the right and beginning
to ascend gradually, until you come out at a house on the
right, Casa Lungagna. Keeping the house to your right, pass
by it and bear immediately left onto a wider stone track.

Follow this road uphill, ignoring deviations.

After passing a small sawmill operation on the right, the
road turns to asphalt again, soon makes a left-hand hairpin
turn and continues up to the *osteria* in Badia Montemuro.

3 ■ RADDA RING WALK
via Volpaia

A 45-minute bus ride from Siena, Radda sits on a high hill
at the heart of the comparatively rugged part of the region known as the Monti del Chianti. It was the capital of
the old League of Chianti and still has its old concentric
streets circling the historic Piazza Ferrucci, where there's a
stately old Palazzo Comunale encrusted with shields.

This is a very pretty walk, much of it along old farm
tracks, with wonderful views over one of the loveliest
parts of Chianti. Points of special interest are the twelfth-
century Romanesque parish church of Santa Maria
Novella and the beautiful fortified hill village of Volpaia
with its extraordinary little maze of covered stone passage-
ways and its church, the Commenda di Sant'Eufrosino,
designed by Benedetto da Maiano.

The Volpaia to Radda portion of the walk is the same
as the route used in the Chianti Excursion, p. 69.

S.L. 96

Food

RADDA

There are a couple of new restaurants here (one of them another *Relais* establishment), but your best bet is still probably the popular Da Michele Pizzeria, which has expanded its menu to include a lot of venison and boar in the form of hams, sausages and pasta sauces. The paper-thin pizzas from the wood oven are simple and good, as is the Moretti beer on tap. Service can be slow, and it's a good idea to reserve.

The combined butcher/grocery story in the main square as you enter town sells excellent cheeses and salamis (their wild boar salami is particularly good). They also stock some organic staples (such as dairy products) and treats (such as blood–orange juice).

VOLPAIA

See food review for Volpaia in the Chianti Excursion section, p. 62.

LOGISTICS

RADDA RING WALK, VIA VOLPAIA

Radda–Volpaia, about 3 hours, unless using shortcut, in which case about 2¼ hours; Volpaia-Radda, about 2½ hours.

ⓘ   Miscellaneous info

🚌   Transport

Ⓜ   Maps, guidebooks and trail info

🍴   Eating

▦   Accommodation

ⓘ

RADDA

Piazza Castello, 6
Tel. 0577-738494
e-mail: proradda@chiantinet.it

🚌

SITA
Tel. 055-47821 (or toll-free from inside Italy: 800-373760)
www.sita-on-line.it
Florence
NOTE: If you're based in Flor-
ence, it's easier to take the bus to Greve and begin from there. However, if you want to start from Radda (perhaps spending the night there before you go), see below for frequency of buses.

Route 345
ATW three per day from Radda to Florence (none on Sun.). 7:10, 8:45 (neither Sat. nor Sun.), 18:15. ATW three per day from Florence to Radda, 7:00, 13:35 and 17:00.
Length of journey: 1½ hours

NOTE: These buses all stop in Greve.

TRA-IN

Tel. 0577-204111 or 204245 or 6
www.trainspa.it
Siena: Note that intercity buses usually leave from and return to the Siena railway station, just outside town. The inner-city buses make regular trips

between town and the railway station.

Route 125
Five or six buses per day (except Sun.) in each direction, beginning around 7:00, finishing around 18:00 or so. (ATW there's a later bus from Siena at 19:20.)
Length of journey: About an hour

TAXIS:

Signore Colella: 335-5647475
Signore Ansalone: 335-5237021
His is actually a limosine service for airport transfers, day tours around Chianti, etc. But he might take you if he's available.
You can also ask the tourist office.

Ⓜ
The tourist office in Radda has the Chianti Progetto Integrato Turismo maps and other 1:25,000 maps. Radda's newsstand/stationery stores also usually carry 1:25,000 maps.

🍴

VOLPAIA

Bar Ucci
Piazza della Torre (Volpaia's main piazza)
Tel. 0577-738042
Price: Inexpensive
Closing day: Monday
Open for lunch, and usually for dinner until at least 20:00 or

20:30. It's best to call ahead to be sure of dinner. Also, if you have a group, they'll stay open, but in that case you need to reserve ahead of time.

La Bottega
Piazza della Torre, 2
Tel. 0577-738001
e-mail: labottega@chiantinet.it
Price: Moderate
Closing day: Tuesday
Open for lunch and dinner.

BETWEEN VOLPAIA AND RADDA

Il Terreno
See IGM map
Tel. 0577-738312
fax 0577-738400
www.podereterreno.it
Price: 35 euros per person, includes their wine
Closing day: None
This is an *agriturismo,* at which you can have dinner (even if you're not staying there) if you book ahead—certainly no later than early morning of the day you wish to eat there. An article written in 1998 by the *San Francisco Chronicle*'s travel editor, John Flinn, about the Chianti Excursion describes Il Terreno. If you're interested, here's the Web address:
http://www.sfgate.com/ cgi-bin/article.cgi?file=/examiner/archive/1998/08/23/ TRAVEL15290.dtl

CHIANTI

RADDA

Da Michele Pizzeria Trattoria
Viale XI Febbraio (down the
steps behind the bus stop—ask
anyone)
Tel. 0577-738491
fax 0577-738784
e-mail: da.michele@virgilio.it
Price: Inexpensive
Closing day: Monday

Make reservations here,
because the restaurant is small
(unless they're using the outside
patio too) and they fill up;
without a reservation there's
a good chance you won't get
in without an extremely long
wait.

⊞

BETWEEN RADDA AND VOLPAIA (ON THE WAY UP)

Castelvecchi
See IGM map.
Tel. 0577-738050
fax 0577-738608
www.castelvecchi.com
Price: 83 euros per night for a
double room with breakfast,
and upward from there

This is a big operation in
beautiful old buildings, with a
restaurant for guests, cooking
classes, horseback riding, a pool
or two, tennis courts, and all
manner of accommodation
arrangements.

La Locanda
Loc. Montanino (see map)

Tel. 0577-738833
www.lalocanda.it
Price: Expensive

Lovely place, and they serve
meals for guests.

VOLPAIA

Podere Vergelli
Just on the edge of town
Tel. 0577-738382
Price: There are two apartments, both have kitchens, and
you can eat in her small garden.
(You can also eat in Volpaia, a
few steps away.) We saw the
apartment for two persons,
and it was nice.

Apartment for two persons,
65 euros.

Apartment for four persons,
100 euros.

Loriana and Lina Carusi
(*affittacamere*)
Volpaia. To find her: Facing
the *enoteca* di Castello di Volpaia, turn right and walk
about 20 m, then make
another right. Watch (in less
than 100 m) for a door with
lots of flowers and a sign,
"Casa Selvolini." If you have
any problems, you can ask
someone at the *enoteca*
or at one of the restaurants.
Tel. 0577-738626
fax 0577-738329
Price: Apartment for two persons, with kitchen and bath, 60
euros per night.

Apartment for four persons,

with kitchen and two baths, 100 euros.

BETWEEN VOLPAIA AND RADDA (ON THE WAY DOWN)

Il Terreno (*agriturismo*)
See IGM map.
Tel. 0577-738312
fax 0577-738400
www.podereterreno.it
Price: 90 euros per person per day, includes dinner

Il Terreno is transitioning to organic, and say they'll be completely organic by the time this book is published. They produce several wines. Dinner there is an experience. For more information, see their listing in the Eating section, p. 91.

Il Pruneto
See map
Tel. 0577-738013
e-mail: pruneto@chiantinet.it
Price: They have a studio apartment for 70 euros per night (or 400 per week) that sleeps a maximum of two or three people. They also have a larger apartment, two bedrooms, two baths, kitchen, at 150 euros per night (1000 per week). During May and June they will probably only book weeklong rentals, but if they're empty they'll accept an overnight.

Farmhouse in a beautiful location. They don't serve dinner,

but you can walk to Il Terreno for dinner, about a 15-minute walk (they'll give you a map).

RADDA

Le Fraschette
Loc. Le Fraschette (see map)
Tel. 0577-738106
fax 0577-749242
Price Double rooms, 60 euros. They also have an apartment.

Our walk passes this beautiful old stone farmhouse, only about ½ km from the town center, yet in a rural setting. They don't serve dinners, but you could have a lovely stroll home in the evening after dinner in town.

Campo agli Olivi
About ¾ km outside Radda
Tel. 0577-738074
www.campo_agli_olivi@ hotmail.com
Price: Two persons, 75 euros; four persons, 98 euros

Three apartments. Pool, garden.

Convento di Santa Maria
5-minute walk from center of town. See beginning of Radda to Valgliagli or San Sano walk directions, p. 77.
Tel. 0577-738065
Price: Double room, 75 euros, includes breakfast; apartment for four people, 95 euros. Two-night minimum.

Directions

*Note that the long description encompassing points **G** to **F** is actually a shortcut and only takes about 30 minutes, despite the lengthy directions. It needs rather detailed directions because it's not a defined path. But along with being shorter, it cuts out a lot of road walking.*

Leaving Radda from the southwest corner of town by the Enoteca/Bar Dante, take the main asphalt road (Via Pianigiani) **G** leading west toward Castellina; pass the four-star Relais Fattoria Vignale on your left.

ATW they're building a sidewalk on the right-hand side of the road here (a real improvement, as heretofore you had to share this busy road with cars and hope for the best), so we don't know what the ultimate configuration here will be. However, there will in any case be a turnoff on the right, probably signed for "Le Fraschette." Take that. (This turnoff will come *before* you reach the first houses built on the right side of this main road—the first house being about 200 m past **G**.)

Follow the main gravel road downhill toward Le Fraschette, and at its entrance bear left; when the track then immediately forks, take the left fork steeply downhill through an olive grove (ignore a hairpin right off the track 50 m or so beyond the grove), staying on the main path skirting the top of the vineyard.

The path then bends around to the right, heading toward a new house, vineyard on right, olives on left, and in about 50 m comes out on a gravel road. Turn right, toward the new house.

In about 60 m (at the end of the vineyard on the left) turn left off the gravel road onto a farm track, vineyard to your left, heading downhill. The track turns left; on your right is the lush vegetation of a streambed. Just as you reach the end of this lush vegetation the track turns right, away from the vineyard, and you'll see two stone houses

50 m above you. To the right of the houses you'll see a small dirt track (emerging from the cypress grove) coming down toward you; head over toward that track and take it steeply downhill to the right.

In another 30 m or so the path turns right, crosses through a gap in the lush vegetation and into a field (which could conceivably be planted with grapevines in the future). Turn left and go all the way across the bottom of the field, keeping the lush vegetation of the streambed to your left and ignoring a track off to the left about ¾ of the way across. At the end of the field, turn left through a big gap in the hedges, and drop straight down to the asphalt road on a small but well-worn single track **F**.

Turn left on the asphalt road and cross the bridge with the brick guardrails. Just beyond the bridge there's an asphalt road on the right; take that road.

Stay on this road for 600 m (about 10 minutes) until you come to a junction, signed for "Castelvecchi" and "Santa Maria Novella" on the left and "Volpaia" on the right. (This is a CAI route shown on the IGM map Monti del Chianti, but it simply follows the road and is not our route.) Just before you reach this major fork, watch on the left for a dirt road. Take this road.

Almost immediately (20 m) you'll see a dirt track uphill on your right. Take this track **E**.

Follow the track uphill for 5–10 minutes, when it ends at a vineyard. Turn right, skirting the edge of the vines, up toward the house (Casa Selvale). The path bends to the left in front of the house, staying between the vines and the stone wall that runs in front of the house. At the end of the wall bear left, keeping to the wide track that now leads between two large vineyard plots, with beautiful panoramas on both sides.

When you get to the end of the vineyard, the path reaches the beginning of a wood, where it winds left into another section of vineyard, through the opening in a wire fence. (Just where the path begins to turn toward this vineyard, there is a very narrow track into the woods, and also a wider track around the right side of the woods. Ignore both of these.)

Take the path that bends left into the vineyard and then immediately turns right along the edge of this vineyard, with the woods to your right. Carry on straight along here until, at the end of the vineyard (about 5 minutes), you see an old stone and terra-cotta tabernacle **D**, where the path turns right. Follow along with the vineyards to your left and a hedge and olive groves to your right.

Ahead to the right and below you, the Pieve di Santa Maria Novella, a twelfth-century Romanesque church, becomes visible. After a couple of minutes you'll reach a break in the fence and hedge, and a stone road turning off to the right **C**. If you want a quicker route for Volpaia (about 40 minutes from here, vs. about 1½ hours for the longer way), you can take this right, down to Santa Maria Novella, and pick up the directions at the end of this section for Santa Maria Novella to Volpaia Shortcut. (To visit the church, see directions from Volpaia to Radda, p. 69.)

Continue on past the turnoff **C** for Santa Maria Novella, following the path as it continues along the vineyard, then bends left and climbs toward a stone building now used as a garage for tractors. Bear right past this building and follow the path as it leads up to a group of old stone buildings—Castelvecchi, now an *agriturismo*.

Bend left behind the buildings, and continue along the track as it wraps around Castelvecchi and comes out on a quiet asphalt road. Turn left.

Almost immediately you'll come to a tabernacle with a gravel road leading downhill to the right (ATW signed "Vignamaggio"). Take this road.

In 5 minutes, just before the gated entrance to the driveway of a house **H**, you'll see a somewhat overgrown path leading uphill to the left. Take this path. This path, although it may be overgrown, was part of a European Community

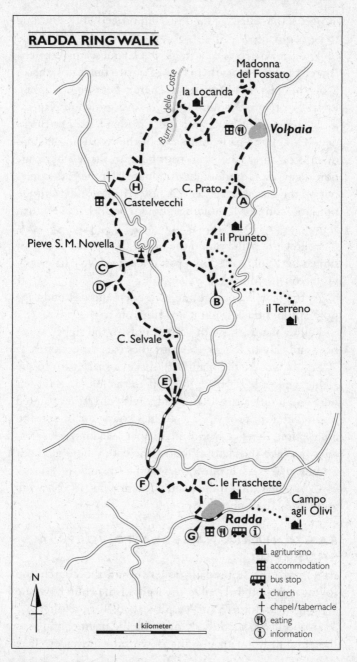

RADDA RING WALK

Madonna del Fossato

la Locanda

Burro delle Coste

Volpaia

(H)

C. Prato

(A)

Castelvecchi

il Pruneto

Pieve S. M. Novella

(C)

(D)

(B)

il Terreno

C. Selvale

(E)

(F)

C. le Fraschette

Campo agli Olivi

Radda

(G)

N

1 kilometer

agriturismo
accommodation
bus stop
church
chapel/tabernacle
eating
information

project some years ago, and will almost certainly continue to be maintained.

The path narrows to a single track almost immediately. After a minute or two there's a fork of two tiny paths (there's a big boulder in the pathway here); bear right, uphill. Lovely footpath, though somewhat overgrown in places.

In about a half hour, just after crossing a stream (Burro delle Coste), the path comes out of the woods into a little open, stony area; the main path bears to the left here; ignore a deviation to the right. A minute later the path comes out on the gravel driveway of a hotel (La Locanda; altitude point 614 on IGM, buildings shown, but not name); turn right.

Follow the path around the hotel, then bear left (ATW signed for "Volpaia") down past olive trees, Volpaia clearly visible off to your left.

As the path swings around to the left and descends, ignore another track leading downhill off to the right.

Follow the track (with Volpaia now to the right). Wide now and easy to follow, the path goes back into woods.

Still in woods, the main path makes a sharp turn to the right, while a lesser track goes off to the left. To your left here you'll find a large flat boulder with directions painted on it. The fork to the left leads in a couple of minutes to a charming derelict woodland chapel, Madonna del Fossato. (To take this detour, follow the path where in about 50 m it makes a hairpin left across the stream.)

Continue right on the main track, arriving in Volpaia in another 5–10 minutes.

SANTA MARIA NOVELLA TO VOLPAIA SHORTCUT

At **C**, take the stone path down toward the church and follow it around the wall to the right of the church, where it brings you out to a small asphalt road. Turn left here.

In about 100 m, directly opposite the main entrance to the church, is a path heading down into the valley. Take

this path. It may (or may not) look rough at firs
tually a well-maintained, shady footpath.

After about 5 minutes you'll cross two branches ɔ.
small stream, and winding along for another 2 minutes,
you'll pass a path forking steeply up to the left; ignore this,
and continue straight on. After 5 minutes a farm track
crosses the path; ignore it.

Follow the main path until you come to a T-junction
B. Go left (ATW signed toward "Volpaia"). In about 50
m, ignore a track branching off to the right.

Follow along this farm track, which soon affords a view
across the valley to Santa Maria Novella. You'll pass in
front of a house, Pruneto.

The thirteenth-century tower of Volpaia itself soon
comes into view. Climb steadily toward it on the main
path, ignoring all digressions to the right or left.

Bear left **A** (ATW signed on a boulder to "Volpaia") as
you enter a row of cypresses. A couple of minutes later
you'll pass a large stone tabernacle on your left before entering the elegant avenue of cypresses leading to Volpaia.

VOLPAIA TO RADDA
Use the directions for the Volpaia to Radda portion of the
Chianti Excursion, p. 69.

4 ■ LAMOLE RING WALK

This is one of the best walks in the region, taking you up
into the high ridges of east Chianti, with fine panoramic
views in both directions, then down blackberry-bordered
footpaths and ancient stone roads through a classically picturesque and unspoiled piece of the Tuscan landscape. As
an added incentive, the tiny hamlet of Lamole has one of
the most pleasant restaurants in Chianti.

Food

The Ristoro di Lamole was one of our favorite restaurants nine years ago, and it still is, having gone from strength to strength while keeping its friendly atmosphere and moderate pricing. The setting, with its westward view over mountains (and fabulous sunsets), is spectacular, and the beautifully prepared food is rare in that it manages to be far more imaginative than the usual rather circumscribed fare without seeming in the least bit contrived or fussy. Unlike most places that venture away from the basics, the originality here is clearly motivated by a genuine love of cooking rather than an attempt to justify inordinate prices. Among the appetizers, we particularly enjoyed the buffalo mozzarella with rosettes of marinated artichoke. The pasta dishes were easily the best we ate in Chianti—a mouthwatering one with shaved truffles, and an inspired ravioli stuffed with pecorino, ricotta and pear. Meat dishes include an excellent casserole of pork with pickled onions, and if you feel your day's exertions have earned you one of the massive steak *fiorentinas* that the region specializes in, the tender, superbly flavored chunk of Chianina beef they serve here is as good as it gets. The vegetables and salads (often the weak point in otherwise good restaurants) meet the high standards of the other dishes. There's a good wine list, and of the delicious desserts we still recommend the amazingly light, creamy, thin-crusted cheesecake, though this is now rivaled by a possibly even more sensational *panna cotta* with white chocolate and coffee beans.

For diners with children, there's a little playground just below the dining terrace, on the other side of the quiet road.

And to preserve (or anticipate) the memory of your delicious meal, attached to the restaurant is a small store where they sell all the makings of a superb picnic.

LOGISTICS

LAMOLE RING WALK,
about 3 hours
(1½ up, 1½ down)

ⓘ   Miscellaneous info

🚌   Transport

Ⓜ   Maps, guidebooks and trail
       info

🍴   Eating

🏨   Accommodation

ⓘ

See Greve Tourist Office listing
in Greve to Parco San Michele
portion of the Chainti Excursion,
p. 54.

🚌

SITA
Tel. 055-47821 (or toll-free from
inside Italy: 800-373760)
www.sita-on-line.it
Florence
Route 345 (Firenze–Greve–
Radda–Castellina–Gaiole)
   Buses between Florence and
Greve are fairly frequent, but
there are only about three buses
a day from Greve to Lamole. On
through connections from Flo-
rence there's a 10-minute lay-
over in Greve; from Greve to
Lamole is another 20 minutes.
Length of journey: Florence–
Greve, about an hour; Greve–
Lamole, about 20 minutes

NOTE: The village of Casole lies
between Greve and Lamole, and
is given in the walk directions as
a shorter version on the return
portion, in case you're headed
back to Greve or Florence by
bus and need a shortcut. Remember to check the bus times
before you leave.

TAXIS

Sirabella, *Tel.* 055-8546309
mobile 347-6949496
Gemini, *Tel.* 055-852025

Ⓜ

Maps are widely available in the
newsstand-type shops in Piazza
Matteotti. Do yourself a favor
and get one that has a scale of
1:25,000. Multigraphic is one
company that puts these out
(Carta Turistica e dei Sentieri).
   Also available for free from
the tourist office are the Chianti
Progetto Integrato Escursionismo maps, also 1:25,000. There
are four of these, covering the
various areas of Chianti. You'll
need the one called Tavola 2 & 3.

🍴

LAMOLE

Ristoro di Lamole
Lamole
Tel. 055-854-7050, 055-8547034
www.ristorodilamole.it
Price: Moderate
Closing day: Wednesday
   The Ristoro di Lamole also
has a small store attached to it,
open from about 9:00, that sells

everything you would need for a delicious picnic. Also serves as a small café, their terrace being a splendid place to have a coffee before you set off.

SAN MICHELE

Villa San Michele
Parco Naturale di San Michele
Tel. 055-851034
Price: Inexpensive
Closing day: April 1–November 3, open every day; December 23–January 3, open every day; March, open Sat. and Sun. only

⊞
LAMOLE

Marcello Bernini (*affittacamere*)
Lamole, loc. Il Poggio
Tel. 338-9089252;
fax 055-8561956
e-mail: alprato@lamole.info
Price: Whole house (8–10 people), 275 euros. Apartment 1, ground floor: two persons, 60 euros; four persons, 110 euros. Apartment 2, first and second floors: six persons, 180 euros.

Conveniently located about 500 m from the Ristoro di Lamole, this house, Casa al Prato, can be rented as a whole, sleeping eight to ten people, or as two separate apartments. They prefer to rent by the week (which is slightly less expensive than the daily prices given here)

but will rent by the night if they're not full.

Le Volpaie
Tel. 055-8547065
www. Fattoriadilamole.it
Price: 130 euros for double room, includes breakfast; discounts for stays of more than three days

They have a pool and a beautiful view. Walking distance to the Ristoro di Lamole.

SAN MICHELE

Villa San Michele
Parco Naturale di San Michele
Tel. 055-851034
Price: Double rooms with breakfast, 52–68 euros; with extra bed, add 11 euros. Apartments for two people, 78 euros (or 516 euros per week); for four people, 103 euros (or 670 euros per week).

Room in the hostel, with breakfast, 15 euros.

Meals can be added at 16 euros for the first one and 10 euros each additional.

This is really a very lovely, relaxed spot. In addition to the front building with the hotel rooms, which are themselves quite simple (one exceptionally nice room in the front—slightly more expensive—has its own terrace with table and chairs; others have access to communal terrace), there is a large building in the back that serves as a hostel. It, too, is perfectly nice, and a great option if you're on a tight budget.

AGRITURISMO

Fattoria Poggiarelli
Via di Petriolo 55-56
Tel. 055-853414
fax 055-289356
www.poggiarelli.it

Price: Double room, 76 euros, includes breakfast. No minimum stay. Apartments, which have a three-night minimum stay, available from 85 euros (for two people) up to 110 euros (sleeps six people).

This *agriturismo* is on the way up to Lamole; you would need a car.

Directions

From the bus stop, with your back to the church **A** and facing the Ristoro di Lamole restaurant, take the left up-hill track, passing on your right the brick steps leading up to the restaurant. ATW asphalt gives way within view (about 40 m) to a dirt track.

Soon this comes out on a small asphalt road; turn left along it.

After about 100 m (and ignoring a smaller track off to the left just before it), a dirt track leads directly uphill to the left, opposite the gateway of a house with a terra-cotta tiled patio. Take this track **B**.

In another 100 m this comes to a T-junction **C** with another dirt road in front of a stone wall and vineyard. Turn left.

After 2–3 minutes you'll pass a shed housing a water pump (or some similar thing) on the right, and the path climbs into the woods. After about a minute's climb you'll pass a boulder on your right with CAI marks (CAI 30).

Very soon after this the path skirts to the left of a vineyard, then passes the tail end of a stone wall. Ignore a small path to the right here (parallel to the wall) and instead continue straight on.

Staying always to the main path (which is easy to follow),

another 20–30 minutes' climb will bring you to the entrance of a pine wood. Ignoring a minor fork to the right, continue on the main path, which bends left into the pine wood. There's a CAI sign on a tree to the right as you enter.

In a few minutes this path reaches a T-junction **D** with another dirt track; turn left. (It may comfort you to know at this point that all the serious climbing is finished now, and it's basically all downhill on the way back.)

Very soon the track comes to an intersection in a more open area **E**. Take the left-most path, uphill, toward the pine trees.

There are really nice views up here. In the morning the whole valley to the east can be filled with a level plain of white clouds below you. To the west is a wide view of the Chianti countryside.

Follow the main path, which bends to the left as you reach the pine trees and skirts to the left of them. In a few minutes you come to a T-junction **F**. Go right, downhill.

Ahead on the hilltop beyond, and also off to the left, are two beautiful views of Italy's ubiquitous mountaintop cell phone towers, one of the ravages of human development. After a few minutes the path makes a steep descent, joining another path that comes in from the right **G**. Keep going straight on.

The next intersection, soon reached, presents four major paths ahead of you. Take the one straight ahead (second from the left) and level. This is CAI 00.

Arriving at the next T-junction **H**, bear left, and so in to Villa San Michele, about 1½ hours after leaving Lamole.

LEAVING SAN MICHELE

Standing in front of the pagoda-style gate **I**, with your back to it, immediately turn sharply left on the path that drops below the gate. Follow this path down the hill, ignoring lesser deviations. There is a tremendous view of Chianti below you. In a few minutes you'll reach an intersection **J**; the main path goes straight on, but we turn right.

(Immediately after you make this right turn, if you look closely you can see CAI paint marks on the two trees to your right.)

The path begins to descend, bending around to the left (where a smaller fork goes off to the right) and continuing downhill.

The path descends steeply here, leveling out alongside a stream at the bottom. (Ignore a smaller track off to the right here **K**.)

Continue following the path along the left side of the stream (dry much of the year).

A little further on, the path can get fairly overgrown (don't hesitate to do some clearing as you pass through), but the way remains obvious, and you continue to descend.

After no more than 5 minutes of this, the path levels out, crosses the stream and bends to the left.

As you begin a gradual climb (on the right side of the stream now), notice the fine old stonework along the left side of the path.

The path is very easy to follow now (ignore a deviation coming in sharply from uphill on the right), and after 15 minutes or so comes out to a T-junction with a gravel path **L**. Turn left. (This is about 40 minutes after leaving San Michele.)

Follow this path downhill, passing three houses, and with very wide views over the valley to Lamole. Just stick to the main path as it winds downhill, ignoring deviations (including one big one, downhill to the right with a big wooden cross, ATW signed "~~Ceppeto~~").

After about 15 minutes this gravel road starts bending sharply to the left around a house. Just *before* this bend and the house, there's a hairpin left-hand turn **M**. This smaller road has ATW a little sign, "Il Terrato." Take this road.

(NOTE: Alternatively, you can continue along the main path, down to Casole, about ½ km away, where you can get a bus back to Greve, if you've timed your walk to so coincide.)

LAMOLE RING WALK

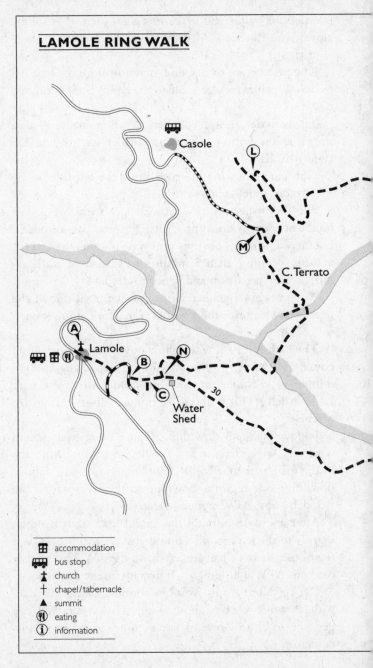

Casole

L

M

C. Terrato

A

Lamole

B

N

C

Water
Shed

30

⊞ accommodation
🚌 bus stop
⛪ church
✝ chapel/tabernacle
▲ summit
🍴 eating
ⓘ information

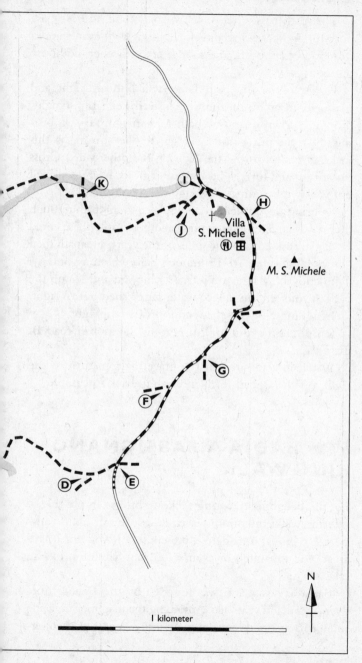

Villa
S. Michele

M. S. Michele

1 kilometer

N

electric fence, abandoned

This path passes between two old stone houses (Casa Terrato) and carries straight on, through vineyards and a stone wall on the left, and soon reaches another old house on the right.

Don't follow the path here (which turns right and passes in front of the house); instead keep on straight, dropping down on a tiny path to a stream. (Try to bear slightly right just before you get to the stream, as this makes it easier to find the path on the other side.) Cross the stream and turn right, toward Lamole. There is a small but well-worn footpath through the woods here.

Ignoring any smaller deviations, keep to this path through the woods, in 5 minutes crossing another brook (these could be dry streambeds at some times of the year). The path then climbs for another 10–15 minutes before coming out at a T-junction **N**. (Here you'll face a vineyard and see up the path to your left the alleged water pump shed.) Turn right.

In a minute or two the road forks **C**; bear right.

Drop down about 100 m here to the asphalt road **B**. Turn right.

Watch in a minute for the gravel hairpin turn to the right, off the asphalt road, and take it, back to Lamole.

5 ■ BADIA A PASSIGNANO RING WALK

For this delightful new ring walk, we broke our old rule of offering walks only from places accessible by public transport. No buses come here at present, but if you don't have a car, you can hitch or even walk from Sambuca, or else take a taxi.

Badia a Passignano was founded by the Benedictines over a thousand years ago. Absorbing the neighboring castle (hence its fortified look), it grew into a center of theological and scientific studies. In 1588 a well-known student of the then Abbott of Passignano taught mathematics there. His name was Galileo. There are fine frescoes inside, including Domenico Ghirlandaio's masterful *Last Supper*. The buildings have been much transformed over the centuries, but they still retain an almost startlingly picturesque appearance, the crenellated towers rising in medieval splendor above their ring of black cypresses.

The walk winds through stunning countryside, passing some beautiful abandoned farmhouses, which will no doubt be bought up and turned into super-deluxe holiday homes in due course, but which at present lend a melancholy beauty to the excursion. There are also some very pretty working farms, including the hilltop farming hamlet of Poggio al Vento, which boasts some very ancient and fine buildings of its own (beyond the main house).

The view across to the abbey on the way back is spectacular.

Food

There are two restaurants in this little village. The Osteria di Passignano is the fancier and more expensive, having serious aspirations toward that dubious entity, a Tuscan haute cuisine. As is usually the case, the result is an unpredictable mixture of refreshing originality and annoying pretentiousness. At the very least it's a pleasant place to sit—a pretty terrace outside and a surprisingly grand vaulted space inside, full of well-heeled diners, and yet remaining friendly in atmosphere. There are various tasting menus at 25 euros, and a 40-euro "Today at the Osteria" special, or you can order à la carte. The style is somewhat nouvelle-ish, small things prettily arranged on large plates. Antipasti include a delicious fava bean flan with pecorino and balsamic vinegar. Steer clear of the over-refined *farro* soup—the kind of rustic dish that vehemently resists being dolled up.

Among the unusual pasta and primi are a subtly flavored salt-cod gnocchi and a surprisingly good risotto of wild greens and saffron (surprising because risotto is usually to be avoided in Tuscany). If you're in the mood for meat, there's a succulent (and relatively substantial) roast baby pig, a goat casserole with asparagus, and the newly fashionable rabbit wrapped in lard, served with artichoke. The *dolci* we tried were ridiculous confections, but there's a good cheese selection, and the excellent wine list features many *vin santos* as well as some very good (and expensive) super-Tuscans.

If all that sounds like too much of a production, then go to the Scuderia, where you can eat a simple, inexpensive, well-cooked meal in low-key surroundings. No lard-wrapped rabbit here, but you could make a light lunch of the delicious garlicky *bruschetta* with green *fagioli,* or the earthy pecorino and honey appetizer. For pasta there's a rich truffled *tagliarini* dish and a very acceptable spaghetti picante. Meat dishes include steak, sausage and a tasty veal scallopine.

LOGISTICS

BADIA A PASSIGNANO RING WALK, about 2½ hours

ⓘ   Miscellaneous info

🚍   Transport

Ⓜ   Maps, guidebooks and trail info

🍴   Eating

⊞   Accommodation

ⓘ
TAVARNELLE

Tel. 055-8077832 or 055-805081
fax 055-8076685

www.comune.tavarnelle-val-di-pesa.fi.it

🚍
There are no buses to Badia a Passignano. If you haven't got a car, you can take a taxi from either Greve or Sambuca (closer). If you're coming from Florence, you can bus to Sambuca and get a cab (or hitch) from there. For Greve bus info, see Chianti Excursion: Greve to Parco San Michele, p. 54.

SITA
Tel. 055-47821 (or toll-free
from inside Italy, 800-373760)
www.sita-on-line.it
Florence, Sambuca
Route 349
Several buses per day, some
changing in Tavarnelle Val di
Pesa.
Length of journey: About an hour

TAXIS

From Sambuca/Tavarnelle:
Signore Mariotti,
Tel. 335-423249; or ask at Tavarnelle tourist office, *Tel.* 055-
8077832

FROM GREVE

Sirabella, *Tel.* 055-8546309
mobile 347-6949496
Gemini, *Tel.* 055-852025
   Rates from Greve should be
about 18–25 euros. Or ask at
tourist office: *Tel.* 055-8546287
fax 055-8544149
e-mail: info@chiantiechianti.it

Ⓜ
Maps are widely available in the
newsstand-type shops. The
maps with a scale of 1:25,000,
which are based on the old
IGM (military) maps, are infinitely more useful than those
with a scale of 1:50,000. Multigraphic is one company that
puts these out (Carta Turistica e
dei Sentieri).
   Also available for free from

the tourist offices are the Chianti Progetto Integrato Escursionismo maps, also 1:25,000.
There are four of these, covering the various areas of Chianti.
You'll need the one called Tavola
2 & 3.

🍴
La Scuderia
Via Passignano, 17
Tel. 055-8071623
Price: Inexpensive
Closing day: Wednesday night
and Thursday

Osteria di Passignano
Via Passignano, 33
Tel. 055-8071278
e-mail: marcello.crini@tin.it
Price: Expensive
Closing day: Sunday

⊞
AGRITURISMO

Casale La Selva
See map.
Tel. 055-8071090
www.casalelaselva.it
Price: Double room, 75 euros;
dinner, 20–25 euros, includes
their own wine and olive oil
This *agriturismo* isn't on our
actual route, but it isn't far. In
fact, the IGM shows a shortcut
to Casale La Selva just across
the road from our map point **G**.
That would be worth trying.
We include it because they
serve dinners.

Podere Torcilacqua
See map.
Tel. 055-8071452
www.torcilacqua.it
Price: Rooms are 28 euros per person; the apartment is 32 euros per person. They'll rent rooms for one night if they have the space.

Note that this *agriturismo* isn't actually on the walk route, but it is very near the abbey and restaurants (about a 5-minute walk), and thus quite an easy walk home after dinner in town.

Podere San Brizzi
See map.
Tel. 055-8071325
Price: For three days and two nights, 58 euros per person, includes breakfast; children under 10 stay for free

This *agriturismo* is on the walk route, but has a two-night minimum, doesn't serve meals, and isn't very close to town. However, if you have a car, this would be an option as a base for two days. They also have a large apartment that sleeps ten for 750 euros per week.

Fattoria di Rignana
Loc. Rignana
Tel. 055-852065
www.rignana.it
Price: See the Web site.

While Rignana is not on the walk, it is in the area. It's a nice place to stay if you have a car (or if you're an ambitious walker: it's only about 1 km from our map point **E** and you could experiment with some of the paths shown on the IGM. Alternatively, you could take the real paths shown going off from our map points **E** and **F**, both of which would join up to the road to Rignana, about another 2 km.). Five apartments; also nice big rooms furnished with country antiques in the old farmhouse. Forty beds in total. Pool. Restaurant on the premises, Cantinetta di Rignana.

Directions

As you enter the hamlet of Badia a Passignano on the road coming from Sambuca (i.e., the southwest side of the hamlet, and the opposite side from which you'd enter if you're coming from Greve), turn right at the Osteria di Passignano, passing it on your right, and with the crenellated western wall of the abbey on your left.

Just past the restaurant entrance (not to be confused

with the *enoteca* entrance, which is on the main road), turn right, passing to the right of a house (ATW #30).

About 30 m ahead of you you'll see a track leading downhill; take this track.

Keep to the main path (ignoring what ATW seems to be a new driveway being built off to the left in 30 m), bending steeply down to the left in 50 m.

In another 50 m bear to the right downhill, where a couple of paths lead off to the left. The path (rugged here) winds steeply downhill.

About 7–10 minutes from the top of the trail, you'll cross a small stream **A** at the bottom of the valley and begin to climb. Ignore a turnoff to the left 70 m after the stream; 5–7 minutes later, ignore another sharp left, continuing along the easy-to-follow main path.

About 15 minutes from the stream **A**, the path bends sharply to the right, then in 100 m bends up to the left between the two boarded-up buildings of Casa Vignola, then bends right again as it leaves the property.

In another 5 minutes the driveway of Casa Vignolina goes off to the right. Ignore this, bearing downhill to the left.

Keeping to the main wide dirt track, in about 15 minutes you'll come to a junction **B** (ATW signed right to "Molina dell'Abate," left to "Casa Brizzi"). Take the left.

Ignore a lesser track off to the right, 50 m from **B**, staying on the main path. In another 3–4 minutes the path forks **C**. Take the left, more rugged path, climbing and ignoring turnoffs.

In 5–10 minutes you'll come out at a junction. The right is the driveway to Casa San Giustino. Follow the main path forward and round to the left. Ignore a minor fork to the left in 30 m.

A pretty walk of 10–15 minutes brings you to a junction **D** at Casa San Brizzi, where you turn left, passing Casa San Brizzi on your right.

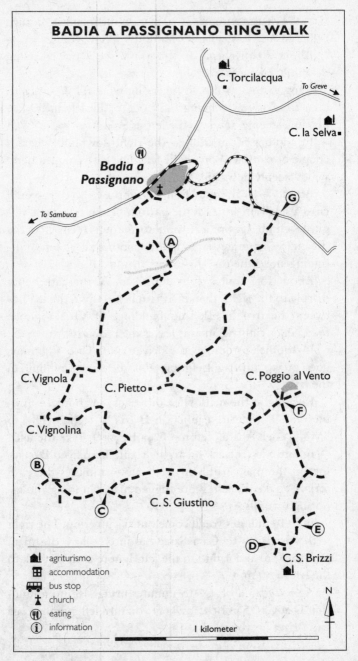

BADIA A PASSIGNANO RING WALK

C. Torcilacqua

To Greve

C. la Selva

Badia a Passignano

To Sambuca

G

A

C. Vignola

C. Pietto

C. Poggio al Vento

F

C. Vignolina

B

C

C. S. Giustino

D

E

C. S. Brizzi

agriturismo
accommodation
bus stop
church
eating
information

N

1 kilometer

A minute or so past Casa San Brizzi you'll see a smaller track leading off to the left **E**; take this track. (ATW signed with a green "4" on a yellow circle background on a tree on the right side of the main road, and with a yellow "3" on a tree to the left.)

In 5 minutes you'll come to a junction with a path coming up from the right. Continue on up to the left. In another minute or so you'll come out of the woods and continue up a straight raised stone track bordering an olive grove to the left.

At the top of this track you'll come to a junction **F** marking the entrance to the hamlet of Poggio al Vento ahead of you. Turn left, away from the hamlet (after you've had a look around it if you're so inclined; there are some beautiful old buildings here), following the main path gently downhill and keeping to the right of the olive grove.

Cross over a vague intersection with a track crossing from behind you on the right and leading ahead down left through the olive grove.

In about 30 m (about 175 m from **F**) bend sharply to the right at the entrance to a vineyard on the left, and fork immediately right again. Just after this fork you'll see the house you're heading for (Casa Pietto) down to the left (about ½ km away).

A stony road with great views of the Badia winds you gently down to Casa Pietto. In 10–15 minutes, where the road enters their yard (ATW at the left of a tall cypress), a right fork leads downhill. Take this fork, and in another 30 m fork right again. This well-defined track leads you in about 15 minutes down to the road **G**.

When you reach the road, turn left, but before you start walking up the road, look ahead of you, toward the abbey. (This path may no longer be there by the time you read this, though we think it will; if it's not, just follow the road from here into Badia a Passignano, a little over 1 km.)

Ahead of you, just where the road bends right, you can see a big pathway up the hill, between two vineyards.

Take this path to the top of the vineyards, where you'll encounter the olive grove above it (visible from the road). Bear right at the top of the vineyards, then curve left around the olive grove, keeping the olive grove to your left and on your right a stone wall and drain sluice. Follow along this wall all the way to the end, where it meets the taller stone wall just beneath the abbey. Cross over the drain here, now with the big wall on your left, and follow along the big wall right out to the road, which takes you into Badia a Passignano.

6 ■ GAIOLE RING WALK, via Badia a Coltibuono

The variety of the Chianti landscape is well displayed on this walk, which takes you through woods and vineyards with views of hilltop castles, up through the lovely little hamlet of Montegrossi, past a huge cement works and a strange, rather desolate mineral quarry, and on to the stunning monastery of Badia a Coltibuono. The Vallombrosan

monks who took over this monastery in the twelfth century established a tradition of expert viticulture that is continued by the present owner, Giannetto Catinari, who has combined it with a more modern expertise in public relations. The result is one of the most fashionable vineyards in Chianti, with its own restaurant and estate shop as well as a cooking school run by Lorenza de' Medici.

Much of this walk is without shade, so spring and autumn are the best times to do it.

Food

The delightful arbored setting and the aspiration to a much higher culinary standard than usual (along with its position on this walk) make the restaurant at Badia a Coltibuono well worth a visit, even though it is now on the coach-tour wine and food circuit. The menu suggests a highly inventive approach to Tuscan cuisine that is largely borne out by the dishes themselves, and it isn't as wildly expensive as you might expect. We had superb croquettes of zucchini and mint with goat cheese, a good *millefeuille* of eggplant and buffalo mozzarella, the best rendering of *pici al ragu* we'd eaten anywhere, an indifferent *panzanella* (the curious addition of a quail's egg notwithstanding), and a minimal but tasty roast rabbit. Other main courses included venison, tuna steak in a white pepper crust, and "crispy young rooster with chestnut honey and sauteed scallions." Among the excellent desserts are some risky-sounding but startlingly good sorbets of lemon and basil, pear and sage, as well as some more conventional flavors.

If none of this tempts you, you can eat in Gaiole. Lo Sfizio di Bianchi in the main piazza is a modest, friendly restaurant/*gelateria* where you can also buy sandwiches.

LOGISTICS

GAIOLE RING WALK, VIA BADIA A COLTIBUONO:

Gaiole–Badia a Coltibuono, 2½–3 hours; Badia–Gaiole, under an hour

---

(i) Miscellaneous info

🚌 Transport

(M) Maps, guidebooks and trail info

(Ⅱ) Eating

🎗 Accommodation

(i)
GAIOLE

Via Ricasoli, 50
Tel. 0577-749411 or 0577-749405
e-mail: prolocogaiole@libero.it

🚌
TRA-IN

Tel. 0577-204225 or 204111 or 221221 or 204246
www.trainspa.it

Siena
Five buses per day in both directions, between 7:00 and about 18:00
Length of journey: About 40 minutes

SITA
Tel. 055-47821 (from inside Italy, toll-free, 800-373760)
fax 055-4782272
Mon.–Fri. 8:30–18:30; Sat.–Sun. 8:30–12:30
www.sita-on-line.it

Florence
Two buses per day from Flo-

rence, ATW 13:35 Mon.–Sat. and 18:55 Mon.–Fri. One per day from Gaiole to Florence, ATW 6:55.

Length of journey: About 2 hours

TAXIS

Michele Colella, *Tel.* 335-5647475

Other taxi services listed by Gaiole Tourist Office: *Tel.* 0577-749355 and 335-5237021.

We were quoted 15 euros for Badia a Coltibuono to Gaiole.

Ⓜ

The 1:25,000 map Chianti Progetto Integrato Escursionismo is available at the tourist office. Other 1:25,000 maps are available at the newsstand-type stores in town.

🍴

Ristorante Badia a Coltibuono
Badia a Coltibuono
Tel. 0577-749424
fax 0577-749031
www.coltibuono.com
Price: Moderate to expensive
Closing day: ATW, during tourist season, open every day

Guided tours every half-hour between 14:30 and 16:30, May–

October (excluding August and Bank Holidays). Also, daylong and extended-stay cooking classes. See the Web site for details.

Try to book ahead, as they sometimes have large groups of people, and there's no other place to eat there.

Lo Sfizio
Gaiole, in the main (pedestrian) piazza
Tel. 0577-743501
Price: Inexpensive
Closing day: Tuesday

▦

There is a hotel in Gaiole called La Fonte del Cieco (Tel. 0577-744028).

ATW no *agriturismo* along the route.

ⓘ

AZIENDA AGRICOLA RIECINE

This vineyard has established a fine reputation for its Chianti. The Gioia di Riecine red *vino da tavola* (one of the super-Tuscans) is aged in *barrique,* while the white is fermented in small wooden barrels. English spoken. If you're walking down from Badia a Coltibuono, stop in here; we thought their wine better than Badia's.

Directions

The street just behind the bus stop at Gaiole is Via G. Marconi **A**. As you face it, from the bus stop, take it to the right, away from town.

This opening stretch of road-walking is at first decidedly plain (an occupational hazard of town environs), but things do pick up. About 1 km past **A**, the tiny and perfect hill town of Barbischio appears off in the distance, capable of distracting your gaze from the pavement.

About 1½ km past **A**, the road bends around to the right across a little stone bridge over a stream. Take the dirt road off to the left **B** immediately before the bridge. Bear left, uphill, past the first fork (in about 200 m), a smaller path that goes downhill to the right.

When the path forks again at a stream **C**, take the right fork, which crosses the stream over a culvert. Ignore the left fork, which more or less parallels the stream.

Stay on the main track, noticing the deviations to the left (ignore any on the right), as you are going to turn off on the third (ATW) of them. The first is a fork uphill to the back, coming about ¾ km after the stream **C**; the second is a good-sized fork about 1½ km past the stream **C**. Soon after this (perhaps 25–30 minutes past **C**, because the ascent makes for slow progress), there is a good-sized fork (nearly comparable in size to what we've been on) making a hairpin turn to the left and behind, and uphill. Take this **D**. If you miss it, you'll come in a minute or two to a stone house (Frabecchi) on the right of the path, with the path basically ending in their yard. (NOTE: The IGM map shows the path, CAI 56, continuing on past Frabecchi, but in fact it doesn't. If you are in any doubt that you've got the correct turnoff, you can always check to see if the house is up ahead.)

After a climb of 15–20 minutes (during which you should ignore lesser turnings to the left), there is a similar-sized path turning off to the left **E**, north and steeply uphill, at what appears to be the top of the hill we've been climbing. It is a wide, steep, stony path. Take this path.

In another 8–10 minutes you'll see a path on the right leading off at a 90-degree angle uphill, the same size but rougher. Ignore this. Just after that, you'll enter a stretch of the walk with a dense evergreen forest on the right and beautiful chestnuts on the left.

The path becomes dense pine forest on either side, making a very dark passage. Ignoring logging trails down to the left and another path down to the right, continue straight ahead.

A couple of minutes later, the path slopes down to a T-junction **F**, where there's a fence straight ahead of you. Turn left here. This is CAI 00.

This is a beautiful hilltop path, with occasional views of Badia a Coltibuono ahead of you on the distant hillside.

Keep following the main path, ignoring deviations off it. Soon you will see the ruined castle of Montegrossi on a hill off to the right. There's a fine view as you come into the hamlet of Montegrossi.

Follow the road through the middle of the hamlet, ignoring two forks to the right just as you enter. The road turns to asphalt here, but there's nobody on it.

Following along the road, a short way after Montegrossi you will pass a large cement works on the left and on the right a road up to the ruins of the castle.

Passing the little tower Cancelli, the road drops down to a junction **G**. Cross straight over the main road, and turn in immediately on the right for the Badia a Coltibuono *osteria* (shop). Following the road on which the shop is located for another ¾ km, you will come to the Badia itself, and its restaurant.

Leaving Badia a Coltibuono

Passing the Coltibuono shop on the left, drop down to the main junction **G** and turn right there. In 100 m or so you will see a dirt road branching off to the left and downhill.

GAIOLE RING WALK

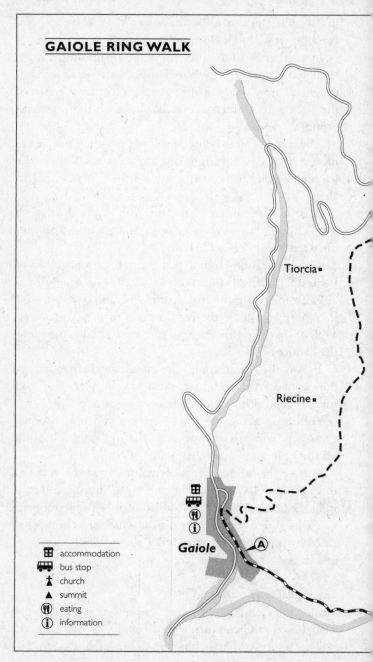

Tiorcia ■

Riecine ■

Ⓐ

Gaiole

▦ accommodation
🚌 bus stop
✝ church
▲ summit
🍴 eating
ⓘ information

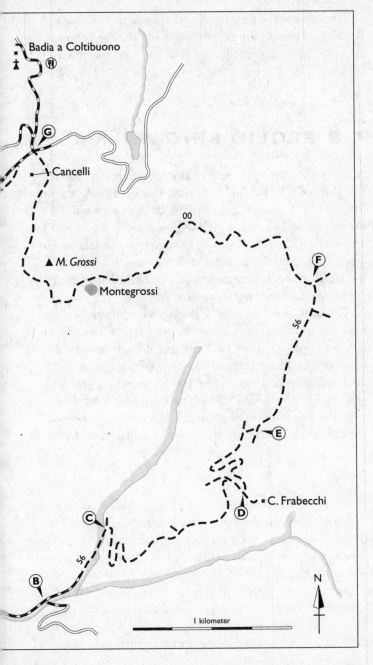

Badia a Coltibuono

G

Cancelli

▲ M. Grossi

Montegrossi

00

F

56

E

C. Frabecchi

D

C

56

B

N

1 kilometer

Follow this road all the way down, passing the Tiorcia and Riecine estates on the right. Eventually the road turns to asphalt, Via B. Bandinelli, and leads on into the town of Gaiole.

7 ■ BROLIO RING WALK

A good walk through some of the most delicately attractive parts of Chianti, and a pleasant way of turning a visit to the famous winery and castle of Brolio into a full day's outing. Little hamlets, a trellised *vitiarium* (vine-covered walkway), and a stream where the intrepid can take a dip (and which even the unintrepid may have to wade across if the weather's been wet) punctuate this fairly gentle meander through serious wine-growing country.

The handsome, turreted Castello di Brolio was bought from the monks of Vallombrosa by the Ricasoli family in 1067, and provided the backdrop for innumerable battles between the Florentine and Sienese factions during the medieval period. It sits in its landscape with a glorious (and highly photogenic) air of permanence. It was here, with the invention of the formula for the wine we now associate with the region, that modern Chianti was born.

Food

You have three choices here (four if you include picnicking, which may be your best bet). The simplest is Trattoria San Regolo in San Regolo, a pleasant enough place with good views of the castle from its glassed-in terrace and an okay way with Tuscan basics. The inexpensive menu includes a decent *tagliatelle* with wild mushrooms, a hearty lasagna, some good local spicy sausages—nothing out of the ordinary, but all fine. Check on the day's specials, as they observe the local tradition of revealing nothing unless pressed.

On the grounds of the castle itself is the fancier Osteria del Castello. The three special menus, including a 38-euro Menu Afrodisiaco featuring fillet of rabbit with truffle and stuffed sage, passion fruit sorbet, and so on, may strike you as dubious, but the food isn't bad, and the atmosphere is quietly elegant. The zucchini blossoms stuffed with ricotta and herbs are tasty as well as pretty to look at. There's a soupy but comforting risotto with green peppercorns and *vin santo,* and they make an appetizing stuffed breast of guinea hen, swimming in sauce. *Tiramisu* buffs will note that in keeping with the generally lubricious nature of the food here, the ladyfinger content of their version of this dish is more or less vestigial, which is one way—if not the most honorable—to ensure a creamy richness.

And then there's San Felice, a picturesque hamlet which has been converted by the Relais chain into a luxury hotel. Here, in an atmosphere of quiet, not entirely benign exclusivity (one has the distinct sense of the original inhabitants of the village having been sinisterly removed) you can dine among the svelte guests on pigeon ravioli, roast sea bass, or guinea fowl supreme stuffed with ricotta and fava bean, at double or triple the usual prices. The food is fine: well presented, impeccably served, not as

pretentious as you might fear nor as interesting as you might hope; if anything, a little bland. There's a simpler "light" menu with a good artichoke and spring salad, a so-so sliced beef with arugula and balsamic vinegar, and a delicious *tiramisu* (it should be, at 13 euros). This is probably the best eating on the Brolio circuit, though only worth it if money is no great concern.

LOGISTICS

BROLIO RING WALK,
about 3 hours

- ⓘ Miscellaneous info
- 🚌 Transport
- Ⓜ Maps, guidebooks and trail info
- 🍽 Eating
- ▦ Accommodation

It lists all the local tourist offices in Siena province. There is also a link to ask them to send you information. One excellent pamphlet they put out (available in English) is "Terre di Siena in bici: Biking Through Siena's Countryside." This 44-page pamphlet makes very exciting reading.

ⓘ
SIENA

Il Campo, 56
Tel. 0577-280551
www.terresiena.it
This Web site is extremely good.

🚌
TRA-IN

Tel. 0577-204111 or 204245 or 6
www.trainspa.it
Siena (train station)
Route 127

From Siena: ATW two buses per day, at 14:00 and 17:50
To Siena: see note below.
Length of journey: 35 minutes

For the intrepid, ATW there's also an early morning bus from Gaiole to Brolio at 6:40, arriving at Brolio 20 minutes later. Ask the driver to let you off at the stop for Castello di Brolio, as the bus sometimes stops only at the Madonna di Brolio stop, from which you must walk up the hill to get to the castello. Unfortunately, on the way back to Siena you have to take the bus to Gaiole, then switch there to a bus for Siena. ATW there's only one bus from Brolio, at 14:35, arriving in Gaiole at 15:00, then a bus from Gaiole at 15:05, arriving in Siena (railroad station) at 15:45.

TAXIS

Siena: Tel. 0577-49222 (or ask at tourist office)

CAI Siena section, Viale G. Mazzini, 95, *Tel.* 0577-270666
e-mail: info@caisiena.it

Ⓜ
Sentieri fra Il Chianti, L'Arno e La Chiana. This is a 1:25,000 map produced by CAI. Most of the 1:25,000 maps do not quite extend all the way down to this walk, but this one does. If you don't want to buy a map just for this walk, don't worry about it;

you can do this walk without a map.

🍴
Trattoria San Regolo
Loc. San Regolo, 33
Tel. 0577-747136
Price: Inexpensive
Closing day: Monday

Note that they are only open for lunch, beginning at 13:00, except on Sat. and Sun., when they are open for both lunch and dinner.

Ask for the specials.

Osteria del Castello
Loc. Brolio
Tel. 0577-747277
e-mail: info@seamuschef.com
Price: Expensive
Closing day: Thursday
Reservations recommended.

Relais San Felice
Loc. San Felice
Tel. 0577-3964
Price: Extremely expensive

⊞
Podere Le Boncie
Loc. Le Boncie
Tel. 0577-359383 or 359116
fax 0577-359383

This is an expensive apartment that sleeps four people, in the hamlet of Le Boncie across from San Felice. No dinners, but an option if you're interested. Perhaps they'll expand at some point.

Directions

From the bus stop, go up through the Brolio entrance (across from the Madonna della Brolio church) and arriving at the top **A**, turn left for the trail, or right to visit the castle.

From **A**, follow this cypress-lined road downhill.

After nearly 1 km, there's an intersection with a house (La Grotta) on the right. Ignoring the road most to the left, ahead of you the road forks: take the left fork, passing a small tabernacle on the right.

Very soon you will pass a small chapel on the right, and then reach the dwellings of Podere Colle. Stay on the road as it passes between these two houses; just beyond them (about 100 m) there is a fork **B**; take the left, downhill, slightly smaller one. (CAI signed.)

This path skirts a field (ATW plowed up); follow the hedge on your left. After angling down to the right (with the hedge), the perimeter of the field becomes a path veering left out of the corner of the field; take that path.

Ignoring a minor deviation leading almost immediately to the left, keep to the main stony track, downhill all the way to a T-junction with a small asphalt road, across from a tabernacle **C**. Turn right here. In a few minutes you'll reach the Borgo San Felice.

Follow the little asphalt road you've been on, which now passes to the right of the buildings of San Felice and soon reaches a parking lot on the right. (There's a gravel road here to the right signed for "Le Boncie" and "Poggio Rosso," but don't take it.) Continue along the asphalt road a bit further, until you come to a couple of brick pillars on the right, marking the entrance to the *vitiarium,* **D**. This is a vine-covered trellis that cuts across the vineyard from San Felice in a straight line. Take this covered way.

(NOTE: If this walkway is closed for some reason, go back to the parking lot and take the gravel road signed to "Le Boncie" and "Poggio Rosso." Take the first left turn (after about 75 m), soon passing La Ca' del Guagliumi on the right, and getting a long panorama toward Siena. Follow this road as it bends left and passes between vineyard and olives and more vineyard, until you reach a T-junction with the vine-covered trellis walkway **E** that comes across the vineyard from San Felice. Turn right here.)

At the very end of the walkway (not the gap in the middle of it) **E**, continue straight on, passing a path to the right. Very soon you enter some woods where, bearing to the left, the path dwindles to a footpath that descends gently through the woods. Follow this footpath, which is narrow but well-defined, descending to a stream (about 10–15 minutes past **E**).

(NOTE: As you near the stream at the valley bottom, there's a small deviation—a hairpin turn to the left—just where the footpath begins to level out after descending all this time. If you follow this hairpin left turn for about 55 paces, you'll come to a very tiny footpath bearing sharply down to the right. There are little pools in the stream here, for taking a dip. The path is quite overgrown, however.)

Cross this stream and turn right on the path you will find on the other side of it. Immediately the path goes through a break in the shrubbery and comes out in a small open area, where it forks. Go right here.

Stay on this stony, ascending footpath, which is narrow but well-defined. After 5–10 minutes the view on the left begins to open out and there's a little fork dropping down to a vineyard; take this fork, turning right at the vineyard.

Follow this farm track to the end of the vineyard (20 m or so), where it turns left along the top of the vineyard, below the house **F**, then curves to the right before coming out on a driveway, where you turn right. Follow the driveway away from the house, out to the small asphalt road **G**. Turn right on this road.

(NOTE: The next section concerns a vineyard the configuration of which has changed since our original edition—as these things often do. In the unlikely event that it changes again, you can use the alternate route given in parentheses immediately following this description. It is, in any event, a very short stretch.)

Ahead of you on the right is the old church of Nebbiano (now a private residence). Just before you come to its main entrance, there's a path on the left that runs atop a stone wall terracing the height difference between the two large vineyards there. This path cuts down through the vineyards to the lowest point of the field (the bottom of the shallow valley) and there forms a T-junction **H** (ATW there's a big, solitary tree growing there) with a track that runs the entire length of the vineyards, along the bottom of the field. Take this path, and when you reach the T-junction at the bottom of the field, turn right and follow the track all the way to the end of the vineyard, where the trees grow along the edge **I**. Turn left along the farm track at **I**, with the vineyard now to your left, trees to your right.

(ALTERNATE FROM NEBBIANO: Continue past Nebbiano, with the vineyard to your left. Walk on the farm track flanking the vineyard, and stay on it as it bends left (away from the road) at the corner of the vineyard. Now with the vineyard on your left and trees on your right, follow the track to **I**.)

About 20 m past **I** take a path forking off to the right. Follow this track (which runs just about parallel to the asphalt road) for about a minute, at which point it comes out on the road **J** (ATW signed "La Torricella").

Cross over the asphalt road to a small path directly opposite.

About 50 m after beginning on this path you'll come to a fork. Bear right here, onto a single, well-trodden path.

After about 5 minutes of descent the path crosses a little stream and begins to ascend as a wider, steep stony path. Near the top it narrows again to a single track, and just after that it meets with a wider dirt track on which you turn left.

Stay on this track, ignoring deviations (including a large track joining us from the left after about 5 minutes).

BROLIO RING WALK

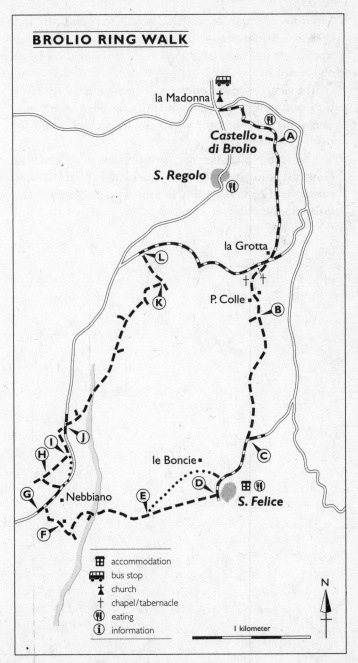

la Madonna

Castello
di Brolio

S. Regolo

la Grotta

P. Colle

le Boncie

Nebbiano

S. Felice

accommodation
bus stop
church
chapel/tabernacle
eating
information

N

1 kilometer

About 15 minutes past the asphalt road at **J,** the trail ends at a T-junction with a similar gravel road. Turn left uphill, and in a minute or two you'll come to the edge of a vineyard **K**.

Turn left on the track here, skirting the edge of the vineyard, and walk down to the line of evergreens at the bottom of the hill, where the track will come out on a main dirt road. Turn right **L**.

Stay on this main dirt road, which takes you back to the crossroads you passed earlier at La Grotta. Turn left here, passing La Grotta and climbing the road back to Castello di Brolio the way you came.

AROUND FLORENCE

For obvious reasons, the immediate environs of Florence don't make for particularly pleasant walking. We had hoped to find interesting routes linking some of the great Renaissance villas such as Poggio a Caiano or Petraia with nearby Etruscan sites, or with one or two of the more celebrated outlying restaurants such as Da Delfina in Artimino, but despite pleasant stretches here and there, these areas are pretty dreary, and the proximity of the industrial plain just beyond doesn't help. Curzio Casoli, from whom we've adapted some of our other walks, does have routes connecting these places in his excellent booklet *Trekking and Mountain Biking Around Florence and Siena,* but you'd have to have quite a tolerance for boring suburbs to enjoy these particular itineraries.

Still, you don't have to go far to find unspoiled countryside. From the hill town of Fiesole, a short bus ride from the center of Florence, there are pleasant walks that can give you at least the illusion of being deep in the heart of the countryside. Better still, take a day off to picnic in the Mugello—the pretty area of farmland and wooded slopes stretching between Florence and the Apennines. A little further afield are the forest and abbey of Vallombrosa, something of a resort area, but nonetheless attractive as well as cool and shady—desirable qualities in the Tuscan summer.

FLORENCE

🚌 Transport

🍴 Eating

ⓘ Miscellaneous info

🚌

Bus Station: Via Santa Caterina da Siena; opposite the train station. English spoken. The main bus company serving the area is SITA. *Tel.* 055-47821 (or toll-free from inside Italy: 800-373760)
www.sita-on-line.it

Train Station: Santa Maria Novella. English spoken. Train information, tel. toll-free inside Italy: 848-888-088
www.trenitalia.it

🍴

There is no shortage of restaurants in Florence (a city that, after all, caters to millions of tourists every year), and all the travel guides will have substantial lists of these. What we can offer are three restaurants that were still unknown to tourists when we wrote this book originally and are still reported by readers to be excellent. All three are well above average and each has its own unique atmosphere. Two of them are on the "other" side of the river (the Pizzi Palace side),

but only a 5-minute walk from it, which makes a lovely stroll of an evening.

Cavolo Nero Trattoria
Via dell'Ardiglione, 22
Tel. 055-294744
www.cavolonero.it
Closing day: Sunday
    Open for dinner only. We almost hate to give this one away. Tucked away in a quiet side street (in the same neighborhood as I Raddi), this tiny place with its young, creative chef was a real find. They also have a garden out back with a few tables. The chef made something special of *pici* with zucchini and ricotta. A terrine of baked cheese and pepper was rich, but great if you're in the mood for cheese. Good pasta with clams. The menu also had departures from the old standards that you find day after day in Italian restaurants, and the food was always imaginatively handled.

Trattoria I Raddi
Via Ardiglione, 47/r
Tel. 055-211072
www.iraddi.com
Price: Low to moderate
Hours: 19:00–22:30
Closing day: Sunday
    The romanticized version of the old-style trattoria come true.

The menu is fairly basic, the food done reliably, honestly, well.

La Giostra Club
Borgo Pinti, 10/r
Tel. 055-241341
email: la_giostra@hotmail.com
Price: Rather more expensive than our usual recommendations, but not extravagantly so
Hours: Open every day for lunch and dinner, except Saturday and Sunday lunch

This "dining club," fairly invisible if you're not looking for it, is something of an adventure. A complimentary glass of good sparkling wine and *bruschetta* kick things off. The kitchen is more or less open, and you watch beautiful plates of food go by: a huge mozzarella, basil, radicchio and lettuce salad; penne with zucchini flowers in an interesting reduced onion sauce; paper-thin slices of roasted beef on a dish full of fresh herbs; superb, smoky *tiramisu*.

PICNICS

Check out the huge Mercato Centrale (Central Market), not only for putting together a picnic, but as an experience in itself.

ⓘ
There are two main tour offices in Florence.
APT Firenze
Via Cavour, 1r
Tel. 055-290832 or 055-290833; *fax* 055-2760383.
This is the main tourist information office.

APT Firenze
Via Manzoni, 16
Tel. 055-23320;
fax 055-2346286.
This is the principal office for administration and correspondence, as well as being a tourist information office. Open 8:30–13:30 Mon. through Sat.

BOOK STORES

There are a few book stores in Florence specializing in travel books and maps.
Libreria Stella Alpina
Via F. Corridoni, 14 B/r
Tel. 055-411688
www.stella-alpina.com

Libreria il Viaggio
Borgo degli Albizi, 41 (near Hotel Mona Lisa)

Libreria E.P.T.
Via Condotta 42r

WALKS FROM FIESOLE

of Florence, the little hill town of
mer retreat for rich Florentines ever
his aristocratic storytellers up to its
villas to escape the plague that was devastating the
city below. With its aerial views over Florence, fine buildings, well-preserved Roman and Etruscan ruins, and cool
breezes, Fiesole has become an obligatory day's outing for
tourists in Florence. A short walk through the town leads
to the park-like slopes of Monte Ceceri, where Leonardo
experimented with his flying machines and the dark *pietra
serena* used in old Florentine buildings was once quarried.

FIESOLE TO PONTE A MENSOLA

Considering how close you are to Florence, this tranquil
walk has a remarkably bucolic feel to it, offering a taste of
classic Tuscan countryside with olive groves, poplars and
old farm buildings. After crossing Monte Ceceri (a 40-
minute climb, mostly quite gentle), the well-marked track
descends through farmland with immense views, passing
the crenellated tower of the eleventh-century Castel di
Vincigliata, and finishing at the suburb of Ponte a Mensola where you can get the bus back to Florence. Ponte a
Mensola itself isn't particularly interesting, though Boc-
caccio spent his childhood there; some good Trecento
works are to be found in the church of San Martino.

Food

Rather than eating in one of the flossy, overpriced Fiesole
restaurants, we suggest buying a picnic at the *rosticceria* just
off the Piazza Mino, at 21 Piazza Garibaldi, which makes
gourmet sandwiches, excellent grilled vegetables and good
salads.

LOGISTICS

FIESOLE–PONTE A MENSOLA, 2–2½ hours

🚌

FROM FLORENCE:

ATAF bus #7 from the station, the Duomo or Piazza San Marco
Length of journey: 20 minutes

GETTING BACK TO FLORENCE:

Pick up ATAF bus #10 in Ponte a Mensola.

ATAF Bus Information
Tel. toll-free from inside Italy:
800-424500
www.ataf.net

ⓘ
IN FIESOLE:

Piazza Mino, 37
Tel. 055-598720;
or toll-free inside Italy
800-414240
fax 055-598822
www.comune.fiesole.fi.it

Directions

Take Via Giuseppe Verdi **A** at the lower left corner of Piazza Mino as you're facing down from the cathedral. Passing some pretty houses and a panoramic view of Florence, you pick up red and white CAI 1 signs; follow these. At Via Adriano Mari, the route branches down to the right toward Monte Ceceri, through cypress woods. Take this route.

Keep an eye on the signs, as the route to the top of Monte Ceceri takes a sharp left at one point, off the main path; take this left. (It is 40 minutes from Fiesole to the summit at a slow stroll.)

After admiring the view, cross the summit and take the *left* trail 1. In 15 minutes you'll come out on Piazza Prato al Pini **B**. Turn right, again following route 1 (Via Peramonda). Here you glimpse real rural Tuscany: olive groves, old farmhouses. Florence, though just the other side of Monte Ceceri, seems a million miles away. At the end of the road, go right **C**. Follow this somewhat busy road (marked CAI 1, red and white) for 100 m to the STAM bus stop on the right **D**. CAI 1 trail goes off down a little track (by the bus stop) ~~by the green recycling containers~~; follow it. Well marked, it is a lovely path with immense views. The crenellated tower of Vincigliata is visible over distant poplars.

Pass through a farm ~~with horse~~s and olive groves, continuing gently downhill all this time. After 45 minutes, the path comes out on a little road **E**. Turn right toward the tower of Vincigliata. ~~Though not~~ open to the public, you can see enough of this eleventh-century ruin to get a sense of its brooding, monumental qualities.

Coming around the tower, take the dirt road **F** that branches off to the left through olive groves. ~~Pick up red and white markings again at a farmhouse~~, and go on. There is a fine, almost eye-level view of the Duomo to your right. Pass to the right of the gates of a villa, and then, where the path splits into 1 and 2, take 2 **G** to the right, a rugged little path down through oaks and laurels. This comes out on a small road. Turn right to Ponte a Mensola, where you can take the ATAF bus #10 back to Florence from the ~~STAM~~ bus stop.

FIESOLE TO MAIANO

A short, pretty walk through the cypress woods of Monte Ceceri and down a rugged mountain path (wear strong shoes) with gorgeous views over rural Tuscany. Maiano has two outstanding restaurants; it is well worth timing your walk to arrive there for lunch or dinner.

Food

Le Cave di Maiano in the quiet little village of Maiano has been attracting gourmets for years. A peaceful, unpretentious place with a terrace, this is the perfect setting for a long relaxing meal of northern Italian cooking at its best: beautifully prepared pastas and risottos, mouth-watering roasts of

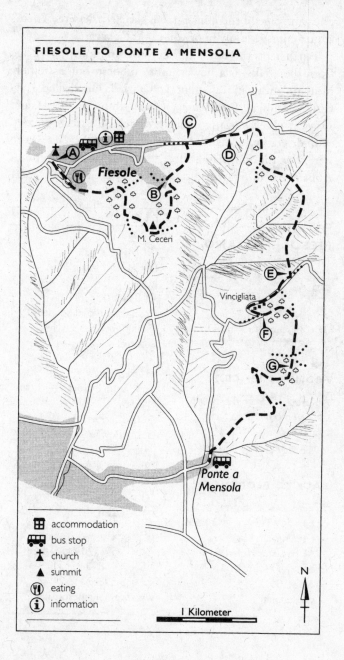

FIESOLE TO PONTE A MENSOLA

Fiesole

M. Ceceri

Vincigliata

Ponte a
Mensola

accommodation
bus stop
church
summit
eating
information

N

1 Kilometer

pheasant, pigeon and guinea-fowl, excellent desserts. There's a four-course set lunch, or you can eat à la carte.

Further up the hill—just as you come into the village from the walk—is a newer, more modest, but extremely pleasant Sardinian restaurant, La Graziella (also called Trattoria Casalinga). *Pane carasau,* a paper-thin fried bread, and *spaghetti alla bottarga,* a delicately flavored pasta sprinkled with dried, grated fish roe, are among the delicacies served here. For the full island effect, get a bottle of the robust Abbaia, but don't expect to do much walking afterward.

LOGISTICS

FIESOLE–MAIANO,
1–2 hours

🚌 Transport

🍴 Eating

ⓘ Miscellaneous info

🚌
FROM FLORENCE:

ATAF bus #7 from the station, the Duomo or Piazza San Marco
Length of journey: 20 minutes

BACK TO FLORENCE:

You can walk all the way back, or take an ATAF bus #17 back into town from Salviatino. ATAF Bus Information. Tel. toll-free from inside Italy: 800-424500
www.ataf.net

🍴

Le Cave di Maiano
Maiano
Tel. 055-59133
Closing day: Monday lunch
Price: Moderate to high
Reservations advisable.

La Graziella
Via Cave di Maiano, 18
Maiano
Tel. 055-599963
Closing Day: Tuesday
Price: Moderate
Reservations advisable.

ⓘ
IN FIESOLE:

Piazza Mino, 37
Tel. 055-598720; or toll-free inside Italy 800-414240;
fax 055-598822
www.comune.fiesole.fi.it

Directions

Take Via Giuseppe Verdi **A** at the lower left corner of Piazza Mino (as you're facing down from the cathedral). After passing some pretty houses and a panoramic view of Florence, you pick up red and white CAI 1 signs; follow these. At Via Adriano Mari, the route branches down to the right toward Monte Ceceri, through cypress woods. Take this route.

Keep an eye on the signs, as the route to the top of Monte Ceceri takes a sharp left at one point, off the main path; take this to the summit, which is about 40 minutes from Fiesole, at a slow stroll.

Cross the flat area at the summit to the path at the far left corner; almost immediately the Maiano path branches off to the right **B**. (It's signed.) Follow this; it's marked with CAI red and white signs (it's route 7, though no numbers are visible at this point). The path winds steeply down. BE ALERT: watch for a sharp left turn where the path levels after 70 m. Take this turn and you'll soon see CAI 7 marked. Ignore the many side tracks; the path is well marked in red and white.

After 10 minutes, as you reach a concrete telephone pole, there's a path down to your right **C**: take this path (there's a sign on a rock indicating that this is the way to Maiano), immediately branching right again at the fork. After another 10 minutes, there's another well-marked turn to the left **D**. Take this turn.

After 10 minutes, you'll come out on a dirt road; go right **E** (still marked 7). In a few minutes you'll come to an iron bar across the road marking the entrance to Maiano.

There is no bus to Florence from Maiano itself, but you can walk straight down the road for about 15 minutes, to Il Salviatino, where you'll find a 17 bus stop.

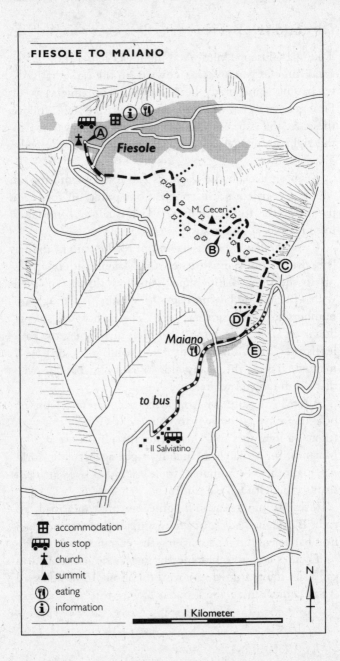

FIESOLE TO MAIANO

Fiesole

M. Ceceri

Maiano

to bus

Il Salviatino

accommodation
bus stop
church
summit
eating
information

N

I Kilometer

9 ■ MADONNA DEL SASSO RING WALK with Optional Spur to Santa Brigida

This is a perfect day walk from Florence, in the area of farmland and wooded slopes between the city and the Apennines known as the Mugello. The route takes you through a forest of massive evergreens and out past the Sanctuary of the Madonna del Sasso (see below). There's an optional spur to the pleasant old village of Santa Brigida with its small but exquisite Romanesque church, well worth seeing. A somewhat rugged 40-minute climb on the way back rewards you with an excellent shaded walk through chestnut woods and sweeping views over the Mugello.

The Madonna del Sasso

In the year 800 a pilgrim (St. Andrea) built a small oratory at Madonna del Sasso. Several centuries later, in 1484, some local shepherdesses had a vision of the Virgin Mary while praying for the recovery of their sick father. The father was cured, and in 1490 a church was built to commemorate the miracle. Wealthy Florentines adopted the church, hence its elegance. The altar contains a stone from the original oratory. Stairs to the right lead down to the chapel of the apparition and the cell of St. Andrea.

Food

Not a gastronomic outing. There's a cheerful pizzeria opposite the bus stop at Vetta le Croci (where you get off the bus from Florence), and a bar with food in Santa Brigida. For something more substantial you could try Dino, a popular restaurant (also a hotel) in nearby l'Olmo, serving Tuscan basics at reasonable prices. Otherwise this might be the occasion to visit the great produce market in Florence (the Mercato Centrale) and put together a picnic.

LOGISTICS

MADONNA DEL SASSO RING WALK (WITH OPTIONAL SPUR TO SANTA BRIGIDA), 3½ –4½ hours

🚌 Transport

🍴 Eating

🚌

FROM FLORENCE AND RETURN:

From Santa Maria station in Florence, take SITA bus #308 (Firenze–Grezzano). Make sure the bus you're taking stops at Olmo, as not all of them do.

NOTE: The place where you actually want to get dropped off is about a kilometer further on

from Olmo. Ask the driver to drop you at Vetta le Croci. To return to Florence, either use the same bus or take the optional spur to Santa Brigida, where there are many buses to Florence.

SITA
Tel. 055-47821 (or toll-free from inside Italy 800-373760)
www.sita-on-line.it

🍴

Dino
Via Faentina, 329; Olmo
Tel. 055-548932
Closing day: Wednesday, between October and May

PICNICS

The Mercato Centrale, a few blocks east of the train station

Directions

After getting off the bus at Vetta le Croci **A** (see Logistics section), turn back, taking the Fiesole road **B** (left), and then go first left again, following the sign to Madonna del Sasso. After a few minutes, coming to the brow of the hill, turn off the road onto a stony track on the left. You can leave your car here if you're driving. You'll see the red and white CAI marker here.

Follow the track around to the right to CAI route 8 **C** (iron bar across the path); take this route.

The route is shady (nice in summer), fairly gentle and fairly well marked in red and white. Ignore turnings unless otherwise stated.

After a while you enter a wood of massive evergreens, very somber and pleasantly cool. Passing a ruined house, you'll come in a few minutes to a T-junction; follow the red and white markers to the left. The path narrows and then soon after meets a small road **D**. Turn left on this road—the path merges with it. Look out for some bizarrely distorted chestnut trees on your right, survivors of the 1939 chestnut blight.

This road leads to the sanctuary of Madonna del Sasso, about an hour's walk from the start.

At the sanctuary the road ends and path 8 resumes. Follow path 8, looking out for a branch that leads off to the right down steps. This is route 8; take it **E**.

The steep, downhill, stony path goes out through an old stone gateway and passes a very pretty farmhouse. Continue straight on, joining a dirt track that leads through an olive grove. At the end, it comes out at a tarmac road **F**.

If you don't want to do the Santa Brigida spur, turn left here, and pick up the directions after spur.

MADONNA DEL SASSO RING WALK

Vetta le Croci Ⓐ

Ⓒ 00

Ⓑ

l'Olmo

🏢 accommodation
🚌 bus stop
✝ church
🍴 eating

SANTA BRIGIDA SPUR (and buses to Florence).
From **F***, go straight down the road for 50 m. At the bot-*
tom, turn sharp left, continuing straight on into the village
(45 minutes to here from the Madonna del Sasso).

    There are SITA buses from Santa Brigida to Florence.

    Leaving Santa Brigida, go back to where the CAI 8
dirt track came out on the tarmac road **F** *and turn right up-*
hill on route 5. You would have turned left onto this if you
hadn't gone into Santa Brigida.

TO CONTINUE WALK. After a steep 100-m climb, turn left
off the road onto a path **G** (well-marked CAI 5 to Ri-
paghera); there's a fine view back to Madonna del Sasso. A
40-minute fairly rugged climb follows, and then a fairly
level passage through a chestnut glade. After another 20
minutes, follow the path left along the ridge.

    In 5 minutes your path meets path 00. Take this left

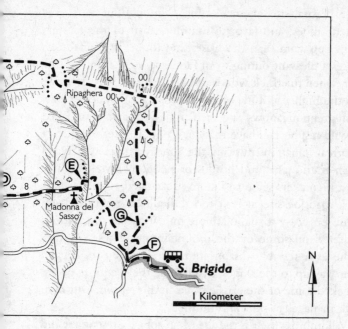

toward l'Olmo (signed). Your climbing is now more or less over. There are sweeping views and good places to picnic, though mostly wooded and shady with cool breezes.

Once your descent begins, continue along CAI 00, ignoring a turn to the right and other deviations. Once you get back to where route 8 started, you'll see an easy short-cut across fields to the bus stop and pizzeria.

10 ■ VALLOMBROSA/ SALTINO RING WALK with Optional Spur

Fifty km southeast of Florence, at the edge of the Prato-magno (a range of mountains stretching between the Florentine Valdarno and the Casentino), lies the forest of

Vallombrosa, site of an eleventh-century (but much restored) abbey, and favorite summer resort of the Florentines. Less wild than the Casentino forest, it nevertheless makes a pleasant outing from Florence, especially in summer, when the thick woods of beech and fir provide shade and the higher altitude offers the chance of a cool breeze. Lush green meadows, spectacular views and an abundance of wild raspberries have made it a popular area for one of the great Italian institutions, the Sunday Picnic, which can mean traffic jams and hordes of people. However, since most picnickers seem to like to stick together and to prefer a roadside site, it isn't too difficult to get away from them. Less easy to avoid are the military radar installations clustered on some of the mountaintops. These eyesores come as a terrible disappointment after you've slogged your way up to the ridges, and frankly they've more or less wrecked some of the classic walks in this region. Our own walk manages to skirt around them

Vallombrosa itself is the site of an abbey, a restaurant and not much else. The main resort center is Saltino, a reasonably attractive village 2 km from the abbey. The tourist office here can give you a trail map, but even though the trails are generally well marked, it's worth getting the real *sentieri* map. There's a ridge walk that runs from Monte Secchieta (1450 m) to Croce Pratomagno that many people recommend. However, you'd need a tent as there's no place to stay at the end other than a rudimentary shelter, Rifugio Buiti.

The Abbey

The abbey was founded in 1038 by a Florentine, Giovanni Gualberto. The story goes that after his brother was murdered, Gualberto caught the murderer but decided to show him mercy, whereupon a crucifix (now in the church of Santa Trinità in Florence) miraculously bowed down to him. In 1193 Gualberto was canonized, and the Vallombrosan Order then became a powerful presence in Tuscany for several centuries. The abbey has been extensively rebuilt and is no longer of great architectural interest, though the setting remains impressive. It still houses the Vallombrosan monks, and also functions as the arboretum for the Arezzo forestry institute, cultivating more than 1500 species of forest plants. To arrange a visit, call either the Vallombrosa Forestry Office or the Sede di Vallombrosa (see Logistics section).

The Walk

This is a half-day ring walk from Saltino, returning via the abbey at Vallombrosa, with an optional spur to Croce di Cardeto, well worth taking if you have the time (it adds about another 1½–2 hours to the itinerary). Much of it is through deep, somber woods of beech and fir, though once you reach higher ground the woods give way to lush clearings with stunning views over the tree-carpeted hills of Vallombrosa. Wild raspberries and blackberries grow along many stretches of the route. If you set off early in the morning you should have no trouble reaching Vallombrosa in time for lunch. Otherwise there are plenty of excellent spots for a picnic.

Food

Catering to Florentine weekenders and a resort clientele, the restaurants here tend to be a little fancier (though not at all pretentious) than in the nearby Casentino. Ristorante Giacomo in Saltino is a bustling, lively place where the sight of the waiters lofting platters of appetizers such as *tonno e fagioli* or great dishes of wild blackberries and ice cream through the crowded dining rooms, can hardly fail to raise the spirits. Prices are reasonable and the menu changes regularly. The *porchetta* (spit-roast suckling pig) spiced with juniper and lemon peel is well worth trying if they have it. Pizzas are served at night.

In Vallombrosa itself, the inexpensive little restaurant attached to the Pensione Medici serves the usual Tuscan standards, such as the thick vegetable and bread soup (*ribollita*) or ravioli with butter and sage, but done with care. The meats are well prepared, and on request, the chef made a particularly good, rather spicy *spaghetti carbonara* (cream, eggs and bacon). Our walk passes through here, and if you get off to a reasonably early start you should arrive in time for lunch.

LOGISTICS

VALLOMBROSA/ SALTINO RING WALK, WITH OPTIONAL SPUR, 2½ hours without spur, 4–4½ with spur

---

ⓘ Miscellaneous info

🚌 Transport

Ⓜ Maps, guidebooks and trail info

🍴 Eating

⊞ Accommodation

ⓘ

The APT office in Saltino is open April 15–September 15.
Tel. 055-862003

Saltino is part of the *comune* of Reggello. The Reggello *comune* has a useful Web site: **www. comune.reggello.fi.it**

🚌

FROM FLORENCE AND RETURN:

SITA
Tel. 055-47821 (or toll-free from inside Italy 800-373760)
www.sita-on-line.it

Route 321 (Firenze–Saltino)
About three buses per day
Length of journey: 1½ hours

Ⓜ

Carta dei Sentieri e Rifugi, 1:25,000. Massiccio del Pratomagno or any other 1:25,000 map available locally.

🍴

SALTINO

Ristorante Giacomo
Via Carducci, 12
Tel. 055-862185
Closing day: Wednesday

VALLOMBROSA

Pensione Medici
Via Tosi Vallombrosa, 123
Tel. 055-862017
Closing day: Tuesday

⊞

There is a good selection of hotels in Saltino, though in the summer you may have to call around a bit before you'll find an empty room. We liked Hotel Le

Terrazze very much, perhaps just for the novelty of it: very practical, straightforward and modern. Also very clean and bright.

Hotel Le Terrazze
Via della Chiesa, 1
Tel. 055-862030

Directions

Heading downhill, south out of Saltino, pass the Ristorante Giacomo on your right; across from the Giacomo on the left is a big parking lot. Here the main road bends off to the right, and a smaller road continues straight ahead uphill, signed "CAI 13, Secchieta"; take this road **A**.

The road climbs and then bends to the left where, as the asphalt gives way to a stony road, there's a deviation to the right, uphill, on a slightly smaller stony track **B**. Take this track (signed CAI 13 on a stone wall on the left of this road).

The road climbs fairly steeply, passing (about 20 minutes out of Saltino) a big old stone house on the left, Bocca del Lupo. (The IGM map is a little off here as regards the placement of Bocca del Lupo in relation to CAI 13.)

Passing through a very dark stretch of pine forest, you'll come to an intersection of several paths **C**. On the right is a little shrine to the Virgin. The path to the left is signed CAI 11; straight ahead and uphill is signed CAI 13, the path we take.

Another 10–15 minutes of climbing leads to a clearing giving a wide view over Regello, and a very nice pathway along the ridge (with many raspberries and blackberries) with views. It is very green and lush up here, even in summer, with dwarfed beeches, yellow broom, ferns, flowers and the tree-carpeted hills of the Vallombrosa stretching down into the valley. It is a very gentle, relaxing walk along here, with no climbing.

About an hour after leaving Saltino, you'll see the path being joined by path 12, coming in on the left **D**.

For a ring walk without the spur, turn left (onto path 12) here and skip over the following spur directions.

VALLOMBROSA/SALTINO RING WALK

Saltino

Vallombrosa

- ⊞ accommodation
- 🚌 bus stop
- ✝ church
- ▲ summit
- 🍴 eating
- ⓘ information

SPUR: Rather than turning left where the path is joined by path 12, continue straight ahead here, quickly reaching a fork by an old casetta forestale, forester's hut. Take the right fork, signed; "A1 CAI 14"; there is also a yellow sign for San Antonio.

*Watch on the left, in 50–100 m or so, for a smaller path off to the left where the bigger path we've been on makes a hairpin turn to the right. The bigger path (with the hairpin turn) is signed "CAI-FI-14 CR. CARDETO." Don't take this. Instead, take the smaller path off to the left **E** (which is CAI path 14 on trail maps).*

About 30–40 minutes after beginning the spur you'll pass a promontory/lookout and then an old stone hut on the left, with some stone seats outside, as you re-enter the woods. Just past here, there's a little turnoff leading to CAI 15. Ignore it and stay on the main path.

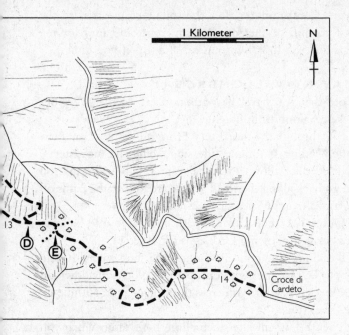

In another 20 minutes or so, you will pass a gate across the path (to stop cars). You now come out on a hilltop with a big wooden cross, the Croce di Cardeto, and a splendid view.

Return the same way you came, passing the forester's hut and reaching the fork where the spur began **D.** *CAI 13 is now on your left, CAI 12 on your right. Take the right-hand path (CAI 12) signed for "Vallombrosa."*

Continue along this way until you reach, after more than 1 km, a fork downhill to the right (CAI 10); take this fork **F**.

Stay on this very old path, descending toward Vallombrosa (ignoring a deviation to the right signed "al 9").

Eventually the path crosses an asphalt road and continues on the other side; soon after this there's a T-junction **G**. Turn right here, reaching the monastery on the left about 20–30 minutes after the spur reconnects with the ring portion of the route (about 3½ hours after leaving Saltino if you took the spur, or 1½ hours if you didn't).

LEAVING VALLOMBROSA

(Note that you have the option of taking the SITA bus back to Saltino from here.)

Pass through the monastery. From the front of the Pensione Medici Ristorante (the side facing the monastery), turn left onto the main asphalt Via S. G. Gualberto. You can go back along the road—there are foot traffic paths off the asphalt, and it's flat but trafficky.

Otherwise, return to the path you came into Vallombrosa on by following CAI signs for 10 & 11.

Reaching (in about 5 minutes) the fork where 10 and 11 split **G**, take the right fork, path 11 (you came down on 10). In a short while you cross the asphalt and continue up the other side.

There's a 10-minute steep climb here, after which you pass a turnoff on the right for 10/a; ignore it and carry straight on.

Shortly you will come to a T-junction **H**; go right (CAI 12), staying on this stony dirt road, bypassing the immediate turn on the left which is the continuation of path 11 (and will lead to path 13 if you want to go back the way you came).

About 45 minutes after leaving Vallombrosa, you'll reach a bar across the road as the path comes out on another dirt road; turn left (12/a).

In another 5 minutes, take a right downhill turnoff (at a lamppost on your left with a yellow sign for Vallombrosa); then take the first left (hairpin) turn you come to. This gravel road winds down in about 10 minutes to the main asphalt road where you turn left and go into Saltino.

THE CASENTINO

The vast forest reserves of the Casentino in the northern Apennines, where the Arno has its source, offer some of the most peaceful and fascinating walking in Italy. In easy striking distance of Florence, and yet utterly remote in atmosphere, the 26,200 acres of heavily wooded peaks running along the border of Tuscany and Emilia Romagna have been largely unchanged since the last Wurmian glaciation, ten thousand years ago.

Franciscan and Benedictine monks were attracted to the area in the late Middle Ages, and the three monasteries of Camaldoli, La Verna and Badia Prataglia are still the only major human settlements. The long association of these monastic orders with the idea of preserving wildlife (even today the monks at Camaldoli, still involved in the stewardship of the forest, observe a rule ordering them to plant five thousand trees a year) seems to have fostered an attitude of quiet respect for the area—not always the case with Italy's wilderness.

The forest is crisscrossed with well-marked trails that follow old mule tracks or paths between the monasteries. There are still traces of the *vie dei legni,* or wood roads, dating from centuries ago when the Grand Duchy of Tuscany used the tallest and straightest trees as masts for its navy at Pisa, dragging the vast trunks (they had to be at least 90 feet high to qualify) through the forest with teams of oxen. Streams, waterfalls (including the famous cascade of Acquacheta, immortalized by Dante in the *Inferno*), green alpine meadows, high breezy ridges with spectacular views, and the deep shade of the forest itself make the area pleasant

for walking even in summer; a perfect antidote to the sti-
fling bustle of Florence in July and August.

From a naturalist's point of view, the Casentino is extraordinarily rich. Italy's first Natural Integral Park, the Sasso
Fratino, was established inside the forest in 1959 as an en-
clave for ecological research. Entry is restricted, but you
don't need to go inside it to experience the wealth of local
wildlife. Populations of red deer, fallow deer, mountain
sheep and the ubiquitous wild boar thrive. The Apennine
wolf has made a comeback here, the most northerly exten-
sion of its territory to date. Woodpeckers—green, spotted and
the rarer black—flit through the trees (the hysterical chat-
ter belongs to the green). From the high clearings you can
see eagle-owls, kites, goshawks and allegedly even golden
eagles circling over the valleys. Up to about 800 m the woods
have a wide variety of deciduous trees: hornbeam, turkey
oak, maple, lime, elm and chestnut (at one time a principal food source for the region). White fir, mountain ash
and beech trees dominate the higher altitudes. The twist-
ing, wind-stunted, silvery limbs of the ridge-top beeches
in particular give the walks there a mysterious, enchanted
quality. The flowers, too, are stunning: anemone, primula
and violets in the woods; gentian and narcissi in the meadows. Rare species of saxifrage grow in the rocks at the top
of Monte Falco, where you can also find black myrtle and
the extremely rare red myrtle. Flower charts have been set
up at one or two of the mountain refuges you pass on your
way, to help you identify the mass of different species.

The Walks

The itineraries we have selected for this area include three
to four days' worth of connected but separable walks, beginning at the monastery of Camaldoli and finishing in San
Benedetto in Alpe. Public transport is available between Florence and all of the main staging-posts (though Campigna
is a bit of a haul; see the Logistics section for more details),

making it easy to do only a particular section of the itinerary, if you prefer.

Also contained in this section are day or half-day ring walks in Camaldoli and Badia Prataglia.

These are mountain hikes of moderate difficulty, steep in places but with a high ratio of reward to effort. Remember to bring food and water, something to keep you dry and, if possible, a compass.

Food

Restaurants in the area go in for simple but robust dishes. The local fauna turn up in stews, salami and *scottiglie* (a form of grilling). Porcini mushrooms, raspberries and wild strawberries grow abundantly in parts of the woods; these are always worth ordering when the restaurant has them in fresh. Waverley Root, an authority on Italian cuisine, recommends the region's small juicy hams and delicately flavoured trout. He notes that the best chickens in Italy are raised in the Arno valley, below the forest, and awards the local *vin santo* (equivalent of the French Sauternes) second prize in all of Italy, after those of the Val di Pesa. Local dishes include *acquacotta* (an onion or vegetable soup thickened with egg) as well as cakes and polentas made of chestnut flour.

11 ■ CASENTINO EXCURSION

The walks in this chapter are now all within the protection of one of Italy's newer national parks, the Parco Nazionale delle Foreste Casentinesi. There are several visitor centers located in the villages lying either within the boundaries or on the outskirts of the park, each with a different theme, some open year-round. New paths have been signed and maps made. Badia Prataglia has become one of the main

*gateways to the park, with a year-round information center
and plenty of good accommodations.*

*Thus, like the next chapter's Garfagnana, the Casentino
will now be much more accessible to walkers and once you
get there, you'll find lots of information and lots of new
walks. We've done a basic update of our Logistics sections,
and the Web sites listed give information—in English—on
all aspects of the park: photographs, descriptions of the visitor
centers, hotel and other accommodation listings, walking itineraries, and much more. The walks we did may have been
slightly rerouted now, and we suggest following the newer
signings, though the basic idea will be the same (that is, the
itineraries will still go from the same starting point to the same
destination). The new 1:25,000 map Parco Nazionale
delle Foreste Casentinesi, Monte Falterona e Campigna
is widely available, and with that in hand, you should find
no end of enjoyment in this vast walker's paradise.*

This three- or four-day route offers some of the best
walking in the northern environs of Florence. If you have
the time, it's a wonderful way to get a rest from the push
and shove of sightseeing and to experience a superb bit of
countryside. The area is of great interest for its enormous
variety of natural vegetation and, because of the prohibi-
tion of hunting, its rich animal and bird life.

The ambience differs from that of other walks in this
book (with the exception of those in the Sibillini) in that
there is less interaction with human settlements. In this
sense, it bears a closer resemblance to the system of hiking
trails found across state and national forest reserves in the US
than most of our other walks, which revolve more closely
around the larger towns. For this reason, you should definitely have one of the trail maps listed in the Logistics
section. The *Parco Nazionale, Foreste Casentinesi, Monte Falterona e Campigna* 1:50,000–scale map covers the entire excursion. The 1:25,000 maps don't, so you will need three
of them (see individual Logistics sections).

The route begins at the monastery of Camaldoli and then climbs through mixed woods and high mountain meadows, eventually crossing the Monte Falterona massif, the highest peaks of the Tosco-Romagnola Apennines and the source of the Arno river. The last day of the itinerary brings you to the Acquacheta Falls and the mountain village of San Benedetto.

If you haven't the time or the inclination to do the whole walk, any part of it can be done on its own (the only difficulty being with the Camaldoli–Campigna and Campigna–Castagno d'Andrea segments, as there is no easy public transport link between Campigna and Florence; though it's not too difficult to hitch between Campigna and Stia, from which there are both trains and buses to Florence.) If you opt for only a segment of the itinerary, we particularly recommend the Camaldoli–Castagno d'Andrea segment, which takes you through the best parts of the forests and over the impressive Monte Falterona massif. If you leave early in the morning from Florence (though you might want to consider leaving Florence late in the day and spending the night in Camaldoli instead) this segment can be accomplished spending only one night (in Campigna) away from Florence, busing back from Castagno d'Andrea at the end of the second day.

Because of the very limited overnight options in this neck of the woods (i.e., if one place is full, you don't have a lot of alternatives nearby), we strongly recommend booking all your hotel accommodations before leaving Florence, unless you're camping. However, don't be overly concerned if you don't reach anyone at the GEA rifugio in Castagna d'Andrea; it is unlikely to be full, and it is the policy of all the mountain refuges to accommodate anyone who shows up.

There is a shop or bar in each of the stopover points that can furnish you with picnic provisions.

Finally, a note on Il Muraglione. While none of the stopovers on this excursion are big towns, Il Muraglione is not a town at all, but literally just the hotel/restaurant. Therefore, unless you're planning to bus back to Florence from Il Muraglione, you may want to consider either taking at a very leisurely pace the walk from Castagno d'Andrea to Il Muraglione in order to arrive there rather late in the day, or on the other hand, getting an early start from Castagno and ploughing on through to San Benedetto. Be forewarned, however, that this latter option is a real haul.

CAMALDOLI TO CAMPIGNA

One of the three great monastic centers of the forest, Camaldoli still draws a fair number of pilgrims and tourists, especially in summer. It's a tiny place, pleasantly set in its densely wooded mountains.

The village consists of the monastery and little else; 300 m uphill is the hermitage (Sacro Eremo di Camaldoli) founded in 1012 by S. Romualdo, a Benedictine monk who wanted to revive the ascetic spirit of the earliest Christian communities and was given the use of the forest by Count Maldolo (thus the name). Despite its remoteness and the austerity of its rule, the place quickly attracted large numbers of visitors—not only pilgrims, but also minstrels, jesters, drunken soldiers and even prostitutes, who drifted there from the nearby court of Count Guido of Poppi. Not surprisingly, these visitors interfered with the solitary meditations of the hermits. Romualdo's solution was to establish a monastery lower down the mountain, specifically to accommodate visitors and look after the forest domains. This has been remodeled considerably over the centuries, but remains interesting for portions of the original cloisters and for its sixteenth-century pharmacy where the monks sell their herbal preparations. Also worth a visit is the church, the Chiesa Maggiore, the interior of which was decorated by Vasari.

The hermitage is as austere as ever. The twenty little

cottages where the hermits still live in silence, each with their own kitchen garden and chapel, remain strictly off-limits. There is a prototype of the cottages, however, which is interesting to visit. There are also a gift shop and a small snack bar.

One of the most enjoyable in the area, this walk begins with a fairly steep climb through fir and beech woods from Camaldoli to the Eremo (you can take a bus) and then climbs again just beyond the Eremo, though this second climb is alleviated in summer by more raspberry bushes growing along the side of the trail than most people will have seen in their lives. After this climb, the path is simply one delight after another, an easy amble through high mountain meadows and mixed woods (predominantly turkey oak but also black and white hornbeams, maples and other oaks), culminating at Poggio Scala, one of the best panoramic points of the park. In the meadows surrounding the knoll, violet crocuses grow in spring, followed later by the big yellow flowers of a rare ranunculus.

From there the trail carries on to Passo della Calla and then a short descent leads you into Campigna and the civilized delights of the eighteenth-century grand-ducal palace, now transformed into an *albergo*.

Food

Attached to the Albergo Camaldoli is the Ristorante Camaldoli, a friendly, unpretentious place with attractive outdoor seating and a menu that makes a good attempt to incorporate the local specialities. For dedicated carnivores, the huge antipasto of cured stag, fallow deer, roe deer and wild boar is a must, though there is no way of telling which meat belongs to which animal. The hare sauce on the *tagliatelle alla lepre* is less a sauce than a stew poured over the pasta—it's tasty and extremely substantial.

The Albergo Camaldoli has a deli that sells the above-mentioned cured hams and salami, and is a good place to shop for a picnic.

The Granduca in Campigna is something of a culinary oasis. The food, though not of huge variety, is extremely well prepared. The salads are excellent. There's a delicious *tagliatelle* with fresh porcini prepared, unusually, with a little tomato. The *tortello* stuffed with potato and onion in butter and sage is also good, and the *panna cotta* with myrtles is wonderful.

LOGISTICS

CAMALDOLI–CAMPIGNA, 3½ –4½ hours

(i) Miscellaneous info

🚌 Transport

Ⓜ Maps, guidebooks and trail info

🍴 Eating

⊞ Accommodation

(i)

There are various visitor centers serving the park. The park's Web site is an excellent source of information (available in English) when planning your trip. It has very useful links as well:
www.parks.it/parco.nazionale.for.casentinesi
Another useful site for the region (again, with good links) is:
www.badiaprataglia.com
Stia Tourist Office, tel. 0575-504106

🚌 **BY TRAIN**

From Florence take the train to Arezzo (frequent service, journey time ¾ – 1½ hours, depending on which train you get), then change for the smaller LFI line (departing from the main railway station) to Bibbieno (Pratovecchio/Stia train, frequent service, journey time to Bibbieno about 45 minutes). At Bibbieno, change for the LFI bus to Camaldoli (about 4 to 6 per day, journey time 20–30 minutes).

Train info (Firenze to Arezzo portion): **www.trenitalia.it**
Tel. toll-free inside Italy: 848-888088

LFI info: **www.lfi.it**
Tel. 0575-39881 or 0575-324294

BY BUS

From Florence take the SITA bus to Bibbieno, then change for the LFI bus as above.

SITA
Tel. 055-47821 (or toll-free
from inside Italy 800-373760)
www.sita-on-line.it
Florence
Route 320
About eight buses per day
Length of journey: About 2½ hours

Getting Back from Campigna

Getting back to Florence
from Campigna is not very
convenient. You have to take the
ATR bus to Forli, a 2-hour ride,
then go from Forli to Il
Muraglione, where you get a
SITA or STAM bus back to
Florence; ATW there are only
two buses a day from Il
Muraglione to Florence, so you
might have to stay overnight in
Il Muraglione.

The only other option is to
hitch from Campigna to Stia
(about 16 km, all on the same
road), from which there are
numerous train and bus connections back to Florence. You
could also try the Stia tourist
office (phone number above)
for a taxi.

Ⓜ
SELCA 1:25,000 Carta Escursionistica: Parco Nazionale delle
Foreste Casentinesi. Available in
the park centers and at local
bookshops.

🍴
CAMALDOLI

Ristorante Camaldoli

Attached to Albergo Camaldoli
Tel. 0575-556073

CAMPIGNA

Granduca
Tel. 0543-980051

Lo Scoiattolo
Tel. 0543-980052
email:
albscoiattolo@hotmail.com

🏨
CAMALDOLI

La Foresta
Tel. 0575-556015
Price: Inexpensive

Albergo Camaldoli
Tel. 0575-556073
Price: Inexpensive

Il Rustichello
Via del Corniolo, 14
Tel. 0575-556046
Price: Moderate

Foresteria del Monastero di
Camaldoli
Tel. 0575-556013
Price: Inexpensive; this is basi-
cally hostel lodging in the
monastery.

CAMPIGNA

Granduca
Tel. 0543-980051
Price: Moderate

Lo Scoiattolo
Tel. 0543-980052
email:
albscoiattolo@hotmail.com
Price: Double room, 52 euros

There are three *rifugi* at or near Passo La Calla; call ahead to confirm bed and meals.

1. Rifugio La Calla (at Passo La Calla); *tel.* 0575-58966
2. Rifugio La Burraia (near Passo La Calla; see your hiking map); *tel.* 0543-980053
3. Rifugio citta Forli; *tel.* 0543-980074
   email: rifugio.citta.forli@comunic.it

CAMPING

Campeggio Pucini, tel. 0575-556006
Fonte al Menchino, tel. 0575-556157

ⓘ
1. Make all hotel reservations before starting this walk.
2. There are a couple of LFI buses daily between Camaldoli and the Eremo (which cuts out some significant climbing).
3. There is a small ornithology museum at Camaldoli, open in the summer.

Directions

Leaving Camaldoli, pass the monastery on your right and continue straight ahead (ignoring the right turn across the bridge), passing PT (post office) on your left. Take the asphalt road here, not the footpath to its left.

Pass a chapel on the right and then cross a stone bridge; 75 m or so after this, take the footpath to the right (by a CAI 72 mark) **A**.

Following CAI marks, the path goes through firs, follows along a stream and crosses an asphalt road. The second time it crosses the asphalt, don't cross over, but turn left onto the asphalt (CAI signed); the path goes off again in about 10 m, to the left. The way is well signed here by the CAI; just follow their marks.

Shortly after this, the path crosses a stream and continues on the left side of the stream, but this isn't altogether obvious as there's a path going straight along the right side too. There's a CAI mark here, intimating that you cross the stream, but no CAI sign on the other side to confirm. You *do* cross however, and the path begins to climb steeply (and soon comes to a CAI mark).

About 40 minutes after leaving Camaldoli, the path comes out on the asphalt again at Tre Croci (three wooden crosses) **B**. Cross over; the CAI mark is just beyond the crosses, though it's not visible from the road. Ten minutes later, you reach the Sacro Eremo di Camaldoli.

Leaving the Eremo, pass in front of it, keeping it on your right. At its edge, take the dirt and stone path leading uphill to the right of the asphalt road and skirting the wall of the Eremo. Follow the wall to the back of the Eremo, where you'll see the path straight ahead signed by CAI (72). (This is also a section of the long-distance GEA trail.)

After a short steep climb, the path turns right **C** for Passo Bertone—well signed—and continues to climb.

About 40 minutes after leaving the Eremo, you'll come out on a dirt road; turn left. There is a level walk along here, shady, which soon passes the beautiful little meadow, Prato Bertone, on the right.

Pass the sign and path for "Batti Locchio, 1.580 km."

About 15 minutes later, after walking through mixed meadows and patches of woodland, you'll come to an open space with several paths serving all directions. This is Giogo Seccheta. Follow the CAI-marked trail ahead to the right and uphill.

About 2 km later (at Passo Porcareccio), CAI 78 leads down to the left. *Don't* take it. In another 10 minutes or so (about 1 km), you'll come to the wayside shrine of the Madonna del Fuoco on your right. As you face it there's a hill to your right with a path up it: this is Poggio Scala, one of the great panoramic points of the park. Don't miss it.

Continuing on through beech wood, you'll reach in another half hour or so the pass at Pian Tombesi, 1403 m

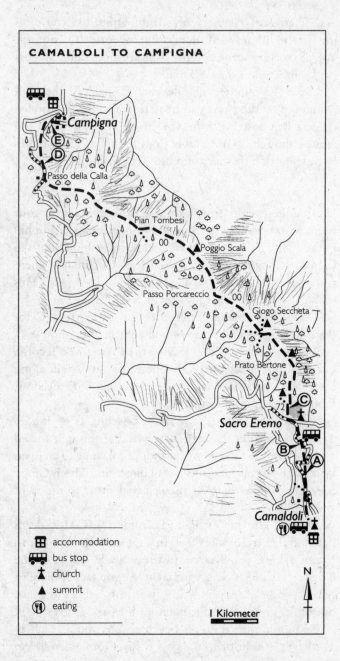

CAMALDOLI TO CAMPIGNA

Campigna

E
D

Passo della Calla

Pian Tombesi

00

Poggio Scala

Passo Porcareccio

00

Giogo Seccheta

Prato Bertone

C

72

Sacro Eremo

B
A

Camaldoli

accommodation
bus stop
church
summit
eating

N

1 Kilometer

(sign on right of path), and another half hour or so beyond here the asphalt road at Passo della Calla.

At Passo della Calla there are several CAI routes marked. Our route is not, at this time, marked by CAI. Turn right onto the main asphalt road and follow it downhill toward Campigna.

About ½ km from Passo della Calla (past a metal guardrail on the right) there's a small path off to the right downhill—you'll see a small wooden sign, "Croce del Piccino 37; Campigna," with red CAI marks too. Take this path **D**.

Follow the CAI marks.

The path comes out on a bend in the asphalt road again (about 10 minutes from Passo della Calla), but don't actually walk onto the road; instead, turn right and walk *behind* the guardrail, following the path as it drops down to the right of the road here.

This is a really pretty path—either cut out of rock, or in the steep parts beautifully built with small slabs of stone driven vertically into the ground. It's shady and all downhill.

The path crosses over a stone and wood bridge and then climbs a bit to the left of a stone basin where the stream forms a pool. Just beyond there, the path comes out at an asphalt intersection—go downhill to the right **E**, reaching the hamlet of Campigna about half an hour after leaving Passo della Calla.

CAMPIGNA TO CASTAGNO D'ANDREA

This walk leads over the principal peaks of the Parco Nazionale di Monte Falterona, Campigna e Foreste Casentinesi, down through chestnut glades and meadows full of wild flowers (poppies, broom, gentians, irises, etc.) to the small town of Castagno d'Andrea.

The Monte Falterona massif divides the plains of the Mugello and Casentino. In reality Monte Falco, at 1658 m, is the highest peak, but because of its fame as the source of the river Arno, it is Monte Falterona's name that has been given to this group of peaks.

The slopes are covered with dense fir groves and beech woods. Anemone, narcissus, black myrtle and the extremely rare red myrtle grow in the clearings near the summit.

In spring it can be foggy up here, but on clear days the summit offers spectacular views over a large part of Tuscany. The cliff of La Verna and the Czhianti valley beyond are visible to the south, to the north the mountains of San Benedetto, and to the west the peaks of Abetone and the Garfagnana.

Food

At present the only restaurant in Castagno d'Andrea is the *osteria,* where you need to let the proprietor know a little in advance that you'll be eating there. The food is plentiful, though a bit rough and ready and more or less limited to what the proprietor happens to have in his cupboard. We had ravioli in a robust tomato sauce and a good *pasta in brodo* (pasta in broth). An otherwise straightforward (and fresh) salad had the perplexing addition of some large raw artichokes. Avoid the steak *fiorentina* unless you enjoy chewing on shoe leather.

There's a kitchen at the rifugio (GEA), but if you don't feel like cooking for yourself, this place is congenial and extremely cheap.

LOGISTICS

CAMPIGNA–CASTAGNO D'ANDREA, 5–6½ hours

ⓘ Miscellaneous info

🚌 Transport

Ⓜ Maps, guidebooks and trail info

🅬 Eating

⊞ Accommodation

ⓘ

There are various visitor centers serving the park. The park's Web site is an excellent source of information (available in English) when planning your trip. It has very useful links as well:
www.parks.it/parco. nazionale.for. casentinesi

Castagno d'Andrea is part of the San Godenzo comune. The comune's Web site has useful information: **www.comune. san-godenzo.fi.it**
Another useful site for the region (again, with good links) is: **www.badiaprataglia.com**

Stia tourist office, *tel.* 0575-504106

🚌

FROM FLORENCE TO CAMPIGNA:

As discussed in the previous walk, getting to Campigna from Florence is not very convenient. If you don't mind hitching, you can take the train from Florence

THE CASENTINO

to Arezzo, then change for the smaller LFI train line that goes from Arezzo to Pratovecchio/Stia, which you take to Stia. Then you have to hitch either to Campigna (about 16 km, all on the same road) or to Passo della Calla (about 13 km on the road to Campigna), where you can pick up our walk directions from the previous itinerary and walk the half hour or so from Passo della Calla to Campigna. Alternatively you could try the Stia tourist office (phone number above) for a taxi.

BY TRAIN

From Florence take the train to Arezzo (frequent service, journey time ¾ –1½ hours, depending on which train you get), then change for the smaller LFI line (departing from the main railway station) to Stia (the Pratovecchio/Stia train, frequent service, journey time from Arezzo to Stia is just over an hour).
Train info (Firenze to Arezzo portion): **www.trenitalia.it**
Tel. toll-free inside Italy: 848-888088

LFI info: **www.lfi.it**
Tel. 0575-39881 or 0575-324294

BY BUS

From Florence take the SITA bus to Stia, then hitch or take a taxi from Stia, as explained above.

SITA
Tel. 055-47821 (or toll-free from inside Italy 800-373760)
www.sita-on-line.it
Florence
Route 320
About four buses per day; this is the same line that goes to Bibbieno, but you usually have to change at Ponticelli for Stia.
Length of journey: Just under 2 hours

FROM CASTAGNO D'ANDREA TO FLORENCE:

NOTE: If you can get your hands on a STAM bus schedule, it's very useful for traveling between Florence and either Castagno D'Andrea or Passo del Muraglione should you be picking up or leaving the itinerary at either of these points. It lists not only STAM buses but also SITA and FS (railroad) schedules. This is particularly useful because SITA and STAM sometimes connect with each other or with the FS in Dicomano or Pontassieve, rather than doing the whole route themselves.

SITA
Tel. 055-47821 (or toll-free from inside Italy 800-373760)
www.sita-on-line.it
Florence
Route 311

Six or seven buses a day. Sometimes you have to change in San Godenzo and/or Dicomano. At Dicomano you can also connect with the train back to Florence if you prefer.
Length of journey: Just over 2 hours

STAM or Florentia
Tel. 055-8490505
www.florentiabus.it
There are STAM or Florentia buses from Castagno to Dicomano, where you can connect with the train.

Ⓜ
SELCA 1:25,000 Carta Escursionistica, Parco Nazionale delle Foreste Casentinesi. Available in the park centers and at local bookshops.

🅿️
Osteria Il Rifugio
Via del Borgo, 7; Castagno d'Andrea
Tel. 055-8374380

⊞
There's a B&B in Castagno, but otherwise it's the GEA Rifugio; very basic hostel-type accommodations.

G.E.A. Rifugio
Via del Borgo, 10
Tel. 055-8375029
Price: Very inexpensive

I Castagni (B&B)
Via di Falterona, 3
Tel. 055-8375077
cell 348-8833281
www.affittaicastagni.it

Directions

The first part of this trail is well marked by CAI.

With the front of Albergo Lo Scoiattolo on your right (the Granduca Hotel down the road behind you) you are facing a fork. The right uphill prong of this fork has a little wooden sign pointing to La Calla. Take this path **A**.

Very soon there's an intersection with a bigger asphalt road; cross over and take the smaller asphalt road leading off the main road on the right, uphill. This smaller road is signed by CAI, and there's also a small wooden sign, "Fangacci 371." The asphalt ends almost immediately and is replaced by a dirt and stone road that leads uphill through tall firs.

When the road forks (after about 100 m), take the right-hand uphill option **B**.

Soon you'll pass on your left a feature of these woods—beehives. The whole forest hums with the sound of the bees, too high overhead to be seen.

Continue on this path (also marked in green and white here), ignoring deviations (including one to the left about 20 minutes out of Campigna and another one 10–15 minutes later, a turnoff to the left over a stone and wood bridge crossing a stream, a CAI path marked by a small wooden sign on other side of the bridge, "371 Strada Provinciale" **C**).

About half an hour later, the path comes out on a big parking lot. Cross to the far end. Across the main road from here you'll see a smaller tarmac uphill road (a military road) whose entrance is marked by the CAI on a tree to the left of it. Take this road **D**.

Following this military road to the end, you'll see a military radar installation. A red-and-white-marked path drops down from the left; take it to the right **E**. This is the long-distance GEA trail.

You may encounter fog along this stretch of mixed beech wood and pasture. A huge structure looms: the top of the ski lift. The path is very clearly marked red and white "00," and sometimes GEA.

At the top of Monte Falco a signpost points right to Fontanella, but we keep going *straight on.*

In about 15–20 minutes, after a rough descent, the 00 path branches up to the right, marked red/white/red on a tree; take this **F**. There is then a steep but mercifully short ascent (about 10 minutes) across a small grassy knoll, back into woodland until you come to a turnoff on the right marked "16"; *don't* take this. The top of Monte Falterona is 50 m past this turning, marked by a rock with a brass plaque noting it as part of the Franciscan way, and a big cross. Be alert here, as it's very easy to take the wrong turn at the cross. Unless you want to go to the mouth of the Arno, DO NOT follow the leftward 00 path marked on a rock just beyond the path. Instead head to your right **G**. The 00 path you do want is in the far right corner of the little pasture. (ATW the marks are painted on saplings.) After 50 m of grass descent, look for the red/white/red sign ahead of you leading into some woods across a wooden fence. Very steep at first, the path then levels off down along a wooded ridge with immense views.

About a half hour from the summit you'll come to a grassy clearing. Path 17 is off to the right. It goes down to the top of the road to Castagno, but you can continue along the ridge by going straight ahead across the clearing, on the same red/white/red 00 trail. It branches to the left almost immediately—you want, not the broad uphill trail, but the narrow, less steep one.

After 15 minutes, you'll come to a long (100 m) grassy area with broom and purple columbines. The path re-enters enters the wood at the end of this on the right. Bear around to the right, as the path goes on in and out of woodland and meadow. It's usually easy to find the red and white marked trees at the end of meadows leading back into woods. The second big meadow is less easy, as the path is tucked away at the far left corner. A steep descent crosses a tiny stream, probably dry in summer.

There is a good picnic spot here, amid a profusion of flowers on a clearing overlooking Castagno.

Continue on 00 until you see a marked tree indicating "18" to the right (very easy to see as it's just in front of you). Take this right turn (18) downhill. The path winds a lot. Keep your eyes open for red and white markers; you should seldom be more than 30 m from one unless you're out of the woods. The path crosses a number of small streams, goes out of the woods across a scrub of broom and dog roses (fewer markings, narrow path) then goes back into the woods. The sound of streams is everywhere in spring, and violets and forget-me-nots.

Continuing on down, the path moves from beech to chestnut *castagno* trees; look for the saw-toothed leaves.

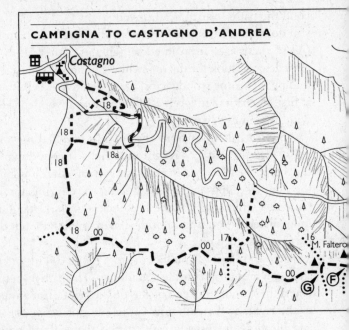

CAMPIGNA TO CASTAGNO D'ANDREA

The flora changes completely as you travel from a lovely chestnut glade full of flowers to an exquisitely fragrant pine grove.

In just over 1 km from the point where you left path 00 for path 18, path 18/a appears on the right. Both paths 18 and 18/a will take you to the road into Castagno (on which you turn left), but 18 is the more direct of the two. However, you may find yourself on 18/a without realizing you ever left 18.

Path 18/a goes down into a valley full of ferns and delicate grasses, and then winds down through a series of small fields; always look for signs on trees, etc., before going too far in any direction. After crossing a little footbridge over a stream, the path comes out at a narrow tarmac road. This is the road into Castagno, to the left. CAI signs direct you to the center of the village, about another 20 minutes from here.

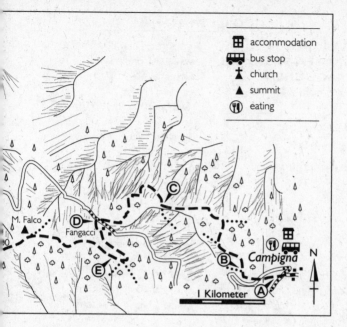

CASTAGNO D'ANDREA TO PASSO DEL MURAGLIONE

This is a rugged, 3-hour walk, much of it through a heavenly valley with streams, ruined cottages overgrown with wild mint and oregano, and beautiful old farm buildings. A steep ascent at the end brings you to the high pass of Il Muraglione, with a memorial wall erected to mark the building of a road across the Apennines connecting the Adriatic and Tyrrhenian seas. It also marks the border between Tuscany and Romagna.

If you're feeling extremely energetic you can go on from here to San Benedetto in the same day, but it's a very long day's match, and it would certainly be more relaxing to stay here in Il Muraglione; though be warned, there's nothing here except the wall, the *albergo* and the landscape.

LOGISTICS

CASTAGNO D'ANDREA–PASSO DEL MURAGLIONE,
about 3 hours

ⓘ   Miscellaneous info

🚌   Transport

Ⓜ   Maps, guidebooks and trail info

🍴   Eating

🎴   Accommodation

ⓘ

There are various visitor centers serving the park. The park's Web site is an excellent source of information (available in English) when planning your trip. It has very useful links as well:
www.parks.it/parco. nazionale.for.casentinesi
   Passo del Muraglione is part of the San Godenzo comune. The comune's Web site has useful information:
www.comune.san-godenzo.fi.it
   Another useful site for the region (again, with good links) is:
www.badiaprataglia.com

🚌

For Castagno d'Andrea, see previous walk's Logistics section.

PASSO DEL MURAGLIONE

SITA
Tel. 055-47821 (or toll-free

from inside Italy 800-373760)
www.sita-on-line.it
Florence
Route 311
Two buses per day (ATW 8:15 and 16:25)
Length of journey: About 2 hours

STAM
Tel. 055-8490505

Florentia
Tel. 055-8490505
www.florentiabus.it

STAM or Florentia run buses to Dicomano, where you can connect with a train to Florence. Infrequent service, so check ahead.

Ⓜ

SELCA 1:25,000 Carta Escursionistica: Parco Nazionale delle Foreste Casentinesi. Available in the park centers and at local bookshops.

🍴

Ristorante-Albergo Il Muraglione
Il Muraglione, 87
Tel. 055-8374393
Price: Moderate
Closing day: Tuesday in winter, otherwise always open

🎴

Ristorante-Albergo Il Muraglione

Il Muraglione, 87
Tel. 055-8374393
Price: Moderate

Rifugio Ferrari
Il Muraglione 82/83
Tel. 055-8373009
Price: Inexpensive;
basic hostel lodging

Directions

Go down the hill from the *rifugio* at Castagno and turn right past the church out of the village.

Turn right at the stop sign, then left on Via San Martino, which is CAI route 14 **A**. There's a sign here with nature walks from Castagno marked out.

The road crosses a stream and winds uphill. At the little cemetery, go left on CAI 14/b. After 25 m, the road forks; take the lower, right fork **B**.

The path climbs down this beautiful valley of woods and wild roses. As you approach the entrance to a stunning cluster of old farm buildings, the path cuts sharply down to the left (look for the sign on a tree) at Serignana.

The trail is well marked with red and white paint blazes. Go on down until you come to a little stone house. Just past it there's an intersection; take a sharp right **C** onto trail 6/b (signed on a little tree) toward Il Muraglione.

For the next 3½ km, follow marked trail 6/b. In case you find it hard to pick up the marks (as always, they tend not to be there when you most need them), the following directions should make it easier.

Cross a narrow footbridge over a stream. Here is another gorgeous valley. Climb up, passing a waterfall down to your right. After about 3 minutes you come to a junction **D**; continue straight over it uphill, keeping to 6/b.

The steep ascent takes you through a little wooden gate. In another couple of minutes, where the path bends sharply to the left, there's a right turn across a stream: take this (you'll soon see a red and white marker).

The path zigzags past a ruined cottage, passing to the

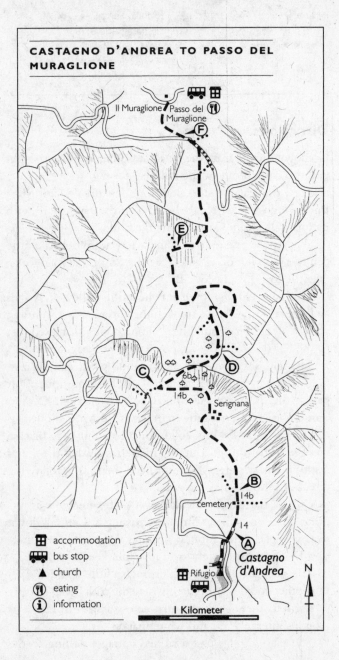

CASTAGNO D'ANDREA TO PASSO DEL MURAGLIONE

Il Muraglione Passo del Muraglione

F

E

D

C

6b
14b

Serignana

B

14b

cemetery

14

A

Castagno d'Andrea

Rifugio

accommodation
bus stop
church
eating
information

N

1 Kilometer

back of it, and then turns left again. Continue on up past some lovely old ruined farm buildings, where the path bends around to the right. You can look back across the valley and see where you came from.

Past the ruins you go through a wide gate, and then up to the *right* (not straight on). At the top, follow markings straight ahead (not right). You come to a clearly marked junction **E**. Go up to the right toward Il Muraglione (marked).

After 1 km you approach the road, with a concrete telephone pole ahead. Before you get to the road, the path forks. Take the left, downhill fork. In 75 m you reach the road. Turn left. Ignoring the first path up to the right, proceed about 100 m to a narrow path marked red and white leading up off the road to the right. Take this **F**. It is CAI 6.

A 15-minute steep ascent brings you to Il Muraglione—bar, restaurant, hotel. Magnificent view.

PASSO DEL MURAGLIONE TO SAN BENEDETTO IN ALPE

A long but exceptionally pretty walk through woods and meadows, ending at the attractive little mountain village of San Benedetto in Alpe. The high point of the walk is the Acquacheta waterfall—a wide veil of water shimmering over high rocks deep in a wooded valley. Dante, who spent part of his exile near here, paid memorable tribute to it in the *Inferno:*

> Straight my guide
> Pursued his track. I followed: and small space
> Had we past onward, when the water's sound
> Was now so near at hand, that we had scarce
> Heard one another's speech for the loud din.
>
> Even as the river, that first holds its course
> Unmingled, from the mount of Vesulo,

On the left side of the Apennines, toward
The east, which Acquacheta higher up
They call, ere it descend into the vale,
At Forlì, by that name no longer known,
Rebellows o'er San Benedetto dell'Alpe, roll'd on
From the Alpine summit down a precipice,
Where space enough to lodge a thousand spreads;
Thus downward from a craggy steep we found
That this dark wave resounded, roaring loud,
So that the ear its clamour soon had stunn'd.

Inferno, xvi, translated by the Revd. Henry Francis Cary

There are some primitive stone refuges you can camp in, as well as some beautiful fields in the last stretch from the falls. The whole falls area is popular on weekends and in summer.

Make sure you have one of the trail maps listed in the Logistics section.

LOGISTICS

PASSO DEL MURAGLIONE–SAN BENEDETTO IN ALPE, about 5 hours

ⓘ Miscellaneous info

🚌 Transport

Ⓜ Maps, guidebooks and trail info

🍽 Eating

▦ Accommodation

ⓘ
There are various visitor centers serving the park. The park's Web site is an excellent source of information (available in English) when planning your trip. It has very useful links as well: **www.parks.it/parco.nazionale.for.casentinesi**

Two helpful comune Web sites for San Benedetto are: **www.sanbenedettoinalpe.it** (On the home page, scroll to bottom and click on "Le strutture ricettive" to see photos and listings of places to sleep.) **www.comune.portico-e-san-benedetto.fc.it** (photos and English version)

🚌
FROM FLORENCE TO MURAGLIONE:

SITA
Tel. 055-47821 (or toll-free from inside Italy 800-373760)
www.sita-on-line.it
Il Muraglione
Route 311
Two buses per day (ATW 6:40, 6:45 and 14:05)
Length of journey: Morning bus, 1½ hours; afternoon bus, 2 hours

FROM SAN BENEDETTO TO FLORENCE:

There are two ATR buses per day from San Benedetto to Il Muraglione, arriving in time to catch the two buses per day from Il Muraglione to Florence (see previous walk's listing for bus info from Il Muraglione to Florence).

ATR
Tel. 0547-21242
www.atr-online.it
Il Muraglione (for connection with SITA bus to Florence)
Route 127
Two buses per day (ATW 7:45 and 15:40)
Length of journey: 20 minutes

Ⓜ
SELCA 1:25,000 Carta Escursionistica: Parco Nazionale delle Foreste Casentinesi. Available in the park centers and at local bookshops.

🍴 ⊞
SAN BENEDETTO IN ALPE

All the hotels in San Benedetto also have restaurants. In addition, there's a new restaurant/pizzeria.

Albergo-Ristorante Acquacheta
Via Molino, 46
Tel. 0543-965314 or 965222
fax 0543-951063
www.acquacheta.it
email: hotelacquacheta@libero.it

Albergo-Ristorante Alpe
Via Molino, 18
Tel. 0543-965316

Ostello-Ristorante Il Vignale
Via Acquacheta
Tel. 0543-965279

Ristorante-Pizzeria Il Laghetto
Tel. 0543-965241

CAMPING

Camping Acquacheta
Tel. 0543-965245

Directions

Go around the back of the Hotel Il Muraglione. Red and white markings on a rock show the steep, narrow uphill 00 path. Take this path.

Continue following path 00, looking out for a sharp left (marked) uphill, which you take. There are various forks beyond here, but the route—a delightful, level trail through woods of evergreens—is generally well marked; just keep an eye out for the red and white trail blazes.

Half an hour from Il Muraglione you'll come to a T-junction. There are pink and yellow paint blazes on a tree at the right corner. Follow 00 up to the left **A**. Walk about 20 m on the track, and you'll come to a grassy opening. Path 00 leaves the track, bending to the right, up the incline.

About 5 minutes after this, the trail converges with an unpaved gravel road, follows it a very short distance and then takes off again on the left side (this is clearly marked), where it runs above the road.

Follow this ridge path for about 2 km through beech woods, until it comes out on a road. Turn right here (CAI 19). This is Colle della Maesta (about an hour or an hour and a half from Il Muraglione). From this point the path is well marked and easy to follow to the falls (Acquacheta) and on to San Benedetto.

After about 20–30 minutes, the road deteriorates a bit, into more of a rutted track. A few cars may be parked here (Il Crocione). There's a sign about Dante's having been there and described the falls in the *Inferno*. To the right of our trail, behind a bar, is a CAI trail to the eleventh-century hermitage visible in the distance away to the right, continuing on to Osteria Nuova and the state road connecting Il Muraglione and San Benedetto. (However, we do not go that way.)

Continuing along the track (crossing the summit of Monte Sinaia) in about 15 minutes you'll see a marked path that goes off to the right **B**. This path (409/a) leads fairly

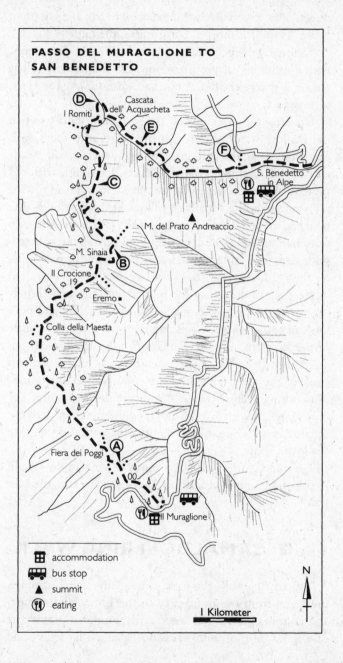

PASSO DEL MURAGLIONE TO SAN BENEDETTO

Cascata dell' Acquacheta

D
I Romiti

E

F

S. Benedetto in Alpe

C

M. del Prato Andreaccio

M. Sinaia

B

Il Crocione
19

Eremo

Colla della Maesta

Fiera dei Poggi

A

00.

Il Muraglione

accommodation

bus stop

summit

eating

N

1 Kilometer

directly (by way of Prato Andreaccio) to San Benedetto in about 4 km. It is shorter, but it misses the falls.

Following the principal track, you now descend steeply, with a series of hairpin turns, into the Acquacheta valley, reaching the river after about half an hour. At the river, turn right **C**.

Crossing the river several times (getting boots wet in the shallow water, unless you opt to remove them each time you cross), the path goes through several small meadows before reaching a bigger pasture, I Romiti, with old monastic ruins on the right just after a ford. Head toward the stone building on a little hillock at the far side of the field and go left. This is the start of the falls areas. The path from here to San Benedetto is extremely well constructed, with steps and some post fences (these latter primarily after the falls).

Keeping to the left of the hillock with the stone building on it, the path descends to a small waterfall and pool with stepping-stones. Cross the river here, **D**, and a little further on arrive opposite the falls, Cascara dell'Acquacheta.

From here to San Benedetto the path follows the left bank of the river (i.e., the river is on your right), sometimes rising well above it. Note that the path, after the falls, is signed with a yellow and red mark, rather than the usual red and white. Along the way the path forks **E**; take the lower route.

Ignore a CAI turnoff (179) about 2½ km past the falls **F**. It is about an hour and a half to San Benedetto from the falls.

12 ■ CAMALDOLI RING WALK

A half-day ring walk, this route climbs fairly steeply through the forest from the monastery to the Eremo (hermitage) and continues along old wood trails through a pretty part of the Casentino, with occasional panoramic views and plenty of wild raspberries along the route in late summer. If your time is limited or you need to finish where you started, this would be a good way of sampling the Casentino's unique blend of the monastic and the primeval. Otherwise, the individual sections of the four-day itinerary (see Walk 11) are generally superior.

For a shorter version, you can walk up to the Eremo and take the bus back down to the monastery (check the bus schedule first, as they not terribly frequent), or vice versa.

LOGISTICS

CAMALDOLI RING WALK,
4–5 hours

For information on transport, etc., see pp. 162–164.

Directions

Leaving Camaldoli, pass the monastery on your right and turn right on the asphalt road **A** leading to Bibbiena, crossing over the stone bridge. Just as you cross the bridge, there's a gravel path on the left, leading to a little log hut with public toilets. Before reaching the hut, however (just about 5 m from the asphalt), there is a small wooden sign for Cotozzo, marked with a CAI sign (trail 68). Take this trail.

Soon you will come to a big wooden cross (behind the monastery) at a fork **B**. Go left here.

The path climbs fairly steeply in this section, through mixed woods of beech, white fir and chestnut; but at least it's shaded, cool and windy even in the middle of summer. Just take it slow if you find it rough going; it's not too bad.

Follow this trail, ignoring smaller deviations and following the CAI markings. About 1 km out of Camaldoli, you'll cross a stream (Fosso del Ghiaccione). Soon after this you have a rather steep climb again, along an avenue of stately maples leading you to the Rifugio Cotozzo.

When you reach the Rifugio Cotozzo on your left, turn right uphill. There is a little wooden sign about 10 m up the hill, "Poggio Tre Confini," with CAI red and white markings. Stay on the main trail, following the CAI marks.

After passing an unmarked fork on the left, you'll come to another small fork to the left—this time, signed both ways. The larger path straight ahead is 68/a; the small one uphill to the left is 68: take this path.

At Poggio Tre Confini (1½–2 hours after leaving Camaldoli), the path turns left (CAI signed) and descends.

Along here you can see the *cippus* (inscribed stones with goblets on them) marking the old boundaries between the holdings of the Grand-duke Leopoldo II and the property of the Camaldolesi monks.

After descending for a short time, you come to a T-junction **C** with a sign on the right to Poggio Tre Confini, and CAI on the left. Turn left, joining with the CAI 00/GEA ridge trail. You may be able to spot raptors along here, as they have a tendency to fly along the line of the peaks.

In 15 minutes or so, the path comes out onto asphalt. Make sure to follow the path to the end, where it connects with the asphalt—by the little wooden sign "Poggio Tre Confini/Fangacci."

Across the asphalt from here (NOT path 70/a signed for Sacro Eremo; though it does lead to the Eremo, the last section of that route is on the road), find a path toward the right, going uphill: this is path 00, with signs for Porcareccio and Poggio Scali, as well as green and white and red and white paint marks on the trees.

Following this stone road you may notice traces of the old Franciscan stonework in it. After 10–15 minutes you'll reach a three-way fork. To the right downhill is signed "Acuti: Lama"; to the left downhill is signed "S. Eremo and CAI 70." Our path continues straight on, but if you're tired, you can drop down to the Eremo from here on CAI 70, which is a more direct route. If you want to go on, there

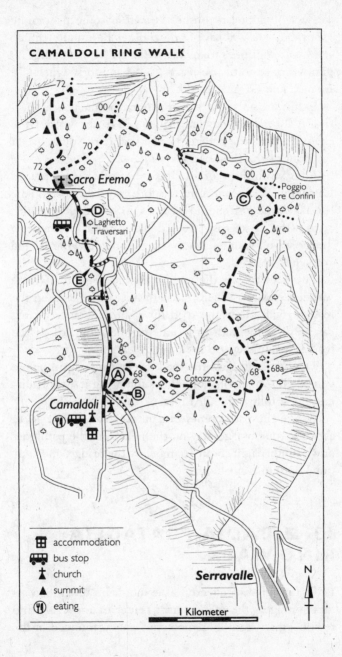

are lots of raspberry bushes as well as some panoramic views, but you will have to do another 10–minute climb.

If you continue, follow CAI 00/GEA for another 20 minutes or so until you reach a left-hand fork signed "72 Eremo" and GEA. Take this.

In this stretch you get your panorama, sun and raspberries. A 20-minute descent brings you to the wall of the Eremo; follow the path along the wall until you arrive at the front of the Eremo.

After visiting the Eremo, take the asphalt road toward Camaldoli. When you come to a fork with a dirt road on the left, take it **D**. You should see the CAI/GEA mark nearby.

In 50 m or so, pass a fork down to the lake, Laghetto Traversari, on your left. Keep straight on, following the red and white markets.

The path crosses the asphalt road at Tre Croci (three wooden crosses). Where the path next comes out on the road, it will follow the road for a short distance; watch carefully for the path to resume on the right side of the road **E** where the road itself bends left.

The path will cross the road several times again before you reach Camaldoli, sometimes following it a short distance. Just follow the CAI marks.

Where the path comes out on the road, about 40 m above a stone bridge, stay on the road until the path goes down on the right about 10 m before the bridge, and continue on into Camaldoli.

13 ■ BADIA PRATAGLIA RING WALK

Badia Prataglia is a cheerful little mountain town (855 m) functioning as the main tourist center of the Casentino region. Apart from its Benedictine abbey, founded in the

tenth century, most of the town is fairly new, but it's pleasant enough and so far seems to have escaped the kind of
tackiness you find at other mountain resorts, such as
Monte Amiata in southern Tuscany.

The Walk

This is a half-day (minimum) ring walk passing through
deep woods of chestnut, fir and beech. Even in summer it
can be fairly cool (and is much cooler than town, so bring
something warmer to wear), especially along the ridge
section, where surprisingly powerful winds blow more or
less constantly. After the initial steep climb above the high
pass at Mandrioli, the going is fairly easy. The relatively
high altitude (about 1200 m mostly) adds a remote, otherworldly quality to the cloister-like atmosphere created by
the tall trees arching over the old woodland paths.

Food

> *The restaurant (which was in nearby Serravalle) that we
> recommended in the original edition isn't there anymore.
> We include what remains of our original food review here;
> perhaps things have picked up since the creation of the Na-
> tional Park. . . .*

Food, unfortunately, is not a strong point here. There's a
good bakery across the street from the Pensione Bella
Vista, where you can buy an excellent blackberry cake.
But the restaurants, many of them in hotels that appear to
double as retirement homes, are pretty unenticing.

LOGISTICS

BADIA PRATAGLIA RING WALK,

4–4½ hours from starting point; add 30 minutes if starting from town

---

ⓘ Miscellaneous info

🚌 Transport

Ⓜ Maps, guidebooks and trail info

🍴 Eating

🏨 Accomodation

ⓘ

There are various visitor centers serving the park. The park's Web site is an excellent source of information (available in English) when planning your trip. It has very useful links as well:
**www.parks.it/parco.
nazionale.for.casentinesi**

Another useful site for the region (again, with good links) is:
www.badiaprataglia.com

Badia Prataglia tourist office
Tel. 0575-559054

Badia Prataglia Visitors' Center
Tel. 0575-559477

🚌
BY TRAIN

From Florence take the train to Arezzo (frequent service, journey time ¾ –1½ hours, depending

on which train you get), then change for the smaller LFI line (departing from the main railway station) to Bibbieno (Pratovecchio/Stia train, frequent service, journey time to Bibbieno about 45 minutes). At Bibbieno, change for the LFI bus to Badia Prataglia (about 6–8 buses per day, journey time 20–30 minutes).

Train info (Firenze to Arezzo portion): **www.trenitalia.it**
Tel. toll-free inside Italy 848-888088

LFI info: **www.lfi.it**
Tel. 0575-39881 or 0575-324294

BY BUS

From Florence, take the SITA bus to Bibbieno, then change for the LFI bus as above.

SITA
Tel. 055-47821 (or toll-free from inside Italy 800-373760)
www.sita-on-line.it
Florence
Route 320
About eight buses per day
Length of journey: About 2 hours

Ⓜ
SELCA 1:25,000 Carta Escursionistica: *Parco Nazionale delle Foreste Casentinesi.* Available in the park centers and at local bookshops.

⊕
PICNICS

Try the blackberry (*moro*) cake and flat oily pizza bread from the bakery across the street from the pensione Bella Vista.

▦

There are lots of hotel options in Badia Prataglia. See the Badia Prataglia Web site (above) for more listings.

Bella Vista
Via Nazionale, 34
Tel. 0575-559011
fax 0575-559440
email:
bellavista@badiaprataglia.com

Hostel Casanova
Tel. 0575-559320
www.peterpan.it (click on "turismo")
Price: Very inexpensive; basic hostel accommodations

Directions

The starting point for this walk is about 2 km out of Badia Prataglia. You can walk or hitch along the road to the starting point, or you can take the bus. You want the bus to Corezzo, which ATW leaves at 6.20, 7.52, 13.30 and 18.40 (but ask in the tourist office for current times). You can ask the driver to let you off. "*Vorrei scendere dove inizia il sentiero per Passo dei Mandrioli*" or, if that's too ambitious, "*Il sentiero per Passo dei Mandrioli, per favore*" should do it. If you want to take a bus all the way to Passo dei Mandrioli and start the walk there, you have the choice of two buses: the ATR bus to Raggio which ATW leaves at 8.05 a.m., and an LFI bus that leaves at 8.45 a.m. Again, check in the tourist office for current information, or call the bus company (see the Logistics section).

Leaving Badia Prataglia toward the east, passing the Pensione Bella Vista on your right, you'll come to a fork just outside town (toward the La Quercia hotel). Take the right fork.

The road soon forks again **A**; take the right, lower one, toward La Verna and Corezzo.

At the next fork take the right, lower one.

BADIA PRATAGLIA RING WALK

Passo dei Cerrini

E

Campo dell'Agio

A

Badia Prataglia

| accommodation |
| bus stop |
| church |
| summit |
| eating |
| information |

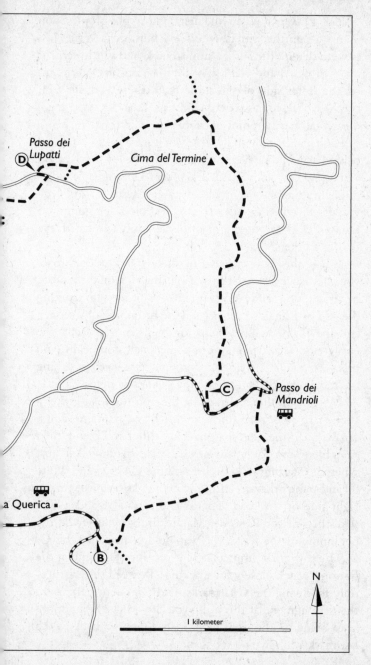

Pass La Quercia on the left (and a bus stop). Soon there's a sign that you're entering Chiusi della Verna. Just beyond that on the left is a stone road **B** and a little cement hut (with CAI and GEA signs on it). Across from the hut, on the other side of the stone road, there's a little sign, barely legible, to Passo dei Mandrioli. Take this stone road, the actual starting point of the walk.

Passing a sawmill on the left, you'll see a path leading up behind it and immediately forking. Take the left, lower, fork.

Follow CAI and GEA markers up to Passo dei Mandrioli. The route passes initially through chestnut and beech woods, and then fir. It's steep, so you won't be going too fast, which gives you plenty of opportunity to keep an eye on the markers.

When the path comes out on a quiet asphalt road, you've reached Passo dei Mandrioli. Turn left on the asphalt, heading toward and passing on your right the sign marking the end of Emilia Romagna and the beginning of Toscana, and the Poppi sign. Passing those signs on the right, the curvy road turns right around some small stone cliffs (and passes on the left an iron cross mounted in stone, marking the car death of a family) and then winds along past a little ANAS hut on the left. Just past the hut, the road makes a very sharp right turn (there are black and white road sign arrows marking the sharpness of this bend), and then straightens out for 50 m or so before bending left. Just where it's starting to bend left, see the CAI red and white 00 and some other green and white marks on a tree on the right side of the road. There's also a small wooden sign (like the one for Passo dei Mandrioli that you saw at the beginning of the walk) for Passo dei Lupatti. Take this **C**.

The path turns immediately left as you start on it at the bottom; watch closely for markings. Proceed slowly, carefully following the CAI marks, fairly frequent here as on the first segment of this walk; you should not be in doubt as to being on the right path. If in doubt, go back to the last mark you saw and try again.

As you begin to climb, you may notice a streambed on the left, maybe 20 meters away. Basically you're climbing straight uphill, parallel with that. It's steep, but just go as slowly as you need to.

Keep climbing up, following the CAI marks. You can see the ridge up ahead of you, and you just keep going toward it.

After passing an area of barren rockiness just before the top, you'll reach the ridge and its tremendous views. Turn left, entering extraordinary-looking beech woods.

Follow along the path, keeping to the ridge (which divides Tuscany and Emilia-Romagna). CAI is pretty spotty here, and there are several little deviations; but just stay on the path that stays closest to the ridge edge on the right. It's very windy and cool, and you can see the valley through the trees.

The path is fairly obvious, and CAI signs do appear intermittently. Keep to the ridge line as much as possible, joining at various points with a slightly larger trail, a logging road. The route through these beautiful, tall beeches is fairly flat, with a bit of gentle up and down. When you notice the path has suddenly become extremely steep, you will be climbing Cima del Termine.

About 10 minutes after this, you'll come to the "corner" of the ridge, where the path turns left (signed).

Always following the CAI route, in about 10 minutes, as you come down toward a more major stone road, leave the main path (which leads down to the stone road) and take the CAI trail that forks to the right. The CAI trail is well marked and runs higher than the main path. After a short while it comes out onto the stone road at its (the stone road's) highest point **D**, Passo dei Lupatti. Turn left on the stone road for a few steps, then turn right again onto the CAI path.

In another 15–20 minutes, there's a turnoff to the left marked with green and white and a "44." On the right side of the path is a stone with pink lettering: ignore the turn; keep on ahead.

After another 15–20 minutes you'll pass another turnoff to the left, marked green and white with "43." Turn left here **E**.

Follow this path down, well marked by CAI. When the path forks about 20–25 minutes into the route, bear left: there's a green and white sign. (Before this there was another path going left and uphill, but you wouldn't take it because it was going uphill.)

Another couple of minutes down there's an unmarked fork; take the left, bigger prong. Don't mind instructions too much—use common sense and just keep on downhill.

About a half hour from the beginning of this descent, the path comes out by a grassy clearing with a wood post fence around it and some picnic tables; this is Campo dell'Agio. Turn right and walk past the field (on your right) and follow the path that leads alongside it, then bends left at the corner of the field; and so into town, winding back and forth so that the descent is gentle.

NORTH OF LUCCA

14 ■ A WALK IN THE GARFAGNANA

The Alpi Apuane, Garfagnana and Orecchiella areas of northwest Tuscany offer extensive hiking opportunities, including two long-distance trails, Apuane Trekking and Garfagnana Trekking. This is a region catering to hikers and as such is well mapped, well marked and somewhat beyond the scope of our book.

On the other hand, you may find yourself up in the northwest corner of Tuscany (on a visit to Lucca perhaps), and if this introduction to the Garfagnana encourages you to go the extra distance, it will have served a good purpose.

We've chosen the Garfagnana rather than the Alpi Apuane because the terrain is milder, better suited to a casual walk; and while less daunting than the Alpi Apuane themselves, the higher Garfagnana trails overlook the splendid, jagged peaks of their better-known neighbors. Moreover, whereas in summertime the high altitudes of the green Garfagnana valley offer a welcome respite from the furnace of lowland Tuscany, the heat can be blistering in the bare rocky summits of the Alpi.

The quiet little resort town of Corfino seems to be frequented solely by Italian families. It's an easygoing place with little in the way of excitement, but at the La Baita hotel you'll get very good food, and if you're in the mood for a low-key environment well positioned for an extensive network of walks, you'll see a side of Italy here that is completely tourist-free.

The Walk

This pretty walk begins amid farmsteads and streams, proceeds to the Botanical Garden of the Parco dell'Orecchiella and then ascends to rocky outcrops, grassy hillsides and the towering cliffs behind them. After climbing to the top of the Pania di Corfino with its splendid views of the Alpi Apuane, the walk leads down to the Visitors' Center of the park (and the Ristorante Orecchiella). The way back to Corfino passes through the tiny farming hamlet of Sulcina; when we passed through they were binding wheat into sheaves.

LOGISTICS

GARFAGNANA WALK 🚌

It is about 4 hours to the Visitors' Center of the Parco dell'Orecchiella, then another 1½ hours back to Corfino. A shorter option is possible that skips the Botanical Garden and the ascent of Pania di Corfino and goes directly to the Visitors' Center, about 3 hours.

🚌 Transport

Ⓜ Maps, guidebooks and trail info

🍴 Eating

🏨 Accommodation

ⓘ Miscellaneous info

FROM LUCCA TO CASTELNUOVO:

By train: to Castelnuovo di Garfagnana from Lucca, on the Lucca–Aulla line
Train info: Tel. toll-free in Italy 848-888088
www.trenitalia.com
Length of journey: 1 hour
Frequency: about ten per day

By bus: CLAP bus to Castelnuovo di Garfagnana; about ten per day
Bus info: Tel. 0583-5411 or 0583-587897; or toll-free in Italy 800-602525

FROM CASTELNUOVO TO CORFINO:

CLAP bus, ATW three per day; the journey takes 25 minutes. *Bus info:* See above.

Ⓜ

Excellent information is available at the Comunità Montana in Castelnuovo di Garfagnana: see below.

Carta dei Sentieri e Rifugi, sheet 15/18, Appennino Reggiano Modenese– Garfagnana, 1:25,000

🅢

CORFINO

La Baita
Via Prato all'Aia
Tel. 0583-660084 or 68680
  Very friendly, family run. Reserve dinner, served at 20:00. Ravioli with ricotta and nuts. Pasta and chick-pea soup—very comforting. Pasta with very fresh, tasty artichoke sauce. Best gnocchi in Italy: homemade with a tomato– pesto sauce. Good garlicky turkey. The pleasant surprise of a tomato and *borlotti* bean salad. Everything beautifully cooked and inexpensive. Decent house red; avoid the white.

PARCO DELL'ORECCHIELLA

Rifugio Ristorante Orecchiella Parco dell'Orecchiella (near the Visitors' Center)
Tel. 0583-619010
Closing day: Friday
  Excellent salad, very good vegetable soups. Unusual *crostini* with a salsa verde and a red salsa piccante. Reserve.

CAMPAIANA

Bar Ristorante il Fungo
Campaiana
Tel. 0583-66680 (or 660158 when the restaurant is closed)
  Very friendly place up in the mountains; you can drive there if you've got a car, or take a day's hike there. (You can also stay overnight, but there is nothing there except this rustic restaurant.) A nice ring walk would be to take CAI 56 to Campaiana, and the Airone I trail back to Corfino (make sure you have a map). Excellent ravioli with mushrooms. Open every day from June 15 to September 30; otherwise only on Saturday and Sunday (as long as the road isn't closed by snow).

🏢

CORFINO

Albergo La Baita
Via Prato all'Aia
Tel. 0583-68680 or 660084

Panoramico
Via Fondo la Terra, 9
Tel. 0583-660161

(i)

Listings for Corfino (in the
phone book or in hotel guides,
etc.) will be found under "Villa
Collemandina."

Tourist office: Orecchiella Park
Center: tel. 0583-619098 or
65169

Open daily July and August;
weekends only in June and
September; and by appoint-
ment for groups October–May.

Next to the Visitors' Center
of the park is a little shop that
sells some local specialities, such
as chestnut flour, honey, etc.
The alpine garden across the
road from the Ristorante Orecchiella is preferred by some to
the Botanical Garden itself,
though the Botanical Garden
boasts the fascinating "animal
feces" exhibit.

**www.parks.it/
riserva.statale.orecchiella**

Directions

Immediately before entering the grounds of the La Baita
hotel in Corfino, take the right-hand turn. In about 10 m
there's a left turn (signed CAI 58) up a path of large
stones; take this, passing La Baita on your left.

Continue to climb up this path, passing a tabernacle
and a fountain, both on the right; ignoring deviations, stay
on the CAI 58 trail.

Passing an old stone farm building on the right (currently a chicken coop), the path forks near a wooden cross.
Take the right fork, signed to CAI 58 and Campaiana.

When you come to a T-junction, turn right.

About half an hour from La Baita, you'll reach the intersection with the Airone trail **A**. (*Airone* is an Italian magazine
similar to *National Geographic,* but perhaps more conservation-
minded; they have created walking trails—several of them
here in the Parco dell'Orecchiella—that are marked in
blue and yellow.) Take a left and follow the Airone trail
(which also, like the CAI route, goes straight on here).

In another 20 minutes or so, you'll reach a hut with a
corrugated roof, currently painted red, just after an Airone
sign (an actual sign, not paint marks), and the path turns

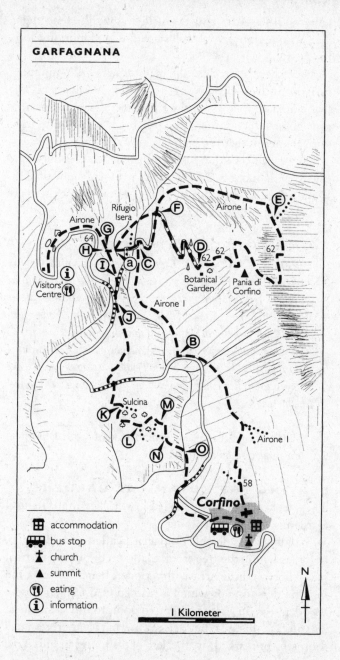

GARFAGNANA

Rifugio Isera

Airone 1

Airone 1

E

F

G

64

H

I

a C

D

62

62

62

Botanical Garden

Pania di Corfino

Visitors' Centre

Airone 1

J

B

Airone 1

Sulcina

M

K

L

N

O

58

Corfino

accommodation

bus stop

church

summit

eating

information

1 Kilometer

N

left. You'll see Airone marks further along the fence here. The Airone trail is very well signed; if in doubt, just look for the marks.

Very soon after this, the path reaches a T-junction; turn right **B**, soon passing a working fountain on the left. The path follows on the right side of the stream now as it climbs. In summer, this area tends to be quite lush, with the result that the path is a bit overgrown in places.

About half an hour past the thatched hut you'll come out to a T-junction **C** with a dirt road and signs of civilization (a fenced-in area with a lot of lampposts, actually a mountain hut, the Rifugio Isera).

*SHORTER OPTION GOING DIRECTLY TO THE VISITORS' CENTER: Turn left on this dirt road **C**, over the bridge, with the picnic area below you on the left. Continue on past a fork sharply up to the right, until you arrive at the footpath marked "Airone 1," **a**, also to the right. Follow this path, which comes out into a field and there joins to a track **G** (you are actually converging with another path called Airone 1 here) that quickly becomes a small path passing between some cottages. From here, pick up directions from **G** on p. 203 to finish the walk.*

Go right on this dirt road, which leads to the Botanical Garden in about 45 minutes.

LEAVING THE BOTANICAL GARDEN

The sheer cliff face to your left as you face the Botanical Garden is where we're going.

Standing outside the Botanical Garden and facing it, before reaching the tree trunk that is on display there, turn left. There's a little area with wooden benches and some big boulders (one of which is marked CAI 62), and also a wooden sign on a tree seeming to point to this sitting area. As you face this area (but before entering it), there's a small footpath, unmarked, to the left of it, going uphill. Take this **D**. (If in doubt, ask someone who works at the gardens where CAI 62 is. There is another way of getting there, but rangers recommend this way.)

There's a tiny wooden sign in the ground, on the right side of the path, near the bottom, barely visible, that says "Pania n. 62." As you climb, you'll see in about 20 m another CAI wooden marker with 62.

Soon you'll reach a hillside completely covered in scree. Begin climbing up along the edge of this, going straight up to where the scree ends and the big rocks begin, where the path turns right.

It takes about 45 minutes to climb this hillside. The ascent is fairly tough going, and though it's marked, the marks are not always obvious. Just keep going along toward the peak you see in front of you; it's pretty clear which direction you want to head in. As you climb this hillside, you can see the Alpi Apuane behind you; the scenery is stunning.

Just below the main peak is a saddle. It's grassy here, and the path is trodden into the grass. Take this grassy track to the right as it leads to the top of the hill, Pania di Corfino.

At the top of the hill, pick up the Airone trail down the back of the hill to the edge of the woods, where there's a T-junction; go right (still Airone).

Follow this Airone trail down behind the hill, through alpine meadows with beautiful scenery and lots of butterflies.

About ½ hour's walk from the summit of Pania di Corfino there's a big wooden cross on a hillside. CAI 64 goes on ahead, re-entering the woods; Airone 1, the path you want, turns left downhill **E**.

In another ½ hour or so, coming out on the road to the Botanical Garden **F**, turn right. In a few meters you'll come to the Airone 1 trail on your right; take this trail.

Follow this Airone trail toward the Visitors' Center, watching for a right turn at the corner of a stone wall (off what looks like a bigger path) that crosses a stream.

———

The shorter walk joins the longer one here **G**. Pass between some cottages (the path is tarmac here); the path comes out on a small asphalt road with a large stone monument to Bruno Segre **H** to the left. Turn right here.

Follow this small asphalt road. About 15–20 m before this little road comes out on a bigger asphalt road, there's a track forking off to the right toward a little wood cabin; take it.

About an hour's walk from the summit of Pania di Corfino, you'll arrive at Ristorante Orecchiella and the Visitors' Center nearby.

RETURN FROM VISITORS' CENTER TO CORFINO

Go back the way you came as far as the stone monument to Bruno Segre **H**. The Airone 1 trail on which you came turns left here. Don't take that. Instead take the unmarked (ATW) path that leads straight ahead, past the monument (which is to your right as you pass it). It is the bigger, downhill path that you want here, not the smaller uphill footpath to the right of it.

Follow this until it comes out on asphalt **I**. Turn right. When you come to the intersection with the main asphalt road, take the first (unmarked) left **J**—about 10 m from the intersection—a fairly wide, grassy track.

Keep on this main path, descending toward Corfino, ignoring any smaller paths.

The path gets quite rocky, and then comes out on an asphalt road. Cross the road and continue on the path on the other side of the road. This path comes immediately to a small asphalt path; turn right.

Follow this asphalt path through the little farm hamlet of Sulcina, passing the Bar Ristorante Luisa on your right. Just beyond here, on the left, is a fountain (working) and a chapel. Instead of following the asphalt road—which turns to the right here—go straight ahead, downhill on a cement track between houses. This leads to a T-junction with the little tarmac road; turn left.

Follow this road as it winds downhill, making first a right-hand bend (maybe 40 m ahead) and then, just before it makes a left-hand bend, look for a gravel track off it to the right **K**, which looks like a driveway leading to a white (ATW) house with red tile roof. Take this track.

This driveway goes past the back of a newish house. Follow it to the right, where it becomes a dirt track, curving sharply left toward Corfino after 100 m. Beautiful old chestnuts line the path.

At the first fork (another 100 m), go left **L**. The path gets a little rougher here. It crosses a stream, and in about 150 m, where the main path bends around to the right, a slightly smaller path goes off to the left, effectively forming a T; (ATW there's a large woodpile here). Go left **M**.

The path bends to descend parallel to and to the left of some telegraph poles. This is a beautiful secluded valley, though the path is somewhat overgrown. In 5–10 minutes the path converges with a better-maintained path coming from the right **N**. Continue straight on, going steeply down to the bottom of the valley, where you cross a stream on a little raised walkway **O** and begin to climb. Look out for the forlorn little abandoned house below you on your right as you climb. (Ignore the downhill fork that takes you down there unless you want to examine it more closely.)

In 2 more minutes you'll come out on the asphalt. Turn right, and go into Corfino. (Go left after passing Hotel California to get to the center.) It is about 40 minutes from Sulcina.

WEST OF SIENA: MONTERIGGIONI AND THE MONTAGNOLA

To the west of Siena, across the Val d'Elsa, lies the hilly, thickly wooded region known as the Montagnola Senese. Sparsely populated, and unlike neighboring Chianti not often visited by tourists, it retains a certain somber flavor from the medieval period, when it formed part of the Via Francigena, the great pilgrim route connecting Rome with northern Europe. Much of the landscape, dominated by the three peaks of Monte Maggio (671 m), is essentially a forest broken by occasional quarries and farms, many of these abandoned. Deer and wild boar roam through the stands of oak, chestnut, maple and hornbeam that roll on for miles at a time. Dark woodland paths (comfortable walking even in summer) come out on clearings that might be filled with a dazzling crop of sunflowers, or might as easily be in the process of reverting to the scrub of broom, myrtle and blackberry that marks the first stage of reclamation by the forest itself.

The hand-hewn stonework of the Via Francigena and its subsidiaries survives for long passages on many of the numerous trails. Painstakingly squared off, the sunken slabs of these little-known ancient roads (which exist all over Italy and are generally referred to as "Francigena" whether or not they formed part of the original route) are surely among the most touching monuments of the medieval period. More prominent survivors of this era are the Cistercian abbey Abbadia a Isola and the stunning thirteenth-century fortified hill town of Monteriggioni, which presides over the northern boundary of the Montagnola, its lovely ringed wall with fourteen sentry towers sitting slightly awry like a tilted crown.

Though Dante compared the fourteen towers to giants in an abyss, the modern eye is likely to find them more charming than forbidding. Both of the following walks have particularly splendid views of the town.

>   Thitherward not long
> My head was raised, when many a lofty tower
> Methought I spied. "Master," said I, "what land
> Is this?" He answer'd straight: "Too long a space
> Of intervening darkness has thine eye
> To traverse: thou hast therefore widely err'd
> In thy imagining. Thither arrived
> Thou well shalt see how distance can delude
> The sense. A little therefore urge thee on."
>   Then tenderly he caught me by the hand;
> "Yet know," said he, "ere further we advance,
> That it less strange may seem, these are not towers,
> But giants. In the pit they stand immersed,
> Each from his navel downward, round the bank."
>   As when a fog disperseth gradually,
> Our vision traces what the mist involves
> Condensed in air; so piercing through the gross
> And gloomy atmosphere, as more and more
> We near'd toward the brink, mine error fled
> And fear came o'er me. As with circling round
> Of turrets, Monteriggioni crowns his walls,
> E'en thus the shore, encompassing the abyss,
> Was turreted with giants, half their length
> Uprearing, horrible, whom Jove from heaven
> Yet threatens, when his muttering thunder rolls.

>   *Inferno*, Canto XXXI, translated by
>   the Revd. Henry Francis Cary

The Walks

When we were in the Montagnola writing the original edition of this book, CAI had recently published a 1:25,000 trail map for the Montagnola Senese and was in the process of clearing and renumbering the mass of old woodland trails to conform to its map. The result is an area with miles of gentle, extraordinarily peaceful walks, all signposted. Perhaps because it is so wooded, we still found ourselves getting lost from time to time. But should you have the desire, there are enough trails here to keep you going for the better part of a month.

Both of our Montagnola walks begin in Monteriggioni; one of them is a ring walk via the Abbadia a Isola and an old pre-Etruscan site; the other ends at the little hamlet (and gigantic villa) of Santa Colomba, where the *agriturismo* Gavina makes an ideal base for further explorations of the region.

15 ■ MONTERIGGIONI TO SANTA COLOMBA

The original edition of this book included a San Gimignano ring walk, which we decided to drop from the book after failing to find a way to rescue it from the various depressing new encroachments of ugliness brought about by mass tourism.

The next day, still somewhat downcast as a consequence of this loss, we came to Monteriggioni to update the Santa Colomba walk. Not more than a half hour into the walk, we passed an old man leading his donkey down the track, accompanied by his dog and six sheep. It was a quiet morning, and a short distance off we could see gorgeous Monteriggioni, set on its hilltop, unspoiled. It seemed little short of a miracle that the necessary precautions had been taken to spare it from the ugly sprawl of houses mangling the hillsides up to the very walls of San Gimignano, whose formerly stately entranceway was now gagged with tour buses. But there it was: one of the most hauntingly beautiful hilltop sights in Italy, the stark simplicity of its ring of towers still unblemished. The lingering pall cast by the San Gimignano disappointment quickly evaporated.

This is a perfect day walk from Siena, or you could stay overnight at the lovely, peaceful *agriturismo* of La Gavina, and next day either take the bus back from Santa Colomba or take your chance with the CAI map to walk another route back to Monteriggioni.

Though longish (4 hours), it isn't a particularly strenuous walk, and much of it passes through deep woods, which makes it an appealing prospect even in summer.

Early on you pass through the organic gardens and meditation center of Ebbio, one of the region's more interestingly offbeat *agriturismo* establishments. A little over an hour later you reach the road to the pretty hamlet of Colle a Ciupe, worth the brief detour to have a look at the little Romanesque church with its recently restored *trecento* frescos and fine views over the surrounding landscape. The Villa di Baldassare Peruzzi, at Santa Colomba, was transformed in the seventeenth century into the vast, weirdly disproportionate monument that broods over the distinctly unmonumental landscape today. It's an extraordinary sight, not exactly beautiful, but impressive. It's private, but the American owner holds an art festival and general "festa" in the grounds every year in late June.

There's a small bar in the village, and you can either get a bus back into Siena (check on times) or stay in the aforementioned *agriturismo* of La Gavina, about a mile away (the owner will pick you up from Santa Colomba).

Food

For Monteriggioni restaurants, see the Monteriggioni Ring Walk.

The bar in Santa Colomba allegedly functions as a trattoria, though by reservation only, which probably means they will require a minimum number of guests. La Gavina, the nearby *agriturismo,* prepares delicious food for people who are staying there, much of it from its own organic gardens. Excellent salads and vegetables, as might be expected, a subtly flavored risotto with wild mushrooms, good local wines, and all of it in abundance, as is usually the case in these establishments.

LOGISTICS

MONTERIGGIONI–SANTA COLOMBA,
about 4 hours
See also Siena Logistics
(p. 230).

(i)   Miscellaneous info

🚌   Transport

(M)   Maps, guidebooks and trail info

(🍽)   Eating

▦   Accommodation

(i)
Castello di Monteriggioni
Tel. 0577-304001
www.terresiena.it
There's also a *pro loco* in Monteriggioni. If you're interested in staying over in Monteriggioni and don't have the 200+ euros to stay in the single hotel there, the *pro loco* has a list of residents renting rooms (*affittacamere*).
Pro loco: Largo Fontebranda 5
Tel. 0577-304810

🚌
TRA-IN

Tel. 0577-204111 or 204245 or 6
www.trainspa.it
Siena–Monteriggioni
Route 130
Fairly frequent buses, and there are even a couple on Sunday.
Length of journey: 30 minutes
Check at Siena bus station for pickup point in Siena. In Monteriggioni, the bus drops off on the main road, which is *below* Monteriggioni.

Santa Colomba–Siena
Route 037
One early bus around 7:10 (check for exact time). Also ATW: 13:40, 14:45 and 20:15. ATW Sunday at 15:20 and 19:55. Ask for location of pickup. Some pick up opposite Villa Tilli. Drop-off in Siena is in Piazza Gramsci.
Length of journey: 30 minutes

Ⓜ
Carta Turistica e dei Sentieri:
Itinerari Nella Montagnola
Senese. This is a 1:25,000 map
put out by CAI. But any other
1:25,000 map covering the
Monteriggioni area or the Mon-
tagnola Senese will be fine.

🍴
For eating in Monteriggioni, see
the listings in Monteriggioni Ring
Walk. For Santa Colomba, see
also the La Gavina *agriturismo*, if
you're staying overnight.

Da Sergio Trattoria
Santa Colomba
Tel. 0577-317105
Closing day: Monday
   This trattoria is open by
reservation only, and it
seems you must have a group of
some kind; the owner didn't
specify any number, so call him
and ask. Meanwhile, during the

day his very modest little store/
café is open for business.

🏠
La Gavina
Loc. La Gavina (see map; just
over 1 km west of Santa
Colomba)
Tel. 0577-317046
email: lagavina@libero.it
Price: 55 euros per person,
includes dinner and breakfast
   Lovely hosts at this *agriturismo*,
with beautiful food from their
organic farm.

ⓘ
In early to mid July there's the
Monteriggioni di Torri Corona,
a ten-day festival celebrating
the history and cultural traditions of the past. Costumed
reenactments in this setting look
pretty spectacular, especially
when they get the torches going
around the perimeter walls.

Directions

Standing in the piazza with the church beside you to your
left, go out through the gate facing you, turning right on
the small asphalt road as you leave the gate. Staying on the
asphalt, walk about ½ km downhill to the main road. Here
turn left for 20 m, and take the dirt road to your right **A**
(ATW signed "Il Mandorlo").

After 150 m the road forks. Go right (ATW signed right
to "Il Gallinaio" and "Il Mondorlo"). A gentle climb of
about 250 m takes you to a wood where the road forks

again. Take the left fork (ATW signed left to "Il Gallinaio" and "Ebbio").

In about 50 m, ignore two lesser paths to the right. Go around the bend and you'll come to an intersection **B**; keep to the main path that curves around to the left (signed to "Gallinaio"), ignoring a sharp left and a right. (CAI trails go down each of these forks, so be sure you have the correct one.)

The path winds gently up, in and out of woods, and after about 5 minutes you'll pass the driveway of Il Gallinaio on the left (ATW has a house number "7"). Continue on, always keeping to the main white stone path. Ignoring a minor fork down to the right after 5 minutes, follow the main path up to the left past the houses of the Ebbio *agriturismo* and meditation center.

Go on upward through the property. The white stone road becomes a smaller path, and 100 m past the house it comes alongside a wood. Ignore an immediate left upward through the wood, proceeding instead on the main path. BE ALERT HERE: the path forks and zigzags numerous times as it climbs through the wood, though on the whole it is very well signed (during this stretch) by CAI, and you shouldn't have to look far at any intersection before you find the red and white CAI markers. Therefore, the following bit of instructions is probably not necessary, but here it is, just in case.

About 100 m after entering the wood, there's a narrow fork up to the left off the main path; the main path turns to the right just beyond. Take the left fork and keep left at the fork that comes in another 30 m. The path is narrow and somewhat overgrown here, but well signed. At the next fork (70 m) go left (ATW there's a CAI sign like this ⌐┐ directing you left, but it could be mistaken for an arrow pointing you to the right). After another 100 m a sign like this ⌐─ on a stone points you to the right, at another fork. After 150 m of winding and climbing, the path comes into a scrubby clearing and passes under a telephone wire. Follow the path across the clearing, bending

MONTERIGGIONI TO SANTA COLOMBA

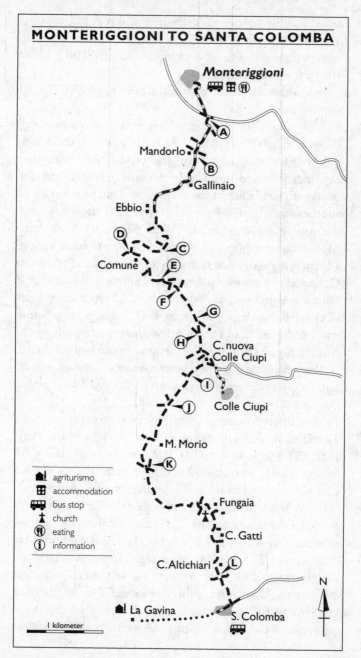

Monteriggioni

Mandorlo

Gallinaio

Ebbio

Comune

C. nuova
Colle Ciupi

Colle Ciupi

M. Morio

Fungaia

C. Gatti

C. Altichiari

La Gavina

S. Colomba

agriturismo
accommodation
bus stop
church
eating
information

1 kilometer

N

around to the right at the far side of this part of the clearing, and continuing again around to the right as the path widens (ignoring a fork backward to the left). This is about 100 m from the telephone wire.

In another 20 m the path forks; turn right (ATW CAI sign on tree).

After about 100 m of climbing, you'll see a stone wall on your right. The CAI-blazed trail follows to the left of this wall for another 100 m, then comes out at another clearing, followed in 20 m by an olive grove. Climb the main path to the left of the olive grove (and to the right of another stone wall). There are fewer CAI signs here, but the path is easier to follow. Wide panoramas back onto Monteriggioni open behind you—be sure to look. Ignore a branch that goes down sharply to your right after 150 m **C**, and climb upward along the main path for another ½ km to a T-junction **D**, where CAI 102 (your trail) joins CAI 105b. Go left (you might hear a dog pound below you on the left), and then, a few meters later, left again, past the house Comune, and straight on out by their drive.

Proceed along the white stone road in and out of woods, ignoring a wide reddish track up to the right after about 200 m.

In another 5 minutes (½ km from Comune) watch for a fork **E** going forward and upward to the right of the main path. (This **E** is where CAI 102 branches off from CAI 105b.) (NOTE: Just beyond **E** on the main path is *another* fork to the right, which will cross over this first fork. Make sure you're on the first fork, otherwise the directions won't work.) Take this right fork and cross over the path that intersects yours in 20–30 m. After 50 m you'll come out on another fork **F**, where you turn right, into the woods.

Ignoring a fork back down to the left after 100 m, go straight on, ignoring another minor left fork in about 3 minutes (ATW trail well-blazed). Keeping to the main path, you'll come to a junction **G** with a major new path going down to the left (this path isn't shown on the IGM map). Turn right.

Almost immediately (about 30 m), you'll come to another junction **H**. Turn left (CAI 109 and 102 converge here, ATW marked on a tree). NOTE: ATW they're clearing on the right here, so we don't know what this will be in the future. In any case, stay on the CAI trail, hugging the border with the thick woods just on your left.

In a minute or two this path passes an old stone wall on the right and narrows to a single track. Then, 5–10 minutes past **H**, you'll reach a T-junction with a bigger track; turn left.

At another T-junction go left again. In a couple of minutes you'll bend around to the right and downhill as you come to a house (Casa Nuova Colle Ciupi), and then left, still downhill, away from the house. In about 40 m this comes out at another junction, a dirt track with a stone wall running along it. Turn right—or, to visit Colle Ciupi, turn left. (Colli Ciupi is a hamlet that has a chapel with *trecento* frescoes inside that have just been restored. Good panoramic views as well.)

The track enters a field and bends around to the left, following a deep ditch and passing a pond. The path enters another field, forking left at the far left corner **I**, onto a stony uphill path. Ignore a right fork after 50 m.

Climbing steadily, you'll come after 10–15 minutes to a little clearing with two paths off to the right **J** (one of them is CAI 107). Go straight on along the main path, passing through an opening in an old stone wall (ATW with a "CAI 102" sign on it) and following the path as it bends to the left, ignoring an overgrown fork to the right 30 m past the wall, and continuing downhill on the main path.

Crossing a narrow meadow and re-entering trees, you'll pass the back of the abandoned, pinkish stone house of Monte Morio. Go around the little pond beyond it and take the left fork. After 5–10 minutes you'll come to an intersection **K** with some new logging trails. Your path is effectively straight on—ATW the second to the right: a stony road going gently downhill (you'll pick up CAI blazes).

After 25 minutes you'll cross a small road with a barrier to the left. A couple of minutes later you'll enter the pretty stone-built farming hamlet of Fungaia. Turning left at the church for 20 m, take the little path that goes right, skirting the side of the first house (the house is on your left). The path winds between two overgrown stone walls, through open countryside, with glimpses ahead to the oversize villa of Santa Colomba. Cross a small road in 200 m and pass to the right of an old house (Casa Gatti) just beyond this. At the fork 70 m after, keep right, following steeply down with the telephone poles.

At the bottom of this steep descent, ignore a sharp left and take the left of the two forks ahead of you. Climb upward, keeping to the main trail. In 100 m you'll come to a junction. Bear left.

In a few hundred meters the path brings you out through the hamlet of Altichiari. In another 200 m you reach a T-junction **L** with a gravel road. Cross straight over, taking the path directly ahead of you into the woods. (CAI seems to turn left here, and there's another half-left fork into the woods, which you ignore.)

In another 5–10 minutes the path brings you out on an asphalt road where you turn right, into Santa Colomba.

16 ■ MONTERIGGIONI RING WALK, with Optional Spur to Montauto

We have had recent feedback on this walk that indicates it is still intact. We didn't revisit the walk on this trip, but have updated the food review and logistical information and made a couple of small changes to the walk directions based on reader information. The ruins of Montauto were being

*renovated in 2000, and the spur path may have been cleaned
up and made easier to follow since we were last there.*

*One reader suggested starting the walk in Abbadia a
Isola in order to reach Monteriggioni in time for lunch. (If
you're using the bus and want to do this, use the Casone stop
and walk the 1 km or so to Abbadia a Isola from there.)*

*The newer IGM maps show a CAI route out the back
of Monteriggioni, and we've had good reports of this route.
Apparently quite a lot of it is through open fields, giving
good views on your approach to Abbadia a Isola.*

This is a fairly gentle, varied walk through woods, farmland and old settlements rich in history.

Abbadia a Isola is a pleasant eleventh-century Cistercian abbey built on what was once an island (hence "Isola")
in the center of marshes. To visit, ask the caretaker (house
to the left of the church) to let you in. A small tip is appreciated. At the southwest angle there remains a little polygonal rampart surmounted by a circular turret with arrow
slits at the summit.

The walk also passes a moving monument to partisan
martyrs of the Val D'Elsa murdered by Fascists during the
last years of World War II. At the Casa Giubileo, next to
the monument, the spur trail to Montauto departs, passing
through deep woods, the path shaded by old holm oaks
bending over it like a continuous gothic arch. When we
were there in 1994, the ruins of a pre-Etruscan castle and
two medieval buildings lay in a state of rather indecipher-
able semi-excavation among the blackberry bushes up
there; they have apparently been restored since then. In any
case, the trip is worth making for the fantastic panorama it
offers over the Val d'Elsa—a great place for a picnic.

Food

We had such warm memories of Il Pozzo that we couldn't
resist going back there this time around, particularly as we

had heard that it was still excellent. Perhaps we caught it on a bad day, but it seemed distinctly tired to us. The service is still friendly and efficient, and we ate some good dishes, among them an excellent gamey stuffed pigeon. But the pastas were bland and cheesy (in every sense) and there was an air of creaky formality to the place that slightly depressed us.

Next door, Il Castello's menu lists an unusually large selection of vegetable dishes and a line in "small meals." We would welcome comments on it for our Web site. There's also an excellent *gelateria* in the far corner where you can buy hot *panini* if you don't want a sit-down lunch.

Meanwhile, in case we did catch Il Pozzo at the wrong moment, here, for old times' sake, is our original review:

The food here is fresh, imaginative, and beautifully prepared. Among the lighter offerings are crisp mixed salads, delicate fried zucchini blossoms, ravioli stuffed with pumpkin, tortellini with truffles roasted in foil, and wonderful mixed cheese pastries. For something more substantial try the wild boar with polenta, or one of the many rich dishes of roast game. The dessert trolley—usually about as enticing as a morgue—is truly tempting here, offering exceptionally good *panna cotta, frutti di bosco* (wild berries) and plums in Chianti. The place is unpretentious and friendly; despite our walking boots and sweaty shirts, we were made to feel extremely welcome.

LOGISTICS

MONTERIGGIONI RING WALK,

about 4 hours

For a shorter walk of about 1½ hours, you could go as far as Abbadia a Isola and take the bus back from there.
See also Siena Logistics (p. 230).

ⓘ Miscellaneous info

🚌 Transport

Ⓜ Maps, guidebooks and trail info

🍽 Eating

🏨 Accommodation

ⓘ
MONTERIGGIONI

Castello di Monteriggioni
Tel. 0577-304001
www.terresiena.it
There's also a *pro loco* in Monteriggioni. If you're interested in staying over in Monteriggioni and don't have the 200+ euros to stay in the single hotel there, the *pro loco* has a list of residents renting rooms (*affittacamere*).

Pro loco:
Largo Fontebranda 5
Tel. 0577-304810

ABBADIA A ISOLA

Tel. 0577-300026

🚌
TRA-IN

Tel. 0577-204111 or 204245 or 6
www.trainspa.it
Siena–Monteriggioni
Route 130
Fairly frequent buses, and there are even a couple on Sunday.
Length of journey: 30 minutes
Check at Siena bus station for pickup point in Monteriggioni; the bus drops off on the main road, which is *below* Monteriggioni.
   If you opt to start or finish at Abbadia a Isola, use bus line 130, as above, but use the Casone stop and walk to the abbey from there, just under 1 km.

Ⓜ
Carta Turistica e dei Sentieri, Itinerari Nella Montagnola Senese. This is a 1:25,000 map put out by CAI. But any other 1:25,000 map covering the Monteriggioni area or the Montagnola Senese will be fine.

🍽
Il Pozzo
Piazza Roma, 2
Tel. 0577-304127
fax 0577-304701
www.ilpozzo.net
Price: Moderate
Closing day: Sunday evening and Monday

⊞

Monteriggioni has only one hotel, the small, expensive four-star, Hotel Monteriggioni (*Tel.* 0577-305009). However, the *pro loco* (see Tourist Office) has a list of people in the village who rent rooms (*affittacamere*)

Directions

Standing in the piazza with the church beside you to your left, go out through the gate facing you, turning right on the small asphalt road as you leave the gate. Staying on the asphalt, walk about ½ km downhill to the main road. Here turn left for 20 m, and take the dirt road to your right **A** signed "Il Mandorlo."

After 150 m the road forks. Go right. A gentle climb then takes you to a wood where the road forks again. Take the left fork.

At the intersection 70 m from here **B**, take the right turn, signed to "Il Mandorlo." (This is about 25 minutes from Monteriggioni.) The middle and left paths here are also CAI trails, so be sure you have the correct one.

Walk straight along this road, which turns into a well-defined grassy path at the rear of the big house on the left and follows alongside its property. The path quickly becomes a dirt one and enters the woods. (This is *not* CAI 101.)

When the path forks **C**, very soon, go right, downhill, keeping straight along this path, ignoring a dubious competitor immediately on the right, uphill. This rugged stone path dates back to medieval times and is well traveled today by *istrice* (porcupines), as the many examples of quills along the way attest.

When the path comes out by a large cultivated field (planted with sunflowers when we were there, like a bright yellow lake), bear right along the edge of it (open field to the left, woods to the right). The path passes through the edge of the woods again, then comes out at the end of the field.

At the end of the field, keep on straight ahead, ignoring a left-hand grassy fork and almost immediately meeting a dirt road, slightly larger, on which you turn right **D**. (This is 50 minutes or so out of Monteriggioni.)

This path in turn comes out on another dirt road **E**. Go left here, between large expanses of field. Follow this road until you come to the asphalt road in about 2 km. Turn left there, and in 100 m or so, come to the Romanesque church of Abbadia a Isola.

The woman who lives in the house to the left of the church is the caretaker. If you want to see the inside of the abbey, she will let you in with a very large key. (A small tip is appreciated.)

Leaving the abbey, turn left onto the same asphalt road, and immediately you'll see a dirt road forking off it to the left. Take this road.

Pass the old polygonal chapel, continuing up the road about 20 m until you come to a junction **F**; bear right here, picking up red and white CAI signs.

Very shortly, the road forks again. Go left. Again, there are CAI red and white markings here.

Follow this stony road, ascending, for about 3 km (about an hour), always staying on the principal track, until you reach Casa Giubileo, a large old homestead on the right (with a green sign "Punto di Sosta" on the corner of it). There is a monument to the partisan martyrs of Val D'Elsa, on the left side of the road here (Ai 19 Martiri il Popolo della Val D'Elsa, 28/3/44–28/3/45) and also, behind the stone wall on the right side of the road, the burial sites of two of them who were gunned down by the Fascists when sleeping here.

Montauto Spur—about 45 minutes round trip

The spur to Montauto departs from here. From the road, before actually reaching Casa Giubileo, you can see a gap between the right rear corner of the house and the stone wall behind it. On the stone wall there's a very visible red and white CAI mark that says 105. Pass through this gap.

Go down alongside the house and you'll see a circular well.

MONTERIGGIONI RING WALK

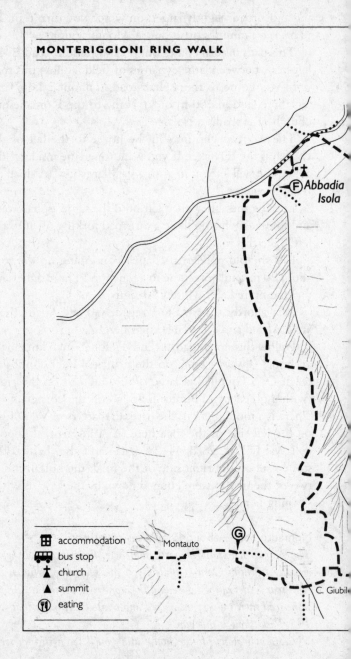

- accommodation
- bus stop
- church
- summit
- eating

Abbadia
Isola

Montauto

C. Giubil

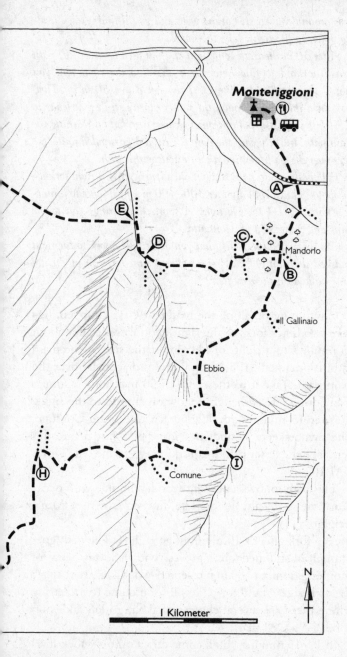

Monteriggioni

Mandorlo

Il Gallinaio

Ebbio

Comune

N

1 Kilometer

Pass around the left side of the well, and you'll find a track leading down to the right. Take this track.

After 30 m the track comes out at a flat area of scrub. The path is a little hard to find here. Look ahead to the right and you should see a red and white CAI sign on a tree 50 m off. Then look for a thin trail through the rather thorny scrub that leads to it. At this point, the path becomes clearer; turn left on reaching the main path. In the woods the path is easy, a deep-shaded route; the trees over the path are like a continuous gothic arch.

Follow the main path straight ahead, ignoring a right fork after about ⅔ km **G**. *In another 300–400 m you'll come to a junction with CAI 105. Go right. A short climb brings you to the ruins and panorama of Montauto.*

On the way back, watch that you don't take a fork to the right (marked with an old CAI sign) after 1 km that you might not have noticed on the way here.

Continuing on along the road past Casa Giubileo, (ignore two lesser forks to the right), you'll come after about 15 minutes to a right fork **H** almost the size of the main path. It's marked "105 B" and crosses diagonally over the main path. Take it to the right. In 50 m it joins a similar road coming from the left; follow on around to the right.

After 15 minutes you'll approach the house Comune. The owner keeps hounds in a large pen. Just before this pen, take the lesser path that forks down to the left. This is CAI 102.

This path follows a pleasant wooded hillside with occasional views toward the delicate, uneven crown of Monteriggioni.

At a fork after 5–10 minutes, go right **I**. The path goes through abandoned olive groves, with a lovely view of Monteriggioni. In 100 m it re-enters woods. BE ALERT HERE: the path zigzags and forks. You'll soon come to a clearing where there are several choices of path; go left and soon you'll see a CAI mark.

In 10–15 minutes you'll come down onto a wider, level

path where you turn right, and then right again soon after. This takes you alongside the organic gardens of Ebbio (see Santa Colomba walk) and down past their buildings, where you come onto a white gravel road. Proceed on this, ignoring a similar white gravel fork to the left 100 m past the main house.

Another ½ km down the main path you'll come to a T-junction with Il Gallinaio on your right (this is about an hour past Casa Giubileo). Go left. After a few minutes you'll come to an intersection **B** with CAI 101. Go across, keeping on the main gravel road.

The splendid appearance of Monteriggioni comes soon on your left.

The gravel road winds down to asphalt (and the stop for the bus back to Siena). To return to Monteriggioni, go left on the main asphalt road, then immediately up to the right.

SOUTH TUSCANY

Less frequented by tourists than Chianti but every bit as beautiful, and in fact superior in terms of its towns and buildings, the area below Siena, stretching from the monastery at Monte Oliveto south to Montalcino, and east to Montepulciano, concentrates some of the most rewarding walks to be had in Tuscany.

Three quite distinct landscapes are linked by the itineraries in this section. Most dramatic is the region of eroded clay hills known as the *crete,* stretching intermittently between Siena, Monte Oliveto and Buonconvento. These strange, pale, barren-looking slopes with their bare cliffs, broken gullies and meadows of white Jurassic limestone look altogether more lunar than terrestrial. A number of elegantly austere farms nevertheless seem to be eking out a living here, grazing sheep and growing crops in the remaining scoops and patches of fertile land. Nature, rather than man, is largely responsible for these eerie monuments to erosion. During the Pliocene age (7–3 million years ago) much of Italy sank below sea level, creating marine basins where quantities of sand and clay were deposited on the land that subsequently emerged. The *crete* never acquired a protective layer of vegetation, and have been quietly disintegrating ever since.

Much of the rest of this area was later covered with lava from the volcanoes at Radicofani and Mt. Amiata. The lava cooled into a layer of permeable black rock known as trachyte, which helped create the fertile farmland around Montalcino and further east around Pienza and Montepulciano. These regions, like Chianti, though with a slightly wilder flavor, constitute what we think of as the classic

Tuscan landscape of terraced vineyards, olive groves, fields of wheat and sunflowers, little orchards, hedges of dwarf maple and small oaks and cypresses planted for their silhouette effects by landowners uniquely conscious of the visual possibilities of their domains. (There were also practical reasons: many of the hilltop trees mark a crossroad in the old bridle paths.) And as in Chianti, the peculiar qualities of this landscape are a direct result of human choice, namely the rejection of the "industrial option" that presented itself as a possible avenue of development as early as the eighteenth century. Instead of pursuing what in the English midlands, say, resulted in slum-filled cities with belching factories and vast mills, the Tuscan ruling class, guided by the Accademia dei Georgofili ("friends of agriculture") made a conscious decision to adopt sharecropping as the best way of exploiting their properties. Whether the rural poor would have been better off as urban wage slaves than under this semifeudal system, whereby a large share of all their labor went to their landlord, is debatable, but the countryside itself certainly benefited. Even today, more than twenty years after the sharecropping system was legislated out of existence (and with it many of the small farms), the overall impression you get as you walk through the hills is of an extraordinarily rich and harmonious relationship between human beings and their environment.

Between Sant'Antimo and Pienza, the itinerary passes

along the Val d'Orcia, a rugged green stretch of mediter-
ranean *macchia* (scrub), gorges and the blue shallows of the
Orcia itself. There are few roads here, and few settlements
apart from the surrounding hilltop castles and fortified
towns such as Ripa d'Orcia and Rocca d'Orcia, some of
them dating back as far as the eighth century. At one time
the route through the valley formed part of the Via Francigena, the chief route linking Rome with the north (hence
the number of castles standing sentinel over it). Nowadays
the only part of this region receiving visitors in any serious
quantity is the little spa town of Bagno Vignoni, though
considering its charms, even this town manages to main-
tain a surprisingly low profile. The delightful spring-fed
pools here belong to a geothermal system that more or less
encircles Mt. Amiata, producing an abundance of natural
springs. Mt. Amiata itself, the only real mountain in southern Tuscany, has plenty of walks and a well-developed trail
system. But unless you're planning to go deep into the
woods and camp out, you can expect big crowds and the
type of establishments that cater to them. Still, if it's mid-
summer and too hot to walk elsewhere, at least you can be
assured of cooler temperatures.

Culturally, almost every one of these walks has something of outstanding interest to offer. The fine renaissance
monastery of Monte Oliveto with its amazing fresco cycle
and intarsia choir stalls, the walled medieval town of Buonconvento, the great hill towns of Montalcino and Montepulciano, the unfinished "Utopian" city of Pienza, the
abbey of Sant'Antimo (surely one of the loveliest Romanesque buildings in all of Italy)—with such a quantity of
gems, all of them set in gorgeous countryside, it would be
hard to imagine a more pleasant or fascinating set of walks.

The Walks

The walks in this section offer anything from an afternoon's
stroll to a journey that could occupy your entire trip.

With the exception of the last one (Murlo Ring Walk), the walks are arranged as a single itinerary that you can join or leave by public transport at any juncture except Ripa d'Orcia. If you have the time, doing the entire itinerary would be an extremely pleasurable way of spending a week or two. Abandoning the bulk of your luggage for even a couple of days and striking out across the countryside can really make the difference—as corroborated by so many of our readers—between a "postcard" vacation and an experience that is genuinely memorable. This area of southern Tuscany would be an excellent choice for a two- or three-day outing, not only because of the exquisite countryside but also because each destination is a small jewel: a point of concentrated interest and pleasure small enough to be thoroughly enjoyed without the pressure of rushing through in order to "see" everything.

Another lure of the itinerary is the presence of so many good *agriturismi* along the route. If you've never tried one before, you might consider it here. Staying in an *agriturismo* can be a less expensive option than a hotel and offers the chance to eat home-cooked meals, which are often better than what you get at most restaurants (to say nothing of the homemade wine). This option is especially recommended for anyone looking to slow down the pace of a trip.

For single-day walks, in addition to the two "official" rings in the chapter, any of the other itineraries can be done as ring walks, using the bus to complete the second half of the circuit. Don't be unduly concerned about using the bus; it's easily done (see the "Practical Matters" chapter for more information and encouragement). Whether or not you have a car, it's easy to set yourself down in just about any of the locations where a walk starts, and it's easy to get yourself back to wherever you want to go when you're done. The distances by road are short (and provide another scenic route through the area), and the buses are inexpensive, easy to use and on schedule. There's also the option of a taxi for those whose pocketbooks permit it, and we've included the phone numbers of local taxi services. It's fun to walk from one little town, across the countryside, to another town beyond, especially when all of the departure and arrival points are so rewarding in themselves.

Finally, some of the walks are fairly long, but few are especially strenuous. The country on the whole is unshaded, which makes these low-altitude walks best in spring and fall.

Food

The clay hills of the *crete* produce excellent white truffles. Montalcino and Montepulciano are, of course, chiefly known for their wines (respectively Brunello and Vino Nobile), but Montalcino also has quite a substantial sideline in good quality honey, while the hand-rolled eggless pasta or *pici* of Montepulciano and Pienza forms the basis for a number of simple, tasty dishes. Superb pecorino and other sheep cheeses are also particular specialties of Pienza.

Restaurants in the area are generally good, keeping for the most part to the traditional Tuscan standards—*ribollita, panzanella, pappa al pomodoro* (a bread-based tomato soup), grilled meats, roast game.

LOGISTICS

SIENA

🍴 Eating

🏨 Accommodation

🚌 Transport

Ⓜ Maps, guidebooks and trail info

ⓘ Miscellaneous info

🍴

Rosticceria Monti
Via Calzoleria, 12
Tel. 0577-289010
   Open at lunch and dinner, a great (and inexpensive) place to drop in for a quick bite. You can sit at a small counter and watch the kitchen through a big plate-glass window. They also do takeaway, a great source for

picnics: prepared dishes, salads, cheeses and salami, as well as bread and wine. They run a restaurant upstairs, serving the same good food as downstairs, but in a more relaxed environment. A nice, inexpensive wine they were serving when we were there was the Casa Nova, Vino da Tavola Rosato della Toscana '93, L.8500.

La Finestra
Piazza del Mercato, 14
Tel. 0577-42093
Closing day: Sunday

Gnocchi with spinach and mascarpone is a dish encountered here and there throughout Tuscany, but to taste it as it should taste, go to La Finestra in the Piazza del Mercato. It's quite a rich dish, but with a full fresh flavour of spinach coming through the mascarpone. Excellent pasta with *porcini* and rocket (*arugula*) seems to be a house speciality.

Good food, appetizing place, moderate price.

Osteria Castelvecchio
Via Castelvecchio, 65
Tel. 0577-49586
Closing day: Tuesday

Largely vegetarian, serving specialities such as couscous, though they also have meat dishes. Interesting *crostini.* Slow service. Good pork with apple.

Osteria Numero Uno
Via di Pantaneto, 32
Tel. 0577-221250

Since the original edition, this restaurant has moved and looks more touristy. The original osteria had a perfect *pasta arrabbiata* (a spicy tomato sauce—ask for it hot and garlicky), good salads, *porchetta* and other hearty meat dishes, and an extremely substantial *ribollita*. They had no menu, really a locals-only joint, where prices seemed to vary according to the whim of the proprietor, but were always low. We hope someone will review the new version of the restaurant for our web site.

PICNICS

See Rosticceria Monti, above

Morbidi, Via Banchi di Sopra, 73/75
Tel. 0577-280268
Closed: Wednesday afternoons

PALIO DINNERS

The city of Siena is divided into districts, or *contrade,* and all of these neighbourhood associations periodically hold dinners, most of which are connected in some way with the Palio, Siena's famous bareback horse race. These dinners occur throughout the year, however, not just at the times of the Palio. Long tables are set out in the street, and the area is festooned with the flags of the district. It's possible to buy tickets for these dinners. If you're interested, contact the Siena Tourist Office.

⊞

Tre Donzelle
Via Donzelle, 5
Tel. 0577-280358

A huge, rambling, fairly inex-pensive place; they are good about letting you leave bags. They have a room where they put them though the security of this room seems not to be of the tightest.

Hotel Athena
Tel. 0577-286313
www.hotelathena.com
A more upscale choice.

AFFITTACAMERE

The Siena tourist office has a good list of rooms for rent.

🚌

BUS

The main bus line in this region is TRA-IN (tel. 0577-204111) **www.trainspa.it**
This Web site has an English version available, and you can get all the current timetable information here.

Once in Siena, there are information points both in town and at the train station. In town, the ticket and information office for the buses between Siena and the towns in the "South

Tuscany" chapter is in Piazza San Domenico: 0577-204245. You can also get bus help at the tourist office.

TRAIN

The station is a short distance out of town (regularly served by local buses). Train informa-tion, tel. 0577-280115; from April to October there is usu-ally someone there who speaks English. Twenty-four-hour left-luggage facilities.

TAXI

Tel. 0577-49222

Ⓜ

Maps and guidebooks: can be bought at Feltrinelli (0577-44009). English spoken.

ⓘ

Tourist office: Piazza del Campo, 56; tel. 0577-280551
APT Siena: Via di Citta, 43
Tel. 0577-280551
Fax 0577-281041
www.terresiena.it
This is a very useful Web site for getting information before you leave on your trip. Once in Siena however, the better office is the one in the Campo at #56. They have maps, accommoda-tions listing, etc., and can help you figure out bus schedules.

17 ■ MONTE OLIVETO MAGGIORE TO BUONCONVENTO

A long but mostly downhill walk through the mysterious landscape of the *crete,* connecting one of the great monastic buildings of early renaissance Italy with the walled medieval town (albeit thoroughly modern in its outskirts) of Buonconvento. The eroded clay and limestone hills of the *crete,* at their most bizarrely lunar on the way from Siena to Monte Oliveto, merge with forest and arable land here to form a dramatic scenery of gullies, rolling hills, thick copses and meadows ending in sudden precipices. A number of handsome farmhouses punctuate the route (which in May and June, when we were there, was a feast of flowers), most of which goes along small paths and little-used dirt roads.

The Abbey of Monte Oliveto stands on the ridge of a hill in a glade of tall black cypresses. A splendid, asymmetrical gatehouse with a Della Robbia terra-cotta leads into the wooded grounds where the simple, beautifully proportioned brick structures of the abbey itself stand in all their original seclusion and tranquillity. Two great treasures are housed in the abbey. First, lining the main cloister is a fresco cycle of the life of St. Benedict by Signorelli and Il Sodoma (who seems intent on imparting as much camp and general homoerotic insinuation into the cycle as he can get away with, including a louche-looking portrait of himself in white gloves and a couple of glimpses of his pet badgers). Less famous, less sensational, but perhaps of finer quality are the wooden *intarsia* choir stalls by Fra Giovanni da Verona, masterpieces of wooden inlay with stunning pictorial detail of musical intruments, landscapes and geometric forms.

The monastery was founded by a group of wealthy, religiously-inclined Sienese merchants, among them Giovanni Tolomei, who started having visions of the Virgin after losing his sight. The group retired here in 1313 with the aim of reviving the plainness and austerity of the original Benedictine rule. Within six years their "Olivetan" order had been officially recognized by the pope. An ambitious building program began, and the monastery grew into one of the most powerful in Italy, a measure of which was the visit paid by Emperor Charles V in 1536 with a retinue of two thousand soldiers. Napoleon suppressed the monastery in 1810, but it was reestablished after World War II and is presently home to a couple of dozen white-robed monks who specialize in restoring old books as well as making wine, honey, olive oil and *Flora di Monte Oliveto,* a herbal tonic, that they sell in the monastery shop.

Contrary to what you might expect from its somewhat unprepossessing approach, Buonconvento turns out to be an exquisite little town, enclosed in the rectangular walls built by the Sienese in 1371. There isn't much to it, but the medieval brick buildings, the ornate gateways (the monumental northern gate opens toward the capital of the province), the squint little alleys and the pretty fourteenth-century parish church (altarpiece by Matteo di Giovanni) have an unusual delicacy. There's a small but very select museum of Sienese religious art, the Museo d'Arte Sacra, with paintings by Matteo, Bartolo di Fredi, Sano di Pietro and others. Buonconvento has been the seat of a *podesta* (head of the *comune,* or "mayor") since 1270, and the coats-of-arms of 25 *podestas* from the old days can still be distinguished on the facade of the fine Town Hall.

Food

La Torre at the Abbazia di Monte Oliveto Maggiore is a rare case of a restaurant in a tourist spot choosing *not* to exploit its monopoly for the purposes of fleecing its captive clientele, but rather to serve them excellent, moderately priced food in a friendly, efficient atmosphere. The menu has been well thought through, fairly traditional but with a wider than usual variety of dishes to choose from, and everything beautifully prepared. Pastas include a perfect *pici* with *aglio* and *olio* (oil and garlic—sounds easy but it's surprisingly hard to get right). The many good vegetable dishes include sauteed chard, fried artichoke (in season), green beans and zucchini. You can have an omelette for a main course, or a wonderfully crisp-skinned grilled guinea hen. If you have room for dessert, try the heavenly almond and lemon *Torta di Nonna*.

A lovely place to sit outside for a leisurely lunch or, if you're staying overnight at the monastery, dinner.

The Osteria da Duccio in Buonconvento, new since we were last here, is a quiet and pleasant place affiliated with the "Slow Food" movement (in this case, "Toscana Slow"—www.toscana-slow.it). The menu is promisingly simple with some intriguingly novel touches, such as the carpaccio of goose breast and a pasta with chicken and saffron. In season they make a deliciously pungent *tagliatelle* with fresh porcini mushrooms. The *Passato di Ceci,* a chickpea soup with pasta in it, is excellent, as is the home-cured *brasaola,* the generous portion of which makes it an option for a main course if you're not feeling up to the *Vera Bistecca Fiorentina* proudly advertised on the door. (We weren't, but judging from the rapturous sounds coming from a group next to us who had ordered it, it can't have been bad.) For dessert there are several home-baked cakes to choose from, and the wine list features a decent selection of Montepulcianos and Brunellos.

LOGISTICS

MONTE OLIVETO MAGGIORE– BUONCONVENTO,
about 4 hours

ⓘ   Miscellaneous info

🚌   Transport

Ⓜ   Maps, guidebooks and trail info

🍴   Eating

⊞   Accommodation

ⓘ

Siena: See listing for Siena tourist office (p. 232). There is also a small tourist office at Monte Oliveto itself, as well as the one in Buonconvento.

Buonconvento:
Via Soccini, 18 (in the building housing the Museo d'Arte Sacra)
Tel. 0577-807181
www.terresiena.it
   Buonconvento's Comune office at Via Soccini, 32, can also be helpful, and they have a fax number as well.
Tel. 0577-806102
fax 0577-807212
www.comune. buonconvento.siena.it

🚌
TRA-IN

Tel. 0577-204245 or 204111
www.trainspa.it

SIENA (RAILWAY STATION) TO MONTE OLIVETO:

Note that intercity buses usually leave from and return to the Siena railway station, just outside town. The inner-city buses make regular trips between town and the railway station.

Route 109
One bus per day, except Sunday. ATW at 13:55 in winter, 14:10 in summer.
Length of journey: Just under an hour
The bus route 109 is Siena to Castelmuzio. NOTE: Double-check the bus time, and get there early; we had some confusion about which bus it actually was. The bus should say Castelmuzio on the front, though you will be going only as far as Monte Oliveto (just before the Chiusure stop). Once on the bus, tell the driver that you're going to Monte Oliveto, as they don't actually stop at the monastery; they let you off at an intersection (see map) from which you have to walk about 15 minutes to the monastery itself.

FROM BUONCONVENTO TO SIENA:

Route 112 (Montepulciano–Siena) and 114 (Montalcino–Siena)

Buses on the 114 line stop at Bivio Buonconvento: ask at the *tabacchi* (where you buy your ticket) to direct you. Buses on line 112 stop in town; again, ask when you buy your ticket. Buses every hour or so. *Length of journey:* About 40 minutes

There are also trains from Buonconvento; the station is just a few minutes' walk from the town center. There are about six trains per day, length of journey is about 30 minutes. See the Trenitalia Web site (with information in English) for exact schedule info: **www.fs-on-line.com.** Or you can call the train station in Siena: 0577-280115.

TAXIS

See Siena Logistics section (p. 232).

Ⓜ

Crete Senesi: I—Val d'Arbia or any other 1:25,000 map available that shows the area from Monte Oliveto to Buonconvento. This map is widely available, including at the tourist office at the monastery (barring unforeseen circumstances, the possibility of which would suggest the prudent walker make this purchase before setting out for the monastery).

🍴

La Torre di Monte Oliveto
Monte Oliveto Maggiore
Tel. 0577-707022
fax 0577-707066
Price: Inexpensive to moderate
Closing day: Tuesday
    Lovely outdoor dining in pleasant weather.

Osteria da Duccio
Via Soccini, 76 (on the main piazza, Matteotti)
Tel. 0577-807042
e-mail: osteriadaduccio@tin.it
Price: Moderate
Closing day: Thursday

Bar Moderno
Via A. Gramsci, in Piazza Gramsci, just on the edge of the old town
    This bar has fantastic pastries (the *riso* when it's still warm from the oven in the morning is unparalleled). It's also open at 6:00, which we found convenient when trying to do walks in weather that reached 100° by 11:00. It's a popular destination with the early-morning working population, and we found it to be superior to the bar Sport in the center of the old town, though that is a nice place as well.

Paradiso Bar Locanda
Chiusure, on walk route
Closing day: Monday
    Open 9:30–23:30. Light

menu of first courses, *salume, bruschette;* nothing fancy.

You can eat at Pieve a Salti restaurant (see *agriturismo* listing below) even if you're not staying there. Reserve ahead.

⊞

Foresteria Monastica di Monte Oliveto Maggiore
Monte Oliveto Maggiore
Tel. 0577-707652
fax 0577-707644
(Hours: 9:30–10:00; 14:30–15:20; 17:30–18:00)
Price: Inexpensive

This is lodging at the monastery itself, and is correspondingly simple. They offer lodging for singles, married couples, and families. Reserve well ahead for busy seasons. Closed in November. No check-in after 19:30. No meals, but unless it's a Tuesday, you can eat at the extremely pleasant La Torre at the entrance to the monastery grounds. (See review above.)

Albergo Ristorante Roma
Via Soccini 14
Tel. 0577-806021
fax 0577-807284
Price: Double room, 56 euros

AGRITURISMO COMPLEX ON ROUTE

Pieve a Salti
Loc. Pieve a Salti
Tel. 0577-807244
fax 0577-809507
www.pieveasalti.it
Price: Double room, 42 euros per person, includes breakfast. They also have half- and full-board options. Also, single, triple and quadruple rates are available. Restaurant prices are inexpensive to moderate, compared to non-*agriturismo* restaurants.

This is a big establishment now, a little too big for our personal taste, but on the other hand it offers lots of extras, for example, its own health spa. Moreover, they advertise themselves as *biologico* (organic), which is a good sign. Rooms and apartments in a number of rustic farmhouses, at a maximum distance from the restaurant of 1 km. Restaurant serves local dishes prepared with their own cheeses, butter, meats, mushrooms and truffles, as well as their own wine. Indoor and outdoor pools, tennis court.

Directions

Leaving the parking lot, wind out the exit road to the junction with the main road, on which you turn right.

After about 400 m, at a left-hand bend in the main road, watch on the right for a path next to red shed with a sign "Sentiero Le Piaggiarelle" **A**.

Turn onto this path, then go up the steps immediately on your left. In a few minutes the path brings you to a quiet asphalt road (by a large wooden cross mounted on a brick base), where you turn right.

Follow this road for another 400 m where, ignoring a hairpin turn back to the left **B**, you continue straight on into Chiusure (on via Porta Senese), almost immediately passing the PT (post office) on your right.

Bear right again as the road forks, and you'll come into a small piazza (with a pay phone) facing the Bar/Alimentari Locando Paradiso. Walk through the piazza, with the bar on your left, and take the left turnoff.

In a minute or two, as the road bends to the left, watch for a small fork forward to the right: take this path. It immediately goes from asphalt to gravel.

Reaching a T-junction in another 30 m, turn right **C**.

About 400 m from **C**, you'll come to another T-junction (near a line of cypress trees) at Casa Caggiolo; go right. Here you get good views on either side of rolling hills with sudden precipices—an interesting mix of forest, farmland and the beautiful clay *cretes,* with a good view of the monastery thrown in.

Keeping to the main path (ignoring a left off the main road about ½ km past Caggiolo), you'll pass the driveway of the homestead Fornacino (a newer-looking house with large pine trees growing all around its borders), about 1½ km past Caggiolo. The road curves left around Fornacino's perimeter where, near the back of the house, there is a smaller dirt track forking to the left. Take this track.

In 2–3 minutes the road forks (with a green gate on the left fork); bear right here **D**.

Keeping always to the main track, in 15 minutes past Fornacino you'll pass to the right of an abandoned house, Casa Nuova di Gre. In another 10 minutes you'll come to

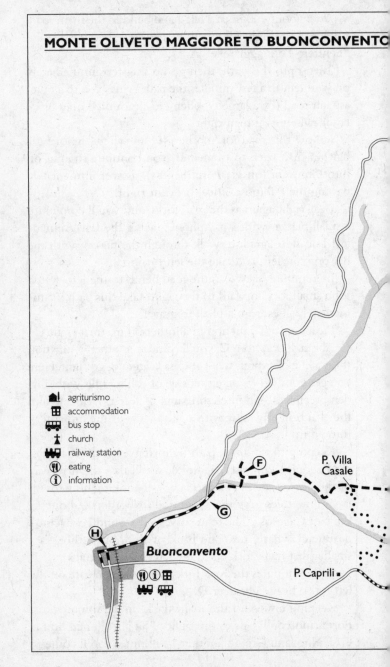

MONTE OLIVETO MAGGIORE TO BUONCONVENTO

Key:
- agriturismo
- accommodation
- bus stop
- church
- railway station
- eating
- information

P. Villa Casale

Buonconvento

P. Caprili

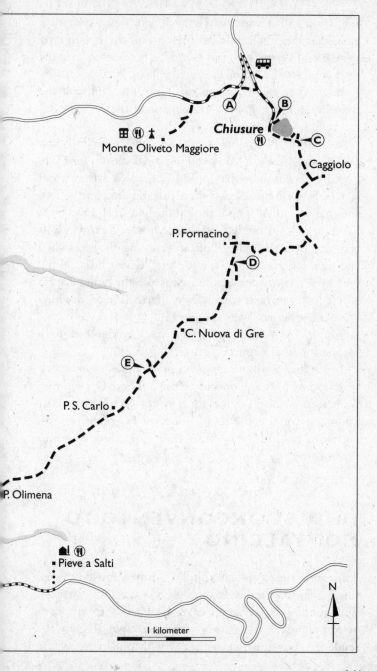

Monte Oliveto Maggiore

Chiusure

Ⓐ

Ⓑ

Ⓒ

Caggiolo

P. Fornacino

Ⓓ

C. Nuova di Gre

Ⓔ

P. S. Carlo

P. Olimena

Pieve a Salti

N

I kilometer

a junction with a larger road (gravel); ignoring a farm track going left downhill, bear left forward on the main gravel road **E**, ATW signed "San Carlo"; 10 minutes later the road winds to the left of the gated villa of Podere S. Carlo.

In another half hour the road goes up a hill past the farm buildings of Podere Olimena, and then begins descending just past it.

In another 10 minutes or so, take the lower fork past villa Casale. [NOTE: If you're taking the diversion for Pieve a Salti, bear left into what looks like Casale's driveway but is actually a dirt road, past their parking area on the left, and then past their house, also on the left. The gravel track bends around to the left below the house, then winds its way down to the valley bottom, crossing the streambed and then climbing up to the top of the next hill, and the road there. As you come out on the road, the house Caprili is just to your right; turn left on the road here, reaching Pieve a Salti in just over another km.]

About 15 minutes later, the road comes out to a T-junction with another road. Go left **F**.

In another 5–10 minutes, this road comes to an asphalt road leading to Buonconvento. Turn left here **G**. (You may want to hitch the 1 km from here to town.) In another kilometer you'll come to a T-junction **H** where you can go left to reach the train station, or enter Buonconvento through the city wall.

18 ■ BUONCONVENTO TO MONTALCINO

Aside from the steep final climb to Montalcino at the end, this is a fairly gentle walk through pretty, rolling farmland with sunflowers and grain crops giving way to vineyards as you approach the valuable (and correspondingly well-tended) wine-growing country of Montalcino, where

Italy's most highly rated and priced wine, Brunello, is produced. You may catch sight of deer, boar or hares, as much
of the walk passes through the wildlife protection zone of
Podere S. Anna.

This is a long walk, along mule tracks but also with a
long stretch along a little-used dirt road. Because of this
long stretch in the middle, if you are doing only one walk
in the area, you may want to pick one of the shorter ones.
Or, you may want to overnight at the *agriturismo* Colsereno,
whose restaurant is also open to the public for lunch and
dinner (see review of their restaurant below).

Coming at the end of a fairly long walk, the final approach to Montalcino high on its hilltop does look rather
daunting, but it's actually less brutal than it seems; and with
its stunning views and avoidance of the usual sprawl surrounding these old towns, it makes an exceptionally pleasant entrance.

The walled town with its impregnable-looking fortress
hasn't changed much since the sixteenth century, when it
offered the besieged Sienese republicans a last refuge from
the Imperial army of Charles V, earning itself the title of the
Republic of Siena at Montalcino and the honor (still ob-
served) of leading the parade every year at the Sienese *palio*.

It's a quiet, affluent, attractive town, with pretty buildings and flower-filled squares, and a number of excellent
shops selling (of course) Brunello, as well as the high-grade
honey the region also produces.

A few readers have told us they did the walk in reverse
wanting to avoid the last steep climb into Montalcino. If
you do that, watch for the very sharp right turn in Bibbiano, toward the Pub/Pizzeria L'Europeo (aka TNT).

Food

An hour or so into the walk, on the outskirts of Bibbiano,
there's a pub/pizzeria with some tables outside, called variously L'Europeo or TNT.

Further along the route, at the *agriturismo* at Podere Colsereno, is Locanda Pane e Vino. This countryside restaurant is as friendly and laid-back as they come, and the inexpensive food is very good. Among its mainly traditional dishes, the menu includes a deliciously zesty *panzanella* (bread salad with tomatoes, onions, basil and peppers) and a hearty *ribollita*. Main courses include stewed wild boar, many grilled meats and a superb *Carpaccio di Chiannina* (slices of raw, tender beef). The house wine and *vin santo* are also well worth ordering. All in all this makes a perfect rest stop, whether for lunch or dinner (you can stay the night), on an otherwise rather long walk.

There are a lot of flossy, overpriced restaurants in Montalcino. Less offensive than most is the Locanda di Piazza Padella in the piazza of that name (which is also called Piazza Garibaldi). As almost everywhere in this town, the prices are above average, but the menu does have some pleasant surprises. There's an excellent fresh egg *tagliatelle* with a pesto made of arugula and pistachio. The much-touted local honey features prominently—we avoided the rabbit in honey and "medicinal herbs," but quite enjoyed a fluffy *sformato* of honey, pecorino and nuts. For a cholesterol blow-out you could try the vast *crostone* with lard and melted pecorino (an appetizer, but it could certainly work as your main course). A less-pleasant surprise (unless you're feeling homesick for American fast food) is the mound of shoestring fries bizarrely served with the *spiedino* (kebab) of fresh mozzarella, tomato and herb pesto.

For something plainer, cheaper, and possibly better, you might try the Trattoria Bar Sciame on Via di Ricasole, an unpretentious-looking place that makes its own pasta, serving Tuscan basics.

LOGISTICS

BUONCONVENTO–MONTALCINO,
4–5 hours

ⓘ   Miscellaneous info

🚌   Transport

Ⓜ   Maps, guidebooks and trail info

🍽   Eating

🏨   Accommodation

ⓘ
UFFICIO TURISTICO COMUNALE

Costa del Municipio, 8
Tel. 0577-849331
www.prolocomontalcino.it and the general Siena area's Web site
www.terresiena.it

🚌
TRA-IN

Tel. 0577-204245 or 204111
www.trainspa.it
Siena: Note that intercity buses usually leave from and return to the Siena railway station, just outside town. The inner-city buses make regular trips between town and the railway station.
Route 114: Montalcino–Siena Frequent buses (about every 1½–2 hours, ATW the last one at 20:30), including a couple on Sunday
Length of journey: About an hour

Ⓜ
The 1:25,000 Val D'Orcia map is widely available at tourist offices and newsstand-type stores. Most of the area covered by the walks in our "South Tuscany" chapter are on this map.

🍽
Pub/Pizzeria L'Europeo (also called TNT)
Segalari/Bibbiano
Price: Inexpensive
Closing day: Tuesday
11:30–14:30 and 19:00–1:00 a.m.

Locanda Pane e Vino
Loc. Colsereno (On walk route: see walk directions and map.)
Tel./fax 0577-847063
cell 339-8598534
Price: Inexpensive
Closing day: Tuesday
Hours: Lunch, 12:00–14:20; dinner, 20:00–21:30 or 22:00
Reservations appreciated.

Ristorante Locanda di Piazza Padella
Piazza Garibaldi, 8
Tel. 0577-846054
Price: Moderate
Closing day: Monday

Ristorante Sciame
Via Ricasoli
Tel. 0577-848017
Price: Inexpensive
Closing day: Tuesday

⊞
AGRITURISMI ON ROUTE

Agriturismo Podere Colsereno
Loc. Colsereno (See walk directions and map.)
Tel. 0577-847030
fax 0577-846542
cell 333-6055480
**www.emmeti.it/Welcome/
Toscana/Senese/Montalcino/
Alberghi/Colsereno/
index.uk.html**
Price: Double room, 47 euros;
apartments, 62–165 euros

They have a restaurant, Locanda Pane e Vino. See listing above.

Pian Pietrucci
Loc. Pian Pietrucci (See walk directions and map.)
Tel. 0577-808304

When we were there, the owners had just sold the place. They said the new owners were planning to fix it up and still do *agriturismo*. If the new owners don't have a Web site, you can contact the tourist office in Buonconvento or the *comune*'s Web site (see listings in previous walk's Logistics section) for an update if you're interested in staying here.

AGRITURISMO SOUTH OF MONTALCINO

La Croce
Loc. La Croce

Tel./fax 0577-849463; in winter 0564-491731.
Price: Double room, 65 euros (includes dinner)

Although you'd need a car to stay here, this is a very friendly place to stay, 3 km south of Montalcino (on the car road to Sant'Antimo; watch for the sign on the left as you're coming from Montalcino). They don't speak much English, but that doesn't seem to matter much. There is a garden where you can have dinner under the pergola, outfitted with a barbecue and tables and chairs; or you can eat with the family, which is a blast. They have great food and their own homemade, extremely enjoyable wine *vin santo* and *grappa*.

MONTALCINO

Hotel Residence Montalcino
Via Soccorso Saloni, 31
Tel. 0577-847188
fax 0577-846477
www.residencemontalcino.it
e-mail: info@
residencemontalcino.it
Price: A wide range of reasonable prices. See their Web site, available in English.

Recommended by a reader who quite enthusiastically described it thus: "Beautiful views, economical, and in the middle of town, but quiet."

Directions

From the front of the train station **A**, cross the main street and follow the street straight ahead of the station, Via Vittoria Veneto.

Take the first right, then the first left, Via di Bibbiano (note that to your right here is the wonderful Bar Moderno). This is the road to Bibbiano, and in about ½ km it crosses the Ombrone River near some distinct *pini marittimi* (maritime pines).

About ½ km past the bridge, take the first left **B**, a dirt road leading to a farmhouse, Pian delle Noci.

Just before reaching the house, and before the stacks of wood and the small brick animal pen, take a right along a farm track heading toward the trees. Where you reach the trees, a cement platform bridge crosses the Stile River.

Continue past the castle tower (just visible up on the right through the trees) and where the track forks **C**, take the right fork, which brings you in about 3 minutes to a junction **D**, where you turn left. (Note that CAI takes you up a little track 50 m before the road forks at **C**, but this looks in danger of becoming overgrown. If you do want to take it, simply go up to the road on the CAI path, go left on the gravel road, and in 100 m you'll come to the junction **D**, where you go straight ahead.)

Pass an abandoned house, and when the road forks by a small pond, take the right branch. About 50 m past the fork, at the end of the hedge, the path meets a fork with a much smaller and somewhat overgrown track. Go left here **E**. (NOTE: Make sure to take the *track,* which is about 5 m in front of a large pine tree as you turn, and effectively between two hedges, rather than the entrance to a field that is directly in front of the tree.)

Follow this track, crossing between two fields with the tower of La Torre ahead of you to the left. Keep on straight, following the path into a second field, which it also

BUONCONVENTO TO MONTALCINO

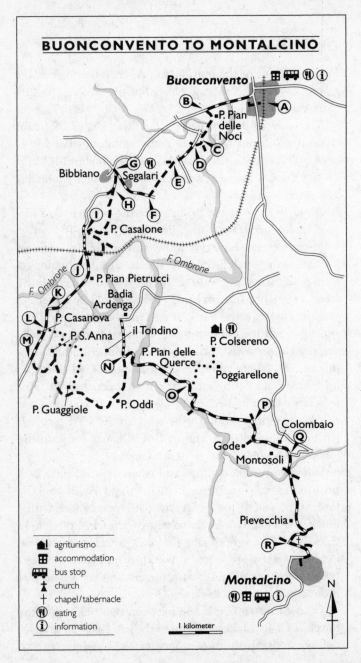

Buonconvento

B

P. Pian delle Noci

A

C

D

G

Segalari

Bibbiano

E

H

F

I

P. Casalone

F. Ombrone

J

P. Pian Pietrucci

K

Badia Ardenga

P. Colsereno

L

P. Casanova

il Tondino

M

P. S. Anna

P. Pian delle Querce

N

Poggiarellone

O

P. Oddi

P

P. Guaggiole

Colombaio

Q

Gode

Montosoli

Pievecchia

R

Montalcino

N

agriturismo
accommodation
bus stop
church
chapel/tabernacle
eating
information

1 kilometer

crosses. (If the track isn't there, just go straight forward and you'll pick it up on your right as you converge with another hedge.)

Follow the path out onto the gravel road that runs along the edge of the cypress trees, and go right on it **F**. Follow this road directly into Segalari, which is visible ahead of you on the right.

Bear right forward and uphill when the asphalt begins, through the little hamlet of Segalari, passing the pizzeria/pub/spaghetteria L'Europeo (or TNT) on your left. At the intersection near a building with a small bell tower, go left on the asphalt road (signed toward Montalcino) **G**.

After passing Via Ombrone on the left, the road soon bends around to the right, and you'll see a smaller dirt track on the left side (but actually leading straight ahead). Take this **H**, ATW signed "Casa di Bibbiano." (This is about 300 m past **G**.)

When this path comes directly in front of the farmhouse of Podere Casalone (in a sort of T-junction, as if it ends there), bear right at the driveway entrance. Follow the gravel path, passing below the house; near the bottom of the hill, about 100 m before you come to a T-junction with the main gravel road (you'll see a small building ahead of you at the junction), turn left on a small farm track **I**. (If you don't want to walk along a railroad track, skip to the note after this paragraph.) When you reach the bottom (about 400 m), rather than beginning to climb the track straight ahead, take the dirt track on your right instead (ATW Siena Province itinerary trail 514), in another minute or two reaching a railroad track. At the railroad track, turn right and walk along the track (be aware that there are—infrequent—trains along here) until you come out at the dirt road **J**. Turn left.

NOTE: If you don't want to walk on the railway track, instead of turning left at **I**, stay on the same path, down to the T-junction with the main gravel road in another 100 m. Turn left on the road, and in about 300 m you'll cross over the railroad track at **J** and continue straight on along the main gravel road.

Stay on this road, passing the *agriturismo* Pian Pietrucci on your left in another ½ km or so.

Another 400 m along this road you'll cross the Ombrone again (here it's a real river, as opposed to the tiny stream it was when we first met it just outside Buonconvento). About ½ km beyond the Ombrone crossing, you'll cross another little bridge, and in another 200 m or so come to a fork: bear left **K**.

About 350 m beyond **K** (and about 100 m before you reach the big stone house Podere Casanova on your right), there's a non-road alternate route that you might like to try; although the road you're on is about to become even quieter than it already is, you can take this part all on farm tracks for a couple of km if you prefer. There are more ups and downs on the alternate than on the road. Either way is nice.

Alternate:

*At the point mentioned above (about 100 m before Podere Casanova), on the left, just before an avenue of cypresses begins along the road, there's a farm track **L**. Take this down to the streambed and up the other side, toward the cypress-lined ridge opposite you.*

When you come out on the cypress-lined gravel road, with some modern farm buildings to your left, turn right onto the gravel road.

Watch on the left for a farm track going downhill through the middle of a field (about halfway down the gravel road, about 100 m). This path crosses another streambed and climbs up the other side. Take this path.

When you reach the top, the path continues straight on down the other side, then up again: go ahead on this. You can see Badia Ardenga to your left on a hilltop, and a little house, Tondino, in the valley.

When you reach the top again, continue straight on, toward a big tree about 30 m in front of you and a vineyard (there's also a vineyard on your right here). Turn right when you reach the vine-yard. In another few minutes the path reaches a little stand of small cypress trees; bend left here, toward the abandoned house Podere Guaggiole. After passing Guaggiole on your right, you'll come out on the main gravel road, where you turn left.

Passing the turnoff **L** for the farm track alternate and staying on the main road, you'll pass a big stone house on your right, Podere Casanova. About ½ km past Casanova, watch for a slightly smaller gravel road, just before another avenue of cypresses begins on the main road. Turn left here **M**.

After about 600 m on this gravel road, you'll come to a fork at a triangle of cypresses with a shrine in them (and the house Casa S. Anna about 100 m to your left); bear right here. In another km or so you'll pass the abandoned house of Podere Guaggiole on your left (which is where the farm track alternate rejoins us).

About 1 km past Guaggiole, you'll pass Podere Oddi. (Note that the CAI trail shown on the Val D'Orcia map is wrong at this point. The path they've marked on the map is no longer in existence.) About 1 km past Oddi the road bends right **N**, at the entrance (straight ahead) to Badia Ardenga. Unless you're visiting the Badia, stay on the main gravel road.

In another km you'll pass the stone houses of Podere Pian delle Querce on your right. About ½ km past Pian delle Querce the road forks **O**. ATW on the left there's a "private road" sign. This road actually goes to the *agriturismo* Colsereno and its restaurant, Locanda Pane e Vino. (The main entrance to Colsereno comes in from the north; this is the secret southern access route.)

To get to Podere Colsereno, take the left private road here, bearing right at the first fork in about 400 m. In another 200 m or so you'll pass the driveway to Poggiarellone on your right; turn left here. You'll reach Colsereno in another 300 m.

Unless you're stopping off at Colsereno, bear right at **O**. In another 600 m bear left, where the right is signed to "Podere La Magia." Another km past that, you'll come to a T-junction **P**; turn right.

Stay on this road, ignoring a turnoff to Gode in 350–400 m. In another 400 m the road changes to asphalt. The asphalt ends in another 300 m or so, at a fork **Q**; go right here.

In about 300 m bear left at a fork (ATW signed for "Le Fonti"), cross a little bridge and fork right just after the bridge.

Pass the old house Pievecchia on your right in another km. The road turns left here, then bends right (ignore a left fork up to an old house).

In another 5 minutes or so, passing an arched drinking fountain recessed into the stone wall, follow the main path as it bends sharply to the right, ignoring a fork off to the left.

After another 5–8 minutes of steep climbing, you'll come out at another gravel road **R**, which you take uphill to the left, passing in 2 minutes a little stone chapel (ignoring a fork back to the right, just before the chapel, and another fork down to the left 100 m after it).

Soon after this, you'll see the stone arch of Porta Burelli, through which you enter the town of Montalcino. For the center of town, turn right at the Hotel Capitani (about 100 m past Porta Burelli), then left past the little park.

19 ■ MONTALCINO TO SANT'ANTIMO

A pleasant walk through farmland and Brunello country, passing some old farmsteads and hamlets that appear completely untouched by the centuries, especially that of Villa a Tolli, a solitary, strange and serene little hamlet tucked away with its little fountain and tall cypresses, crumbling walls, little houses, minuscule cemetery and wood cross at the fork in the road. The slight discomfort of an unavoidable (but very brief) stretch on the asphalt road is more than made up for by the prettiness of the rest of the walk, above all the stunning sight of the Romanesque abbey of Sant'Antimo lying below you in the olive groves and pastures full of white heifers as you come over the ridge of the Starcia valley. Though the abbey is best seen from the other side, even from here it would be hard to imagine a more sympathetic combination of architectural grace and natural setting.

Begun in 1118, the abbey was once home to a prominent Benedictine community. Few of the monastic buildings remain (the chapter house and refectory are now used as barns) but the abbey itself with its rounded apse and perfectly proportioned tower survives in all its glory. Creamy stone bricks, luminous Volterran alabaster, playful carvings and frescoes of animals (copulating pigs in the sacristy) give it a peculiarly sunny air. Note the apse with its little radiating chapels, and the women's gallery—an unexpected borrowing from Byzantine architecture.

A group of French Cistercian monks now runs the abbey, celebrating Mass with Gregorian chant several times a day.

Food

It pains us to say this, and we do so tentatively since it is possible we caught them on a bad night, but Bassomondo seems to have taken a dive since we were last here. The personnel and menu are much the same, but the service has become tired if not surly, and the food decidedly hit and miss. If you stick to the *zuppa di pane* (a variation on *ribollita*) and one of the homemade pastas, you'll probably be all right, but you move on to the boar stew or the rabbit in Brunello at your own risk (ours were almost inedibly salty). Again, this was once a lovely restaurant and even quite recent reports from readers have been glowing, so we may be wrong here, and hope that we are. But be warned.

If you don't want to take a chance, there's a newish trattoria/pizzeria across the road from Bassomondo, called the Locanda Sant'Antimo. It's reasonably priced, with a large but fairly conventional menu that includes many truffled dishes. The cooking isn't inspired—more emphasis on quantity than quality (they make a gigantic mixed salad that includes tuna *and* mozzarella). On the other hand, we had an excellent, steaming, spicy plate of *pennette all'arrabiata* and a pretty good *Caprese* salad. The wood-fired pizza oven is only in service at night, which is probably the best time to come here. They have rooms, so you can relax at a table with a view of the floodlit abbey, then roll on into bed.

You can also buy snacks and sandwiches up in the pretty village of Castelnuovo dell'Abate, either at the bar or further along at the little store.

If you're picnicking at Sant'Antimo, there's a drinking fountain outside the apse end of the church.

LOGISTICS

MONTALCINO–SANT'ANTIMO,
about 3 hours

ⓘ   Miscellaneous info

🚌   Transport

Ⓜ   Maps, guidebooks and trail info

🍴   Eating

🎴   Accommodation

ⓘ

See listing for Montalcino tourist office in previous walk's Logistics section.

🚌

TRA-IN

Tel. 0577-204245 or 204111
www.trainspa.it
Siena: Note that intercity buses usually leave from and return to the Siena railway station, just outside town. The inner-city buses make regular trips between town and the railway station.
Route 114: Siena–Montalcino Buses from Siena to Montalcino aren't as frequent as buses from Montalcino to Siena. ATW one at 7:15, then not again until afternoon. Check the schedule.

Length of journey: About an hour

The bus between Montalcino and Sant'Antimo (Castelnuovo dell'Abate) is privately operated and called La Peschiera. It leaves Montalcino from Piazza Cavour (where the current schedule is posted) and leaves Sant'Antimo from the intersection near the restaurant Bassomondo, where the main road and the road leading down to the abbey meet. Length of journey is about 15 minutes. No buses on Sunday. It's also pretty easy to hitch this stretch, if you're so inclined.

ATW schedule is:
From Montalcino: 7:10, 10:40 (Friday only), 13:45, 14:45, 19:00
From Sant'Antimo: 6:35, 7:45, 11:05 (Friday only), 14:25, 16:45
www.lapeschiera.it

Ⓜ

The 1:25,000 Val D'Orcia map is widely available at tourist offices and newsstand-type stores. Most of the area covered by the walks in our "South Tuscany" chapter are on this map.

🍴

Locanda Sant'Antimo
Via Bassomondo, 8 (just at the top of the road leading down to the abbey)
Tel. 0577-835615
www.locandasantantimo.it
Price: Inexpensive
Closing day: Tuesday
They do pizzas at night.

Ristorante Bassomondo
Via Bassomondo, 7
Tel. 0577-835615
Price: Inexpensive
Closing day: Monday

🏨

AGRITURISMO ALONG THE ROUTE

Le Ragnaie
Loc. Ragnaie (On walk route; see walk directions and map.)
Tel./fax 0577-848639
e-mail: info@leragnaie.com
www.emmeti.it/Welcome/ Toscana/Senese/Montalcino/ Ristoranti/ragnaie.it.html
Price: Double, 77 euros; single, 52 euros; prices include breakfast

They have a pool. Will usually serve dinner—especially if you tell them you're on foot—if you reserve ahead. Make sure to arrange this ahead of time, as there aren't any restaurants within walking distance.

Il Cocco
Villa a Tolli; loc. Il Cocco (On route; see walk directions and map.)
Tel./fax 0577-285086
www.ilcocco.it
Price: See the Web site.

They have two apartments, usually rented on a weekly basis. Staying here will only work if you have a car, in which case you could use this location as a base for exploring the area. At the request of guests, they will serve dinner once or twice a week.

CASTELNUOVO DELL'ABATE

(Sant'Antimo is just outside this village.)
Locanda Sant'Antimo
Via Bassomondo, 8 (just at the top of the road leading down to the abbey)
Tel. 0577-835615
www.locandasantantimo.it
Price: Double, 65 euros (one of the rooms has an extra single bed in it as well)

When we were there they had only two rooms available, which were simple and clean with nice views. They had a shared bathroom. However, their Web site now indicates sixteen beds, so they must have expanded, and probably have rooms with private bathrooms as well.

Attached to the restaurant of the same name (see listing above). This is probably the easiest place to stay, near the abbey.

La Palazzetta
Loc. La Palazzetta (on IGM map, about 1¼ km NE of Casteln-uovo dell'Abate).
Tel./fax 0577-835631
cell 348-9038507
Price: Double, 62 euros

They usually rent by the week, or for three nights mini-mum. However, if they have a vacancy, they will gladly rent the apartments by the night. No meals are served here though, so you'd have to walk down the road 1¼ km to Bassomondo or Locanda Sant'Antimo.

ⓘ
ATW visiting hours at the abbey of Sant'Antimo are 10:30–12:30 and 15:00–18:30. Masses (at which Gregorian chant is sung) are Monday–Saturday at 7:00, 12:45, 14:45, 19:00 and 20:30 (21:00 in sum-mer); Sunday at 7:30, 9:00, 11:00, 12:45, 14:45, 18:30 and 20:30 (21:00 in summer).

Directions

Leaving from the large traffic intersection by the southwest tip of the Fortezza wall, where the car road signed to Sant'Antimo begins, cross over the intersection, heading for

MONTALCINO TO SANT' ANTIMO

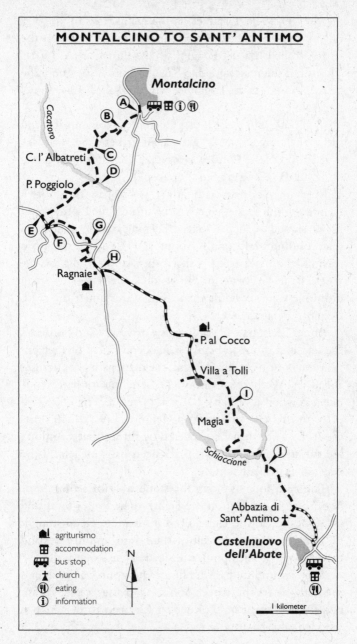

Montalcino

Ⓐ

Ⓑ

Ⓒ

C. l' Albatreti

Ⓓ

P. Poggiolo

Ⓖ

Ⓔ

Ⓕ

Ⓗ

Ragnaie

P. al Cocco

Villa a Tolli

Ⓘ

Magia

Schiaccione

Ⓙ

Abbazia di
Sant' Antimo

*Castelnuovo
dell'Abate*

Cacatoro

agriturismo
accommodation
bus stop
church
eating
information

N

1 kilometer

the bar (ATW Le Terrazze) on the hill in front of you and on the right. Immediately past here the first street on the right is called Via del Poggiolo. Take this street **A**. (NOTE: This is not the road signed to Sant'Antimo. Also, ignore the first right off Via del Poggiolo, which is called Traversa del Poggiolo.)

In about 200 m you'll pass a cemetery on your left and the asphalt gives way to gravel. From here the road descends, and at the bottom forks; take the right fork, going downhill **B** (ATW signed "Pietroso").

Keep on the main path. About ½ km past **B**, ignore a right downhill fork—which is the turnoff for Pietroso and ATW signed as such—instead keeping on the main road that continues left uphill. About 150 m past the Pietroso turnoff, the road makes a sharp turn to the right and on your left, at the corner of the bend **C**, you'll notice a small old stone water conduit channeling water under the road. Begin to be alert here.

About 25 m past **C** you'll pass a driveway and house on the left, and the road begins to descend; 75 m further on, near the bottom of this descent, the main path goes straight ahead (ATW there's an iron gate here, but it's hardly noticeable when it's open), but you turn left. There are two paths to the left: you want the leftmost one, which skirts the stone wall (that is so covered by shrubs that you don't see the stone underneath) that's been on your left all the way along this last stretch.

The path follows along the stone wall for a minute or two (vineyard below on the right), then comes to an old stone house on the right, Casa L'Albatreti. Keep straight on here, passing to the left of the house, and just beyond the house bear left uphill, still skirting the stone wall.

Another minute past the house the stone wall ends and the path enters the woods and soon crosses a tiny stream bed **D** (bear right here). Keep to the main path, which is wooded and shady.

In about 10 minutes the path emerges from the woods at an old stone house, Poggiolo, on your right. Bear left here.

Past Poggiolo the road is wider. Follow it for ¾ km (7–10 minutes), when it comes out on a quiet asphalt road **E**. Turn left.

After about 150 m on this road, there's another asphalt road on the right (signed to "Tavernelle" and other places). Across from this turnoff, on the left side of the road, is a small dirt path **F**; take this path.

This is not the loveliest of paths, but it avoids having to walk on the asphalt road. After about 7–8 minutes, you re-join the asphalt road; ATW the last 50 m before you reach the road is a bit of a scramble over some mounds of bull-dozed earth. It's not difficult though, and it's clear where you're meant to go.

On reaching the main road **G**, cross over and pick up the trail directly opposite.

Where the path forks in about 70 m, go left. Continue on the main path for about 5 minutes until you come to a junction with a gated driveway, where you turn left. Soon you'll come back out on another main road, where you turn right.

Walk about 200 m on this road, until you come to the first left, a gravel road for Villa a Tolli; take it **H**. (Note that the *agriturismo* Le Ragnaie is across the main road from **H**.)

Stay on this main gravel road, through pretty country-side with good views of Mt. Amiata along it. There's little traffic on it, but it is long—about 2½ km—and unshaded.

After about 2 km, you'll pass the entrance for Podere al Cocco on the left, and a little more than ½ km beyond that, you'll reach the hamlet of Villa a Tolli.

Heading toward the bell tower of the little church, you'll come to a fork with a big wooden cross in front of the church. Bear left at the cross (ATW signed "Fattoria La Magia").

Follow the main track, a pleasant, partly shaded walk.

After about 10 minutes (¾ km) you'll come to a fork **I** at the long driveway of La Magia. Bear left downhill here, ATW signed for "Sant'Antimo."

Follow the path, continuing downhill (ignoring a hairpin fork left downhill after about 10 minutes). Soon some glimpses of Sant'Antimo come into view. Stay on the main path, ignoring minor forks; you'll have a sense of where the abbey is, so you'll know which way to go: always keep to the main path.

About 20 minutes past the La Magia driveway you'll cross over a streambed, and about 5 minutes later you'll reach a T-junction with a gravel road **J**. Turn left (to the right here, the road crosses over the streambed 15 m on).

Follow this road all the way to the abbey, less than 1 km away.

(NOTE: To reach restaurants and bus stop, you need to walk up the Sant'Antimo access road to the main road; see map.)

20 ■ SANT'ANTIMO TO RIPA D'ORCIA

A gorgeous and varied stretch of country, the rolling contours of the Starcia valley give way to the more dramatic scenery of the Val d'Orcia, with its knolls, streams, gorges and castle-topped promontories. The view of Sant'Antimo to the left as you set off is magical. The abbey with its agglomeration of slopes and terraces sits like a small stylized hill on a background of fields, cypresses and braille-like arrangements of olive trees that manage to look decorative without showing the fanatical orderliness of overexploited farmland. Meanwhile the colors and contours of the town of Castelnuovo dell'Abate blend almost indistinguishably into its own real hill, forming an unusually harmonious meeting of man and nature.

As you reach the river Orcia (where a small amount of wading may be necessary, depending on recent rainfall) and move into the Val d'Orcia, the pervading atmosphere begins to feel more remote. There are few blacktopped roads around here, and the silence is impressive. Little pathways lead through a characteristically Mediterranean scrub of holm oaks (leaves like a cross between a holly and a regular oak), arbutus and broom, sufficiently dense and abundant to shelter animals such as boars, foxes, porcupines (a good spot for finding quills), hares, roe deer and badgers. Coming out of the woods, you'll see the splendid central keep of Ripa d'Orcia ahead of you, with the fortress of Rocca d'Orcia behind it. The castle and tiny hamlet of Ripa d'Orcia belonged to the Sienese territorial organization in the medieval period, later passing into the hands of the Carli branch of the Piccolomini family, who own it today and have turned it into what must be one of the most peaceful hotels (complete with its own restaurant) in the country.

We've done the walk from here to Bagno Vignoni in both directions, and there are also several walks marked on the IGM, all of which could keep you happily occupied here for a couple of days.

Food

The owners have kept the restaurant in this spectacular place small and low-key—even to the point of subdued. The menu is minimal, the food good but basic. They make a flavorful bean and farro soup, and decent *crostoni* with eggplant or melted cheese and ham. Pastas were fine, and a veal dish with spicy tomato and mushroom was pleasant, as was the strawberry cake that followed. They also produce their own wine, a very enjoyable accompaniment to dinner.

The indoor dining room is a little gloomy, especially as there's a terrace outside with gorgeous sunset views, where you can have drinks but not, unfortunately, dinner. Perhaps with a few more requests than our own, the owners will consider changing this policy.

LOGISTICS

SANT'ANTIMO– RIPA D'ORCIA,

about 3 hours

ⓘ Miscellaneous info

🚌 Transport

Ⓜ Maps, guidebooks and trail info

🍴 Eating

🎴 Accommodation

ⓘ
SAN QUIRICO D'ORCIA

Via D. Alighieri, 33
Tel. 0577-897211

🚌

For buses to Sant'Antimo, see Montalcino to Sant'Antimo walk, Logistics section. There is no public transport (or anything else except the castle) at Ripa d'Orcia.

Ⓜ

The 1:25,000 Val D'Orcia map is widely available at tourist offices and newsstand-type stores. Most of the area covered by the walks in our "South Tuscany" chapter are on this map.

🍴

See listing for Castello di Ripa d'Orcia below.

🎴

Castello di Ripa d'Orcia
Loc. Ripa d'Orcia
Tel. 0577-897376
fax 0577-898038
www.castelloripadorcia.com
Price: Double with breakfast, 110–135 euros
They also have apartments. See the Web site.

The closing day for the restaurant is Monday. Reservations requested. The restaurant is open for dinner only, so you can either picnic or walk on to Bagno Vignoni for lunch.

They normally have a two-night minimum, but if you explain you're on foot, and they have the room, they will make an exception.

Directions

Coming from the abbey, take the steep road, almost 1 km, up to the main intersection **A**. Take the second–most left, passing the Osteria Bassomondo on your right and carrying on along that road, which turns to gravel just beyond here.

This is a small road, very untraveled, with a wonderful

SANT' ANTIMO TO RIPA D' ORCIA

accommodation
bus stop
church
eating
information

Abbazia di
Sant' Antimo

Castelnuovo dell'Abate

P. la F

view to the valley on the left, the abbey set amid patchwork fields punctuated by cypresses. Don't forget to look back!

After about 20 minutes from **A**, you'll pass Podere La Fornace on the right. Wide views on the right out to Monte Amiata.

In 15 minutes or so, you'll pass the two farmhouses of Podere Loreto–S. Pio on the right. The road begins to descend, and you'll soon see the glitter of the river Orcia.

About 15–20 minutes past Loreto–S. Pio, you'll pass Podere Casalta on the left (a relatively new stone farmhouse, and ATW home of three noisy but harmless dogs). Bear to the left after passing the house.

After a continuous descent from Casalta, you'll reach the bottom, having crossed the railway track (probably without noticing it; it tunnels under you, far below), and you'll come to an open space with several paths leading off

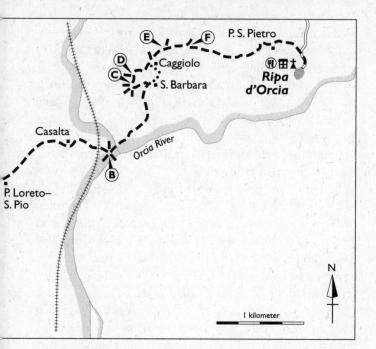

it **B**, and the railroad track above you to the right. The selection of paths is as follows: to your right going under the
railroad tracks; straight ahead downhill to the river; 90° to
the left; and hairpin left. Take the 90-degree to the left
path, which you'll see borders the river.

In another minute the path crosses a stream on a funny
kind of bridge made of big rocks. Beyond the bridge,
continue on the main path, which bears left.

After following the path up and down across open fields
for about 10 minutes, you approach the house S. Barbara
(not shown on IGM map). Here you can follow the CAI
route, which continues up the road to the next farmhouse,
Caggiolo (pick up directions from Caggiolo below), or
you can take a chance with our shady variant, as follows:

Reaching the compound of S. Barbara and standing in
the driveway of the various buildings with the house to

your right, turn left away from the house (ATW CAI mark on tree here), bending back downhill in almost the same direction as you've just come. In about 25 m there's a slightly smaller fork bending uphill to the right; take this path.

Stay on this path for about 5 minutes, until you reach an intersection of paths **C**: there are two to the right and two to the left. Take the first right, which dips briefly, then begins to climb gently.

In another couple of minutes, reach a T-junction with another dirt track **D**: go right.

In about 5 minutes more, the path forks: bear left. Follow this path uphill and in another 2 minutes it bends left and reaches Caggiolo, intersecting another gravel road that wraps around Caggiolo (the CAI route). Turn left, passing the house on your right. Where the road forks just beyond it, take the right fork. In another couple of minutes the path forks again; go right again **E**.

In about 5 minutes you'll come to an open space that looks as if it might have been mined or quarried. The main path goes straight ahead, and a smaller path branches off to the right of that. Take this smaller fork, downhill **F**. (ATW there are two blue and yellow marks in the first few minutes of this branch, in case you are in any doubt.)

This is a very nice, mostly wooded path. The castles of Ripa d'Orcia, and Rocca d'Orcia behind it, appear on the right, and of course Monte Amiata.

Stay to the main path, passing Podere S. Pietro in 20 minutes or so. In another 5–10 minutes the path leads up to a T-junction, with a chapel on your left. Turn right here, and so into Ripa.

21 ■ RIPA D'ORCIA TO BAGNO VIGNONI (and Bagno Vignoni to Ripa D'Orcia)

A pleasant, effortless walk along the Val d'Orcia, most of it downhill, with the bonus of a swim in a spring-fed pool at the end. A sharp descent from the castle of Ripa d'Orcia leads to the banks of the Orcia itself, a clear, shallow, boulder-strewn river at this point, with the ruins of a bridge that was swept away in the great floods of 1929. This was once an important crossing, connecting the castle of Ripa with those of Rocca and Castiglione d'Orcia. An abandoned mill across the river gives this forlornly picturesque area its name: la Mulina. The stones for the impressive pillars of the bridge were brought from a travertine quarry (now derelict) which you'll pass through just before reaching Bagno Vignoni. Shortly after it a clear, gushing, slightly sulphurous stream marks the beginning of the geothermal spring system on which the spa of Bagno Vignoni was built, and a little beyond this you'll reach the cliff below Bagno Vignoni itself, with its warm spring water splashing down into an extraordinary, light opaque blue pool where you can bathe. Up at the top of the cliff you'll be greeted by the surprising sight of a long culvert with a number of generally rather overweight bodies lying in it, reading the newspapers while the curative waters gush over their limbs.

The waters of Bagno Vignoni have been "taken" since Etruscan times, its thirty-six springs gushing from 1000 meters underground. Saint Caterina of Siena is said to have appreciated their therapeutic qualities, as is Lorenzo the Magnificent, whose family built the splendid arcaded *piscina* (swimming pool)—a kind of flooded, bubbling piazza, famously used by Tarkovsky for some of the more surreal passages of his film *Nostalgia*. The *piscina* itself is off-limits for bathing these days, but in addition to the cliff pool you can bathe in the Posta Marcucci hotel, a converted renaissance summerhouse built by Pius II, who also built the nearby town of Pienza.

We've done the walk both ways this time; there are several ring walks here, charted on the Val D'Orcia map, that could keep you amused for a few days' stay in Bagno Vignoni.

Food

Of the many tempting restaurants in Bagno Vignoni, Il Loggiato is the most quirky and delightful. Owned by three graduate students in their twenties and located in an old Capuchin friars' convent, it's perhaps more a kind of Italian tapas bar than a fully fledged restaurant, but its snacks, which include several polenta dishes, twenty different *crostoni* (among them, of course, the now ubiquitous *lardo di colonnata*), wonderful salads, and enough pecorino platters to satisfy the most serious cheese connoisseur, are substantial as well as inexpensive. First-rate ingredients and an inspired simplicity in the presentation made us want to sample every dish we saw passing by, from the plates of wild boar *salumi* to the bowls of steaming *ribollita*. Everything we did eat was excellent, and we particularly recommend the sublimely rich polenta with lard, the *crostoni* with melted pecorino and artichoke, and the unusual chickpea, arugula and onion salad.

LOGISTICS

RIPA D'ORCIA– BAGNO VIGNONI (AND BAGNO VIGNONI–RIPA D'ORCIA), about 1½ hours each way	ⓘ Miscellaneous info
	🚌 Transport
	Ⓜ Maps, guidebooks and trail info
	ⓘⓘ Eating
	⊞ Accommodation

ⓘ

SAN QUIRICO D'ORCIA

Via D. Alighieri, 33
Tel. 0577-897211
www.comunesanquirico.it

🚌

RAMA

Tel. 0564-25215
www.griforama.it
San Quirico–Bagno Vignoni
(See notes below.)
Siena–Arcidosso line
Two to four buses per day
Length of journey: 10 minutes

The Bagno Vignoni bus goes to and from San Quirico, which is the hub for transfer to/from Siena. ATW there are eight TRA-IN buses a day from Siena (stopping in Buonconvento) to San Quirico, and an additional four from Buonconvento to San Quirico. Going in the other direction, there are nine TRA-IN buses a day from San Quirico to Buonconvento, six of which continue on to Siena. (For TRA-IN bus info, see the Logistics section of one of the previous South Tuscany walks.)

The RAMA bus company services Bagno Vignoni. There are two buses a day (except Sundays) from San Quirico to Bagno Vignoni, ATW 9:00 and 15:15. The 15:15 actually originates in Siena, bus # 2056, departing Siena railroad station at 14:15, stopping also at Buonconvento railroad station at 14:55, arriving San Quirico at 15:15, where you change for the 15:15 connection to Bagno Vignoni. From Bagno Vignoni to San Quirico there are buses (Monday through Saturday) at 6:27, 8:50 (8:57 on Sunday), 14:17, 14:50 (goes through to Buonconvento and Siena), and on Sunday a bus at 18:25. This is the schedule ATW, but check again when you travel.

Note that you can also get TRA-IN buses for Pienza and Montepulciano in San Quirico.

Ⓜ

The 1:25,000 Val D'Orcia map is widely available at tourist offices and newsstand-type stores. Most of the area covered by the walks in our "South Tuscany" chapter are on this map.

🍴

Il Loggiato
Via Delle Sorgenti, 36
Tel. 0577-887174
cell 338-2352256
www.loggiato.it
Price: Inexpensive
Hours: Open Friday only from 18:00 until midnight; Saturday and Sunday 11:00 until midnight. During vacations and all of July and August, open every day.

269

⊞

La Locanda del Loggiato
Piazza del Moretto, 30
Tel. 0577-888925
cell 335-430427
www.loggiato.it
Price: Double room with
breakfast, 130 euros

Hotel Le Terme
On the main piazza
Tel. 0577-887150;
fax 0577-887497

Price: Double room with
breakfast, 90 euros

For less expensive accom-
modations, you can check with
the tourist office for *affittacamere* (rooms for rent in
people's homes).
   One current listing is:
Barbara Marini
Bagno Vignoni, 25
0577-887174

Directions

From Ripa D'Orcia, follow the road out, soon passing on
your left a chapel at a fork in the road (where you came
into Ripa if you walked from Sant'Antimo) **A**.

Bearing right past the chapel, after nearly another ½ km
there's a dirt road to the right, across from some cypress
trees (and a drinking fountain with nonpotable water).
Take this right **B**.

Stay to the main path, now well signed by CAI. The
path winds downhill for about 30 minutes of steady descent, when it bottoms out and crosses a small streambed,
then forks **C**. The right fork goes down to the river,
which is very pretty: 50 m down to the right you can see
the ruined travertine pillars of the old bridge.

To continue to Bagno Vignoni, take the left fork at **C**.
(Note that CAI maps this intersection incorrectly on the
IGM map, showing it on the wrong side of the river.)

It may be helpful to know that from here to Bagno Vignoni you are essentially following the course of the river.

Be alert here: after climbing between small trees for
about 100 m, the path comes to a field on the left and after another 20 m or so, you'll see a smaller little track go-

ing down to the right (the first track to the right) **D**. This is your turnoff: take it, following the course of the river.

The track more or less follows the course of the river, winding in and out of scrub.

When you reach a big field (about 10 minutes past **D**), the path bears right, following the bottom edge of the field about two-thirds of the way across, at which point it turns right downhill into a thicket of shrubs and small trees.

In about 5 minutes, emerging from shrubs onto a rocky outcrop, continue ahead, bearing slightly left, back into shrubbery.

In another 5 minutes or so you'll come to a rocky open area with a big fork left and uphill: *don't* take that—instead continue straight downhill.

(Ignore a right fork about 2 minutes later.)

Stay on the path. In another 15–20 minutes you'll pass a waterfall on your left, then reach a gravel parking area **E** with a big cliff face to the left, with newly built iron railings and stone walls. There's a path here leading up toward the cliff. Climb up and you'll come to a light opaque blue pool, very inviting—and you can jump right in. Go on climbing up to the top of the cliff, where you'll see the long culvert full of bathing beauties. This is Bagno Vignoni, a very pleasant place.

BAGNO VIGNONI TO RIPA D'ORCIA

From the top of the old hot springs (i.e., where there's a parking lot, playground, and Bar Il Barrino, just at the end of Via del Gorello), head downhill.

Reaching the big pool near the bottom, go down a little further, to the parking area **E** below.

Alternatively, you can leave from the other parking area above, the one across from the bus stop. In that case, take the asphalt road toward the main road (SS2). Take the first right off here (ATW signed for walking itinerary), a sharp right, downhill, gravel road that leads down to a parking area.

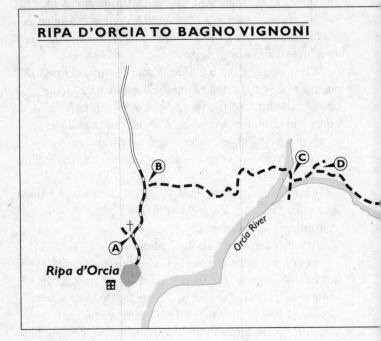

RIPA D'ORCIA TO BAGNO VIGNONI

From the parking area below the pool **E** (whichever way you came to it), with the Orcia River on your left, take the dirt road in front of you that leads out of the parking area, parallel to the river. Stay on the main path, ignoring deviations.

In about 10 minutes you'll pass the old travertine quarry on your left, bearing to the right of it.

In another couple of minutes there's a junction with a right uphill curve into private property (there may be a gate here). Bear left here.

Just beyond here the path forks: bear right (the left fork goes down to the river).

Another minute further on, you'll reach a rocky open area with a bigger fork right uphill and a smaller fork left downhill: go left downhill. Ripa d'Orcia is visible to the southwest here and just beyond.

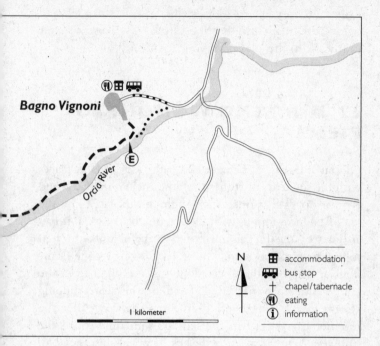

Bagno Vignoni

Orcia River

E

N

1 kilometer

⊞ accommodation
🚌 bus stop
✝ chapel/tabernacle
🍴 eating
ⓘ information

The path gradually narrows, goes through shrubbery, then emerges into the open, where it follows along the bottom of a field.

Reaching a junction **D** a few minutes later (ATW blue and yellow paint blaze on a rock here), bear left, always following the course of the river.

A couple of minutes later you'll come to a T-junction **C** (note that the CAI route on the IGM is not drawn correctly here; it shows the junction on the wrong side of the river). ATW there are walking itinerary signs here. Left downhill goes to the river, and you can see from here the remains of a little suspension bridge crossing it. However, take the right fork here for Ripa d'Orcia.

Cross the tiny streambed, then climb for 25–30 minutes, staying on the main trail, which is well signed by CAI. When you reach the T-junction at **B**, where there's a fountain on your left (don't drink from it), turn left and follow the road into Ripa d'Orcia, first passing (after nearly ½ km) the chapel on your right.

22 ■ BAGNO VIGNONI TO PIENZA

Old farm tracks, dirt roads, and paths still lined in places with the squared-off stones from the ancient medieval and Roman roads that once passed through this area link the spa of Bagno Vignoni with Pienza, one of the great urban artifacts of the Renaissance, in a peaceful walk through rolling fields of corn and wheat. Fortress-like stone farmhouses, many of them abandoned in the flight from the countryside that marked the end of the sharecropping system in the 1960s and 1970s, line the way. After the summer harvest, when the farmers sometimes burn the stubble in artfully contoured black stripes against the gold, the fields and hedgerows are full of pheasants, partridges, rabbits and hares. Black cypresses and large, scattered oaks provide a few choice verticals, completing the classic pictorial effect of this archetypal Tuscan landscape.

As you climb toward Pienza, you'll pass the eleventh-century Romanesque parish church, Pieve di Corsignano, with a cylindrical belltower and two decorated portals. Carved sirens, dragons, a musician and dancer deck the entrance, a scene asserted by some to disclose the existence of an ecstatic cult descended from ancient Dionysian ritual. With its beautiful little sculptures inside and out and the peculiar intimate charm of its primitive interior, this is well worth a visit (ask in the house at the back for the key).

Pienza itself, visible on its hill with its needlelike tower for much of this walk, is an extraordinary mixture of the monumental and the miniature. When the great humanist scholar Enea Silvio Piccolomini became pope, he decided

to transform his birthplace, Corsignano, into a Utopian city, renaming it Pienza after his own papal name of Pius II. He commissioned the architect Bernardo Rossellini, who worked under the tutelage of the great Alberti, who had laid down the principles of art and architecture that governed the Renaissance age. In just three years, 1459–

1462, the cathedral, the papal and bishop's palaces and the central blocks of the town itself were completed. The intention was to extend the town across the hill, but the project ended as abruptly as it had begun: Pius died two years after the consecration of the cathedral, and his successors showed little interest in bringing his plans to completion. What might have been a *citta ideal* along the lines of Urbino froze at little more than the size of a village. Its strange air of grandeur and folly has guaranteed its use as a stage set ever since, most famously by Zeffirelli, who used it as a backdrop for his film version of *Romeo and Juliet*.

In May the town hosts a flower show featuring extravagant floral displays inspired by Renaissance paintings. There's also a renowned cheese fair on the first Sunday in September.

There are two *agriturismi* along the way, the first, Il Rigo coming about two hours past Bagno Vignoni, while the other, Terrapille is only about a 20-minute walk from Pienza. Both serve dinners, so if the idea of an *agriturismo* stay appeals to you, this may be the time to try it. Il Rigo is farmed organically, and offers cooking classes. They also sometimes do a light lunch which, even if you're not staying overnight there, would make a perfect stop along the walk. Call ahead of time to reserve.

Food

As you'll see from the shop windows, Pienza prides itself on its pecorino and other sheep's cheeses. Rightly so; the clayey grazing land around here is full of wild herbs and aromatic plants that give the milk a slightly perfumed flavor, producing exceptionally fine cheeses. Fresh or aged, rolled in herbs, crushed peppers or ashes, these have long been the basis for the local economy. The traditional Pienza pecorino is small and round, and at one time was used in a local ball game known as *Cacio al Fuso,* which is still played at the cheese fair (the *Fiera del Cacio,* held the first Sunday in September).

Other local specialties include the rustic, hand-rolled flour-and-water pasta known as *pici, tagliatini* in broth, bread-based soups, *panzanella* (Tuscan bread salad) also called *salimbecca,* as well as sweet desserts and cakes such as *serpe* and *ricciarelli di Pienza.*

The large number of *alimentari* and *cantine* in Pienza makes it an ideal place for assembling a gourmet picnic.

Just outside the wall, off the circular Piazza Dante Alighieri, Il Prato was our choice last time around. It looked as if it had been seriously tarted up, so we returned on this trip with a certain amount of suspicion. It has been somewhat fancified, but the food is still genuinely adventurous, mostly pretty good, and interesting even when it isn't a hundred percent successful. The *spagliette* (puff pastry) with fava beans and pecorino is an unusual creation—its lemony, cheesy filling doesn't have a discernibly fava flavor, but it is nevertheless extremely tasty. For gnocchi lovers there's an outstanding gnocchi with arugula and pignoli. Some of the meat dishes sounded over the top—turkey breast with melted pecorino and truffles, for example—but the carpaccio of veal with parmesan, arugula and truffles was sublimely good. Skip the stuffed onions and potatoes.

Another restaurant that looks enticing is the Cucina di Fiorella. However, it was shut every time we tried to go, and locals told us that this is fairly typical, but that when it does deign to open, the food is excellent. We would welcome reports for our Web site.

LOGISTICS

BAGNO VIGNONI–PIENZA,
3½ –4 hours

(i) Miscellaneous info

🚌 Transport

Ⓜ Maps, guidebooks and trail info

🍴 Eating

⊞ Accommodation

(i)
Corso Rosellino, 59
Tel./fax 0578-749071
www.terresiena.it

🚌
For Bagno Vignoni bus information, see Ripa d'Orcia to Bagno Vignoni walk.

TRA-IN

Tel. 0577-204245 or 204111
www.trainspa.it
Siena: Note that intercity buses usually leave from and return to the Siena railway station, just outside town. The inner-city buses make regular trips between town and the railway station.
Route 112
ATW two buses a day from Pienza to Siena, at 9:20 and 14:30, and six (spread over the course of the day) from Siena to Pienza. (None on Sunday.)

Length of journey: An hour and 15 minutes

MONTEPULCIANO

Route 112
About seven buses per day from Montepulciano to Pienza, and about ten a day from Pienza to Montepulciano.
Length of journey: 20 minutes

TAXIS:

Tel. 335-5424668 (As always, the tourist office is a good source for additional or current numbers.)

There are also buses to and from Rome, for more connections to Montepulciano or for connections to Montalcino. Ask at the tourist office. There are also occasional buses from Pienza to Chiusi, where you can get a train to Florence or Siena.

Ⓜ
The 1:25,000 Val D'Orcia map is widely available at tourist offices and newsstand-type stores. Most of the area covered by the walks in our "South Tuscany" chapter are on this map.

🍴
Il Prato
Viale S. Caterina 1/3
Tel. 0578-749924

www.ilprato.it
Price: Moderate
Closing day: Tuesday

La Cucina di Fiorella
Via Condotti, 11
Tel. 0578-749095
Price: Moderate
Closing day: Wednesday

Agriturismo Il Rigo
See note in their listing in the
Sleeping category below.

⊞

A good Web site for accommodations (the *affittacamere* listings
are particularly good values) is
www.cretedisiena.com
Check with the tourist office for
information on other lodging.

AGRITURISMO ON ROUTE

Il Rigo
Loc. Casabianca (On walk
route; see walk directions and
map.)
Tel. 0577-897291
fax 0577-898236
www.agriturismoilrigo.com
Price: Double room with breakfast, 91–113 euros; room with
dinner and breakfast, 66–95
euros per person
 You may be able to have
dinner there even if you're not
staying over. Price for dinner is

22–25 euros per person, excluding wine.

Agriturismo Terrapille
Podere Terrapille, 80 (On walk
route; see walk directions and
map.)
Tel. 0578-749146 or 748434
cell 338-9204470
Price: Double room, 88–98
euros; apartment for four, 165
euros; breakfast, 6.50 euros;
dinner, 20 euros (doesn't include drinks)

PIENZA

Camere dal Falco
Piazza Dante 8 (across from the
bus stop)
Tel. 0578-749856
fax 0578-748551
Price: Single, 47 euros; double,
62 euros
 The rooms here (connected
with the Ristorante dal Falco)
fill up quickly.

Affittacamere Mauro e Chiara
Via della Valle, 4
Tel. 0578-748278
fax 0578-748468
cell 339-8274227
e-mail: mauroechiara@
cretedisiena.com
Price: Double room, 62 euros
(16 euros additional for a third
bed); apartment for two, with
kitchen, 78 euros

Directions

Standing in front of the Albergo Le Terme, facing the central piazza (the old pool), turn right. Walk to the end of the street (the corner of the pool), and turn right (heading east) **A**.

Walking along a dirt track with a stone wall on your left, you'll come very shortly to an intersection where you meet with six paths (two of which are gated). Considering them in a counterclockwise direction, ignore the right-most (which leads to asphalt), and the one straight ahead (which passes between stone pillars into a driveway); take the next one, which leads uphill along the stone wall bordering a property to your right. The path climbs a hill (toward the north), following along the left side of the wall, past the house.

Soon the path becomes a single track and a bit overgrown, but still recognizable as a path. Just keep climbing up straight ahead; the path soon levels off and reaches a T-junction with a dirt road **B**. Go left here. (This is about 5 minutes after leaving Albergo Le Terme.)

Follow this road uphill for a few minutes, until you come to the first (an old) house on the right, Tassinaie, with a stone wall in front of it. Just at the end of the stone wall past it, beginning in front of their driveway gate (and following a very short distance along a stone wall connected to the front gate), is a path on the right **C**. Take this path, bearing left where the stone wall turns a corner to the right.

In about 5 minutes the path bends right **D**, and above you you'll see an old abandoned farmhouse Cerrolungo with a big electric power pylon next to it, and some olive trees on the hill between you and the house. Leave the path here and turn left, climbing up the hill toward the house with the hedge to your left, olive grove to your right. At the top of the field you'll come to a T-junction with another farm track; turn right, toward the house in front of you.

Follow the track past the house and beyond, as it curves around to the left and downhill, passing under the electric

BAGNO VIGNONI TO PIENZA

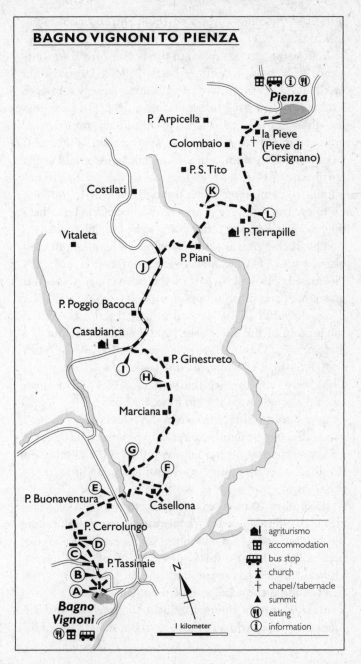

Pienza

P. Arpicella ■

Colombaio ■

la Pieve
(Pieve di
Corsignano)

■ P. S. Tito

Costilati ■

Ⓚ

Ⓛ

Vitaleta ■

■ P. Terrapille

Ⓙ

P. Piani

P. Poggio Bacoca ■

Casabianca

Ⓘ

P. Ginestreto ■

Ⓗ

Marciana ■

Ⓖ

Ⓕ

Ⓔ

P. Buonaventura

Casellona

P. Cerrolungo

Ⓓ

Ⓒ

P. Tassinaie

Ⓑ

Ⓐ

**Bagno
Vignoni**

N

1 kilometer

🏠 agriturismo
田 accommodation
🚌 bus stop
✝ church
† chapel/tabernacle
▲ summit
🍴 eating
ⓘ information

line, then bending around to the right and continuing downhill.

Follow this straight down to the asphalt road **E** (the entrance to San BuonaVentura B&B; Podere Buonaventura on the IGM maps). Cross over and almost directly across the road find a farm track that leads into a field. The path goes left, then immediately right, crossing down toward trees. Follow it into the trees, where it bends around to the right, crossing a little stream, and then climbs across a field to the farmhouse of Casellona. (After crossing the stream and beginning to climb up the path through the field, if you look up to the left you'll see cypresses and an electric line: that's the road up there, and you're going to be heading toward it.)

The track bends around Casellona and comes out on a gravel path (ATW house is being renovated; it looks like this gravel path will be part of their driveway). Cross this gravel path and directly opposite follow an old farm track there, downhill (ATW toward some large shrubs) and at the bottom of the hill (about 100 m) you'll come out at a dirt track **F**. (This is about an hour from Bagno Vignoni.)

A little further along on this track, as in many places along here, you can see the vestiges of the old Roman road, the squarish stones laid in straight lines.

In about 5–10 minutes, when this path comes out on a T-junction **G** with another dirt road, go right, uphill, toward a file of cypresses on the hillside just ahead. Continue on this road, after 5 minutes or so passing a newish house on the right.

In another 10 minutes or so, pass to the right of Marciana, an old stone and brick farmstead, going to the right of its two main, old buildings, and bear right on the smaller farm track just beyond. The town of San Quirico d'Orcia is visible to the left in the distance. Ahead on a distant hillside is the silhouette of the Pienza tower.

Near the top of the first hill you climb (about another 5 minutes), the main track turns left, but there is a slightly more minor track bending to the right, toward some trees. Take that track **H**.

This track heads downhill through trees to arrive at Podere Ginestreto, an abandoned house of red brick with an external staircase to the upper level (a feature found in many of the old farmhouses of the region, the upper level housing the people of the farm, the ground level the animals). Pass to the left of the house, bearing left on the farm track here.

The track drops down, then climbs over a wild hillside. Cresting the hill, in the distance ahead, San Quirico is again visible, and more immediately, the *agriturism* farmstead of Casabianca. (NOTE: Casabianca is the name of the house as it appears on the IGM map; however, they have named their *agriturism* operation Il Rigo.) When you reach the gravel road **I** (Casabianca is to the left here), turn right.

In another 5–10 minutes, you'll pass the simply styled red brick house of Poggio Bacoca.

About ⅔ km (5–10 minutes) past Bacoca, ATW there's a small marble cross on the right. A bit more than 100 m later, there's a path on the right **J**: it's the first right after the driveway of Poggio Bacoca. (Another marker is a low stone wall beginning on the left side of the road, about 25 m beyond where this path goes off to the right.) Take this path.

After about 10 minutes the path forks, about 75 m before a small old stone house (Podere Piani) straight ahead. Take the left-hand fork.

This path leads downhill toward a streambed, which it crosses in another 3 minutes or so, then begins to climb again.

Stay on this path (ignoring a path **K** coming from the left in about 5 minutes from the streambed). As you walk along this path, the house ahead of you on a hill slightly to the right with a line of cypresses leading to it is Terrapille. Pienza is to your left.

The path ends at a T-junction **L** with the driveway for Terrapille. Turn left for Pienza.

Follow the driveway for a little more than 1 km, until it comes out on a road, on which you turn right, passing in front of the chapel La Pieve (Pieve di Corsignano). About 100 m past La Pieve, turn left uphill on a single-lane asphalt road. Climb up this, reaching Il Prato restaurant on the right in about 5 minutes.

23 ■ PIENZA RING WALK

If you're staying in Pienza, or even in Montepulciano, this is a lovely walk; a perfect way to experience the unique landscape of this area. Pienza is *the* place to assemble a picnic, especially if you're into cheese (it's the pecorino capital of Tuscany, and has some of the best food stores in the region). Alternatively, the *agriturismo* Il Rigo sometimes serves a light lunch. Call ahead to reserve. See the Bagno Vignoni to Pienza walk for more information.

LOGISTICS

PIENZA RING WALK, 1½ –2 hours	Please see the Bagno Vignoni to Pienza walk for logistical information.

Directions

From the circular piazza Dante Alighieri, your back to the old town, pass to the left side of the piazza. Passing a playground on the right and Il Prato restaurant on the left,

PIENZA RING WALK

P. Arpicella

Colombaio

la Pieve
(Pieve di
Corsignano)

P. S. Tito

Costilati

Vitaleta

P. Piani

P. Terrapille

agriturismo
accommodation
bus stop
church
chapel/tabernacle
eating
information

1 kilometer

bear left downhill (ATW signed for "Pieve di Corsignano").

This road comes out at a T-junction with another small asphalt road; turn right here, reaching the Pieve di Corsignano (La Pieve on the IGM map) on your left in about 100 m.

Immediately past the Pieve "driveway" is the gravel road (left and downhill) to Terrapille (ATW signed to "Terrapille"): take this road.

In ½ km this gravel road bottoms out near some cypresses; ignore the fork to the right here. The path begins to climb toward Terrapille, reached in another ¾ km (about 10 minutes). However, unless you're going to the actual house, watch about 150 m before the house for a dirt track forking off at a 90-degree angle to the right, downhill **L**. Take this track.

In 600 m (8–10 minutes), ignore a fork to the right **K** as the main path curves left. In another 5 minutes or so the path dips and crosses a streambed. The small old stone house ahead and to the left is Casa Piani.

After a few minutes' climb, the path bends to the right. Ignore the track to the left here, which leads to Casa Piani in about 75 m.

In another 10 minutes or so, you'll reach a T-junction with the main gravel road **J**. Turn right here. (Unless you're going to Il Rigo for lunch, in which case turn left on the road here, and walk about 1½ km to the entrance for Il Rigo on your right.)

In another km or so, there's a road on the left that leads in about ¾ km to the beautiful white travertine chapel Vitaleta, its façade extremely photogenic against the background of *crete* and cultivated fields.

Another ½ km past the turnoff for Vitaleta, you'll approach the next farmhouse, Costilati, on the right. Here, take a smaller track **M** forking off the main gravel road to the right and downhill, about 100 m before the house.

This farm track leads down into the valley between cultivated fields, then up the other side toward Pienza, passing on the right the abandoned Podere S. Tito. About 30 m past here, where the path forks, turn left.

Stay on this path, passing the house Arpicella on your left, with a newer outbuilding immediately after Arpicella's driveway on your right. In about 150 m, after passing a couple of stone sheds with terra-cotta roofs, there's a fork off to the left that you ignore, continuing straight ahead on the main gravel road. Ignore another lesser track crossing yours in another 70 m.

Soon you'll pass the driveway down to Colombaio on your right—there are some cypresses along the driveway—and then a new house closer to the road, also on the right.

In another 5 minutes the path comes out on asphalt, with the Pieve di Corsignano (La Pieve) on the right. About 100 m past La Pieve, turn left uphill on a single-lane asphalt road. Climb up this, reaching Il Prato restaurant on the right in about 5 minutes.

24 ■ PIENZA TO MONTEPULCIANO

Traveling on foot between these two great hill towns gives you a much better sense of their relationship to the landscapes they respectively overlook than the usual 20-minute bus or car ride could possibly do. The slow pace turns the rich arable and grazing land around Pienza and the steep green vineyards of Montepulciano from mere backdrop to intimately experienced context, making one's appreciation of the towns themselves incalculably more vivid and intense.

The route passes near the pleasant walled village of Montichiello, whose crooked watchtower is visible from afar. There's an altarpiece by Pietro Lorenzetti in the thirteenth-century parish church (key available from the house next door), and a tavern-like restaurant with a good selection of Tuscan dishes. Every year in the last weeks of July and first week of August, the village presents its popular *Teatro Povero,* a kind of dramatization of current issues related to the community's traditions, written and performed by the villagers.

About a half hour before Montichiello, the walk route passes two *agriturismo* farms, both of which serve dinner and either of which would make a good place to break the journey, if you're so inclined.

Montepulciano is one of the most attractive towns in Tuscany. Higher than Montalcino, and livelier too, with its many churches and handsome palazzi, its warren of steep cobbled alleys and vine-trailing stone bastions, it is essential viewing for anyone venturing south of Siena, and makes an excellent base for excursions into southern Tuscany. Tourism is well established (aided by the various festivals the town hosts) but it's far from overwhelming, and the real base of the local economy is wine—the Vino Nobile di Montepulciano, an internationally prized wine for over a thousand years.

On a clear day from the top of the town you can see tremendous panoramic views over the countryside, stretching toward the Sibillini mountains, the high peaks of the Gran Sasso, Assisi's Mt. Subasio, Mt. Amiata, the Val d'Orcia, Pienza, and even the towers of Siena. It was up here that the idea for this book was conceived.

Food

As in Pienza, the specialty here is the hand-rolled flour-and-water pasta called *pici* (from *appiciare,* to roll). *Panzanella, ribollita,* and other Tuscan dishes are common, as is the olive oil–based bread known as *caccia.* A soft cheese called *raveggiolo,* presented between two fern leaves, is one of the tastier local products, and there's also a local version of creme caramel known as *lattaiolo.* Capon, rabbit, pheasant and guinea fowl, as well as *nana* (chicken split down the middle) and *ocia* (goose), are served roasted or stewed in Vino Nobile. Various special cakes such as *Ciaccia dei Morti* or *Crogetti* are made for the Day of the Dead and other feast days. Between the many *cantine* (wine shops) and the excellent grocers (many of them nowadays well stocked with natural foods and organic produce), you should have no difficulty assembling an outstanding picnic. Or visit the open-air market held in the gardens outside the Porta al Prato on Thursday mornings.

Just inside the entrance to the pretty walled village of Monticchiello is an exceptionally pleasant little *enoteca/osteria,* La Porta, moderately priced, with a good wine list and a menu that strikes a subtle balance between the traditional and the original. Along with many daily specials, they offer good *bruschette* with tomato, white beans and eggplant; excellent homemade ravioli stuffed with potato and pecorino; and a tasty *pici* with pepper and cheese. Their roast pork with cheese sauce, mushroom and truffle sounded a little over the top for the hot summer day when we visited, and we stuck with pastas and vegetable dishes, among them a light, intensely flavored *sformato* of artichoke and zucchini, one of the best versions of this low-key Italian souffle that we had anywhere. They serve a serious coffee ice cream, which we had *affogato* (from the verb *affogare,* to drown or to suffocate: a *gelato*—usually the *crema* flavor—severed with an espresso poured over it, a delightful afternoon treat deserving of wider renown, available at any bar that has *gelato*); the perfect pick-me-up after a somewhat bibulous lunch.

For a meal of genuine gastronomic interest, Borgo Buio is the place to go in Montepulciano. A rather serious, almost scholarly atmosphere pervades the shadowy, vaulted brick interior, and the menu confirms the sense that food here is treated as a matter of solemn importance. A section of the menu features *Piatti Storici* (historical dishes), which include *carabaccia,* a delicious onion soup with almonds; and home-made *pici* with *cipolloto* (a wonderfully light, fresh scallion sauce) or breadcrumbs (*briciole*). Our daughter, a connoisseur of *pici all 'aglione* (tomato and garlic), declared their version the best ever, and this seemed entirely justified. There are dishes one reads about but very seldom sees, such as the beef casserole known as *peposo alla fornacina;* and for lovers of the internal organs, there is an outstanding *fegattelli all'aretina*: lard-wrapped baked liver with a subtle fennel flavoring. Vegetables are all beautifully prepared, as are the desserts. The place also functions as an *enoteca* and has an excellent wine list (we drank a fine Vino Nobile, a Salchietto '99).

LOGISTICS

PIENZA–MONTEPULCIANO,
3–4 hours

- ⓘ Miscellaneous info
- 🚌 Transport
- Ⓜ Maps, guidebooks and trail info
- 🍽 Eating
- ⊞ Accommodation

ⓘ

Via Gracchiano nel Corso 59a, near Sant'Agostino
Tel. 0578-757341
www.comune montepulciano.siena.it

🚌

There are long-haul buses to and from Rome, which are also useful for connections to Montalcino. Ask at the tourist office.

The Montepulciano train station is 10 km out of town, and the buses that link the station with the town are not always exact connections. If you're using the train, it's easier to use Chiusi Station, which has more frequent main line connections anyway, is served by regular bus service (LFI), and is not much further away (about a 45-minute ride). There are also occasional buses from Chiusi Station to Pienza.

Montepulciano is on the main bus route between Siena and Chiusi. TRA-IN buses do the stretch between Siena and Chiusi, stopping at Pienza and Montepulciano on the way.

LFI (MONTEPULCIANO)

Tel. 0575-39881 or 0575-324294
www.lfi.it
Chiusi–Chiusi Station (railway)
Buses run about every half hour
Length of journey: About 45 minutes

For railway connections, use the station at Chiusi, which is much better served than the Montepulciano station.

TRA-IN

Tel. 0577-204245 or 204111
www.trainspa.it
Siena: Note that intercity buses usually leave from and return to the Siena railway station, just outside town. The inner-city buses make regular trips between town and the railway station. Route 112
ATW two buses a day from Montepulciano to Siena, at 9:00 and 14:10, and six (spread over the course of the day) from Siena to Montepulciano. (None on Sunday.)
Length of journey: An hour and 15 minutes

Bus stops at San Biagio two minutes after it leaves the main stop.

PIENZA

Route 112
About seven buses per day
from Montepulciano to Pienza,
and about ten a day from
Pienza to Montepulciano
Length of journey: 20 minutes

MONTEPULCIANO–
MONTICCHIELLO

Route 113
Two buses on Thursday (8:20
and 12:30) and one on Friday
(9:10)
Length of journey: 20 minutes

TAXI:

Tel. 0578-716081
(As always, the tourist office has
current taxi numbers.)
   If you want a shorter walk,
you could take the bus to
Monticchiello, have lunch, and
walk back to Montepulciano.
You'll miss a lovely stretch of
the walk, though.

Ⓜ
The 1:25,000 Val D'Orcia map is
widely available at tourist offices
and newsstand-type stores.
Most of the area covered by
the walks in our "South Tuscany" chapter are on this map.

🅟
La Porta
Via del Piano, 1; Monticchiello
Tel./fax 0578-755163

e-mail: rist.laporta@libero.net
Price: Moderate
Closing day: Thursday

Borgo Buio
Via Borgo Buio 10
Montepulciano
Tel. 0578-717497
fax 0578-756784
www.borgobuio.it
e-mail: posta@borgobuio.it
Price: Moderate
Closing day: Thursday
   Open 10:30–midnight. Lo-
cated inside the city walls, near
the Torre di Pulcinella.

Agriturismo Casalpiano
Loc. C. al Piano (On walk route;
see directions and map.)
Tel./fax 0578-755060;
cell: 339-3125651 or 333-
7110829
e-mail: agrcasalpiano@libero.it
Price: 25 euros per person,
includes wine.
Closing day: None
   Dinners are available even if
you are not staying overnight; by
reservation only.

⊞
A good Web site for accommodations (the *affittacamere*
listings are particularly good
values) is **www.cretedisiena.
com.**
   Check with the tourist office
for information on additional
lodging options.

AGRITURISMO **ON ROUTE**

Agriturismo Casalpiano
Loc. Case al Piano (See walk
directions and map.)
Tel./fax 0578-755060;
cell 339-3125651 or 333-
7110829
e-mail: agrcasalpiano@libero.it
Price: Double, 80 euros;
breakfast, 6 euros per person;
apartment for four people, 150
euros (breakfast extra, but the
apartment has a kitchen)
   Serves dinners, 25 euros per
person, includes wine. They have
a pool.

Santa Maria
Loc. Podere Santa Maria
(See walk directions and map.)
Tel./fax 0578-755080;
cell 335-8396942
e-mail: az.santamaria@virgilio.it
Price: Double, 60–65 euros;
dinner extra; need to reserve

Casa Frati
Loc. Casa Frati (See walk direc-
tions and map.)
Tel./fax: 0578-749061
www.casafrati.toscana.nu
Price: 50 euros per night
   This is one apartment only,
for two people, with a kitchen.
They don't serve meals.

MONTEPULCIANO

Affittacamere Bella Vista
Via Ricci 25
Tel./fax 0578-716341
cell 347-8232314
or 338-2291964
e-mail: bellavista@bccmp.com
Price: Double room, 49–60
euros
   No one lives here, so you
have to call Gabriella when
you're arriving, and she will
come and let you in.

Directions

Leaving Pienza through the southeastern gate at the bottom of Corso Rossellino (the far end of town), cross over
the main asphalt road (ringing Pienza) and take the small
asphalt road that leads downhill to the left **A**.

This road turns to gravel in about 200 m, taking you
immediately into rolling farmland, with views over the
hills to the Monticchiello tower. Pass the turnoff to Casa
Frati on your left about 10 minutes (less than 1 kilometer)
past **A**.

Take the next left after Casa Frati, ½ km, ATW signed

PIENZA TO MONTEPULCIANO

for the *agriturismo* Stagnino. (If the sign is gone, you can tell it's the correct turnoff by the fact that there are two entrances to this gravel road, first the one you've come to, and then 20 m ahead, another one that hooks up with the first one.)

Follow this gravel road steeply downhill, crossing a streambed in another ½ km or so, and about 200 m past that you'll pass on your left the driveway up to Stagnino.

About 300 m past the Stagnino driveway, you'll pass on the right the driveway down to Casangelo, and another 100 m past that reach a crossroads (ATW signed "tutte le direzioni") **B** where you turn right.

In another ½ km the path crosses the valley bottom, then bears right and is joined by a path coming in from the left. After climbing about 150 m from the valley bottom, the path comes out on a T-junction **C**: go right.

Follow this beautiful, cypress-lined *sterrata* (gravel road) through exquisite countryside for about ½ km, at which

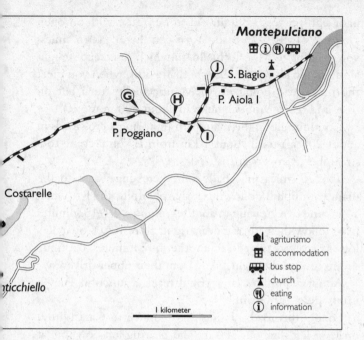

point you'll pass the entrance to Telle on your left (note that the IGM shows a hiking path going up this way, but it doesn't pan out), and just beyond that the *agriturismo* Casalpiano, also on your left.

At Casalpiano's front gate, you'll meet a road coming in from the right **D**. Go straight here.

Unless you are headed for the *agriturismo* at Podere Santa Maria, you can take a little shortcut here: just as the road makes a right before the bridge, keep going straight on instead; you'll see some little steps up to a footbridge. Cross the footbridge and take the path that crosses the field and rejoins the road.

Otherwise, cross the road bridge and bear left at the fork just beyond. About 200 m past the bridge you'll pass on your right the driveway for the *agriturismo* Santa Maria.

Continue to follow the road as it winds uphill. A little more than ½ km past Santa Maria, watch for a small dirt road on the left **E** (ATW marked by one of the Siena Province path signs) across from an old stone house with an open archway facing the road. Turn left here. (NOTE unless you're going to Monticchiello, in which case keep straight along the road for a little more than ½ km, when you meet the main road going up to Monticchiello: turn left on that, and reach Monticchiello in about 300 m more.)

Continue along the main path (ignoring a crossroads in about 200 m) until about 1 km from **E** you'll come to a streambed. Cross over that.

This is a pleasant, shady valley crossing. Keep to the main path uphill, following it sharply up to the left when you come to a clearing in about 5 minutes; 10–15 minutes later, follow the path as it bears right, away from Costarelle's lower driveway (gated). In another 5–7 minutes, continue on up toward the right, away from their upper driveway.

About 5 minutes later you'll reach a junction **F** by a utility pole; turn right.

Follow this road, passing the entrance to Casa Nuova on your left in about 300 m, and bearing left downhill at a junction another 300 m or so past there.

In about another 1½ km, you'll pass the house and not very nice building of Poggiano. About 300 m from there you'll meet an asphalt road **G**, where you turn right downhill.

Meeting the main highway **H** in nearly ½ km, turn right. Walk 300 m on the main highway, which bends to the left past a big octagonal building on the right, then comes to a small road on the right with a bus stop sign. Just across from the bus stop, on your left, is a road, Via Dell'Aiola **I**. Turn left off the highway onto this road, ATW marked with a walking itinerary sign.

In about ½ km you'll come to a junction **J**. Ignoring the driveway on your left and the continuation of the road you're on (straight ahead downhill bordering a fruit orchard), instead turn right (by a kind of modern brick tabernacle for the electric lines), immediately passing a modern house on your left.

Stay on this track, with great views of San Biagio.

In just under 1 km, this road ends at a T-junction with an asphalt road; turn right, underneath Biagio, reaching its main entrance in another couple of minutes.

To continue into Montepulciano, continue on the road in front of San Biagio, making your first right onto Via di S. Biagio, and so into Montepulciano.

25 ■ MURLO RING WALK, via LA BEFA (STAZIONE MURLO), and Addenda:

- *Buonconvento to La Befa (Stazione Murlo)*
- *La Befa (Stazione Murlo) to Murlo*

Originally we included this walk primarily for people who thought they'd enjoy a ride on the gleefully toy-like branch line train. For anyone still drawn to this idea, there's something better yet; from the end of April until mid-June and again from mid-September until the end of October, the *Treno Natura* program—originally (and still) an effort to get people out for hikes and bike rides—takes the old trains (and by old they're talking about some steam locomotives) out of storage and runs them on some of the most scenic rail lines around. Some of the routes have been taken out of regular service, so that it is only on a *Treno Natura* train that you'll ever travel them. The rails and old stations on these routes are entirely maintained by the dedicated volunteers who keep this excellent program alive.

In any case, the Murlo walk can now be highly recommended on its own account. Not only can you get there now (when we wrote the first edition of this book, the closest bus was in Vescovado), by either bus or the four or so daily trains, but the area itself has really come into its own, without being ruined. It still has an off-the-beaten-track feel to it, while at the same time offering the extremely *simpatico* Del Arco restaurant in Murlo as well as the Museo Etrusco, an understated gem of a museum, just small enough to be completely absorbing without being overwhelming.

The town is still quiet—"deserted" would be the correct adjective for the day we were there—but perhaps due in part to the year-round presence of graduate student archeologists, there's a sense that someone has brought a breath of life into the place.

The area's walking itineraries have also been given a major overhaul and, along with a plethora of new picnic tables, have become almost *too* well signed. We've used one of them as the La Befa to Murlo portion of the walk, but have also retained our old (unrevised) version of this part of the itinerary, longer and with a less "managed" feel to it. (See the La Befa [Stazione Murlo] to Murlo addendum, p. 308.) The combination of wide views and pretty fields, an area rich in wildlife (a wild boar trotted straight across our path when we were first there) and the rewards of the village itself make this a highly enjoyable excursion.

There's an *osteria* in La Befa that is reputed to be excellent, and a new B&B. Otherwise, it's the train station (Stazione Murlo) and not much else.

(NOTE: The addendum Buonconvento to La Befa [Stazione Murlo], p. 306, is given in case you want to start the walk in Buonconvento; the initial tract follows the same route as the Buonconvento to Montalcino walk. See that walk's Logistics section for information on Buonconvento.)

Food

The Dell'Arco restaurant in Murlo is a delightful place with an arched terrace looking out onto pretty countryside. The food is straightforward and very well prepared. They make a delicious *sott'olio* (marinated vegetables) of big white beans, olives, mushrooms, artichoke and pickled onion. The pastas include ravioli stuffed with cheese and truffles, *pici* with porcini mushrooms, and a *penne all Etrusca* with a sauce of ham, olive, mushrooms and peas, which may not be altogether authentic historically, but is certainly tasty. A good main course for a hot day would be their plentiful but light *tagliata* (sliced rare beef) with parmesan and arugula. For dessert they make their own excellent *panna cotta* with wild berries, as well as a *tiramisu*. At night they also serve pizzas, for around 4 euros each, which sounds like a bargain.

LOGISTICS

MURLO RING WALK, VIA LA BEFA,
1½–2 hours each way

Addenda lengths:
Buonconvento– La Befa (Stazione Murlo), 2–2½ hours;
La Befa–Murlo, 3–4 hours

ⓘ   Miscellaneous info

🚌   Transport

Ⓜ   Maps, guidebooks and trail info

🍴   Eating

⊞   Accommodation

ⓘ

In the nearby (larger) town of Vescovado, at Via Tinoni, 1
Tel. 0577-814213
www.comune.murlo.siena.it

At the Etruscan Museum
Tel. 0577-814099
The woman at the store La Tinaia is an excellent source of information. See below.

🚌

TRA·IN

Tel. 0577-204245 or 204111
www.trainspa.it
Siena: Note that intercity buses usually leave from and return to the Siena railway station, just outside town. The inner-city buses make regular trips between town and the railway station.
Routes 110 and 111,
Siena–Vescovado
There are a few direct buses in both directions every day, but most of the buses require a change (in Casciano for the 110 line, and in Monteroni for the 111 line). There are about seven buses a day on the 111 line, between Monteroni and Murlo. Service between Monteroni and Siena is extremely frequent and not limited to line 111, so you shouldn't have to wait long at Monteroni in either direction.

Length of journey: About an hour on the direct 111 buses; somewhat longer if you need to change.

TRAIN

Train info: **www.fs-on-line.com**
ATW there are four trains a day from Siena to Stazione Murlo (La Befa), at 6:00, 12:18, 13:20 and 17:39.
Length of journey: About 35 minutes. From Stazione Murlo to Siena there is only one direct train, at 7:15. Otherwise, the trains take 2–3 hours in this direction.

For more information on *Treno Natura,* visit their Web site (in Italian, but you can always look at the splendid Photo Gallery for inspiration):
www.ferrovieturistiche.it

You can also get information from the Siena APT (tourist office), 0577-280551, or directly from Ferrovia Val D'Orcia, 0577-207413 or 338-8992577, or e-mail at: trenonatura@ katamail.com

Ⓜ
Crete Senesi; 1—Val d'Arbia

🍴
Bar Pizzeria Dell'Arco
Via delle Carceri, 13
Murlo
Tel. 0577-811092
Price: Inexpensive
Closing day: Monday

Ristorante Brunello
La Befa
Tel. 0577-806255
Closing day: Wednesday

⊞
La Locanda del Castello
Via Tonda, 36
Murlo
Tel. 0577-814603
e-mail: hio21@libero.it
Price: Between 30–80 euros per night, depending on the season
Nice location in the center of the village.

L'Etrusco
Via delle Carceri, 15
Murlo
Tel. 0577-811102
fax 0577-814046
cell 338-2037677
www.etruscomurlo.it
Price: Double room with breakfast, 65–70 euros

AGRITURISMO

Podere Montorgialino
Loc. Montorgialino (On route: see walk directions and map.)
Tel./fax 0577-814373
www.montorgialino.com
Price: Double room with breakfast, 125 euros
Pool. Dinners available, if you request ahead of time.

Olivello Murlo
Loc. Olivello (on addendum route from La Befa to Murlo)
Tel. 0577-374084
www.olivellomurlo.it
Price: See the Web site

B&B

Il Palazzotto
La Befa
Tel. 0577-808310
e-mail: info@ilpalazzotto.com
Price: Double room with breakfast, 90 euros

Pool. Dinners available, 21 euros per person. Two-night minimum on the weekends only. (As always, it's worth checking; if they're not full, they may waive the minimum requirement.)

(i)

MUSEO ANTIQUARIUM POGGIO CIVITATE (THE ETRUSCAN MUSEUM)

Tel. 0577-814099
Open 10:00–13:00 and 15:00—19:00; closed Monday.

There is also a small tourist office here. See also #2, La Tinaia.

La Tinaia, at Via Tonda 44 in Murlo, has an interesting selection of local products and the helpful owners are a very good source for local information. Among the many biologically grown products on offer in the store is a thoroughly enjoyable, inexpensive red wine, Colombaia.
Tel. 0577-814637
www.latinaiashop.com

Directions

LA BEFA TO MURLO

Walk uphill on the asphalt road out of La Befa (in the opposite direction of the train station). Just past town the road begins to descend; when it bottoms out in about 100 m, there's a gravel fork off the main road, downhill left, ATW signed by Siena Province: take this fork **M** (marked with a red and white "1" along trail).

Stay on the main trail, well marked by the red and white "1," ignoring deviations. Soon you'll cross a stream, Torrente Crevole. Climbing uphill past the stream, you'll pass Molina della Befa down on your left, and just beyond here the road forks; bear right uphill, then turn right at the T-junction just beyond.

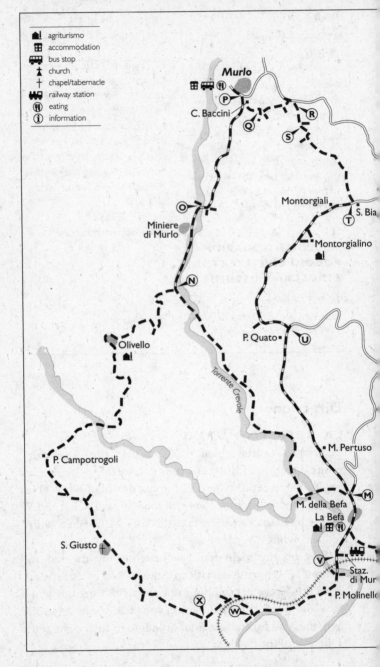

agriturismo
accommodation
bus stop
church
chapel/tabernacle
railway station
eating
information

Murlo

C. Baccini

P

Q

R

S

O

Miniere
di Murlo

Montorgiali

S. Bia

T

Montorgialino

N

Olivello

P. Quato

U

Torrente Crevole

P. Campotrogoli

M. Pertuso

M

M. della Befa

La Befa

S. Giusto

V

Staz.
di Mur

P. Molinello

X

W

MURLO RING WALK, VIA LA BEFA

Addendum: La Befa (Stazione Murlo) to Murlo
Addendum: Buonconvento to La Befa (Stazione Murlo)

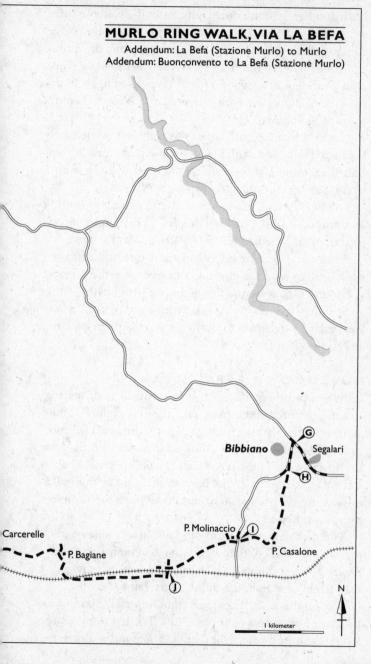

Bibbiano

Segalari

G

H

Carcerelle

P. Bagiane

P. Molinaccio

I

P. Casalone

J

N

1 kilometer

In another 5 minutes the path crosses the Crevole again, where you can see the remnants of the old stone bridge. The path is a train track bed; stay on it, ignoring deviations.

In another 15 minutes or so, where a little railing flanks your path, ignore a right turn and keep on straight. In another 15 minutes the path crosses Ponte Nero, where it's scary to look down.

Coming to a log gate across the path and immediately before a T-junction with a wider stone path, turn left uphill; then immediately reaching another junction with a stone road making a curve, turn right **N**.

Follow the road, which is wide here, passing in another 10 minutes or so the station complex (ATW under reconstruction) and the hamlet of Miniere di Murlo.

At the end of Miniere, bend right out of town on a small asphalt road **O**, crossing a bridge over the Crevole again, and then a second bridge over a streambed.

Stay on the main asphalt road for about 1½ kms, where you reach a T-Junction **P** just below Murlo. Turn left here, and so into Murlo.

MURLO TO LA BEFA

Leaving from the parking lot below Murlo with the two amazing umbrella pine trees, take the first right **P**, about 30 m from the parking lot, signed for "Miniere di Murlo."

In about 100 m you'll come to Casa Baccini on your left. Just past the house is a stone outbuilding with an open archway; take the track that skirts to the right of this building and almost immediately curves down to the right between two hedges.

The path descends, bottoming out in a couple of minutes at a streambed, then beginning to climb very gently. In 25–30 m it comes to a T-junction with a bigger dirt road (right downhill, left uphill); turn left **Q**.

Stay on this path, ignoring a right fork after 50 m or so. In about 5 minutes you'll come to a T-junction by a large farm structure on your right. Turn left here and go out to the asphalt road and turn right. Walk down this asphalt road for about 50 m and turn right onto a small track **R** going up a field: take this track, following alongside a hedgerow to your right, climbing toward some woods at the top of the field.

Reaching the top of the field, the path forks (both sides meeting just inside the woods): take the right side of the fork, which immediately bends left, then in about 15 m meets the left side of the fork. Bend right here **S** (ignoring the path that goes straight ahead paralleling the top of the field you've just left).

In another 2 minutes you'll reach a T-junction with a very deeply rutted track: turn right (Il Casino on IGM).

Stay on the main path here, ignoring deviations (including one about a minute later that goes off to the right where the main path divides and rejoins around a small island of trees; there are several more of these little "tree islands"; always keep to the main path).

ATW they are excavating Etruscan ruins along here, and there are several little footpaths leading to various excavation sites.

Reaching a T-junction **T**, about 20 minutes past Il Casino, turn right. (The left-hand turn leads to a small shrine of San Biagio in about 25 m.)

Soon you'll pass Casa Montorgiali on the right, and another 5 minutes or so further on, the gated entrance to Montorgialino: its *agriturismo* entrance is 100 m further on, where their driveway forks off left of the main road.

Continue on the main track all along here, ignoring lesser tracks.

About 25 minutes past the *agriturismo* Montorgialino, you'll reach a T-junction **U**, (left downhill, right uphill) where there's a stone wall to your right that turns the corner to the right: do the same, passing Podere Quato behind this stone wall on your right.

In 20 minutes, pass Monte Pertuso on the left, then in 10 minutes more reach the intersection with the asphalt road; bear right onto it (passing on your right in 50 m the right downhill gravel path **M** leading back to Murlo), and so into La Befa.

Addendum: Buonconvento to La Befa (Stazione Murlo)

Directions

MAP NOTE: For the first part of this walk (through **G**) use the map for the Buonconvento to Montalcino walk (p. 248). Pick up Murlo Ring Walk map from **G** onward.

(NOTE: You can see an alternate route marked on the IGM map, coming near La Torre just before the hamlet of Segalari, and rejoining our route at Podere Molinaccio. Judging from the map, it looks like a very nice option, while offering a lot of potential for getting lost (it's purported to be a marked itinerary, but don't interpret this as being synonymous with not getting lost). We'd be interested to hear any reports on this route.)

From the front of the Buonconvento train station **A**, cross the main street and follow the street straight ahead of the station, Via Vittoria Veneto.

Take the first right, then the first left, Via di Bibbiano (note that to your right here is the wonderful Bar Moderno). This is the road to Bibbiano, and in about ½ km crosses the Ombrone River near some distinct *pini marittimi* (maritime pines).

About 400 m past the bridge, take the first left **B**, a dirt road leading to a farmhouse, Pian delle Noci.

Just before reaching the house, and before the stacks of wood and the small brick animal pen, you'll take a right along a farm track heading toward the trees. Where you reach the trees, a cement platform bridge crosses the Stile River.

Continue past the castle tower (just visible up on the right through the trees), and where the track forks at **C**, take the right fork, which brings you in about 3 minutes to a junction **D**, where you turn left. (Note that CAI takes you up a little track 50 m before the road forks at **C**, but this looks in danger of becoming overgrown. If you do want to take it, simply go up to the road on the CAI path, go left on the gravel road, and in 100 m you'll come to the junction **D**, where you go straight ahead.)

Pass an abandoned house, and when the road forks by a small pond, take the right branch. About 50 m past the fork, at the end of the hedge, the path meets a fork with a much smaller and somewhat overgrown track. Go left here **E**. (NOTE: Make sure to take the *track,* which is about 5 m in front of a large pine tree as you turn, and effectively between two hedges, rather than the entrance to a field that is directly in front of the tree.)

Follow this track, crossing between two fields with the tower of La Torre ahead of you to the left. Keep on straight, following the path into a second field, which it also crosses. (If the track isn't there, just go straight forward and you'll pick it up on your right as you converge with another hedge.)

Follow the path out onto the gravel road that runs along the edge of the cypress trees, and go right on it **F**. Follow this road directly into Segalari, which is visible ahead of you on the right.

Bear right forward and uphill when the asphalt begins, through the little hamlet of Segalari, passing the pizzeria/pub/spaghetteria L'Europeo (or TNT) on your left. At the intersection near a building with a small bell tower, go left on the asphalt road (signed toward Montalcino) **G**.

After passing via Ombrone on your left, the road soon bends around to the right, and you'll see a smaller dirt track on the left side (but actually leading straight ahead). Take this track **H**, ATW signed "Casa di Bibbiano." (This is about 300 m past **G**.)

When this path comes directly in front of the farmhouse of Podere Casalone (in a sort of T-junction, as if it ends there), bear right at the driveway entrance. Follow the gravel path, passing below the house and continuing down to the T-junction with the main gravel road **I** (you'll see a small building there). Turn left on the main dirt road, then immediately right, at the farmhouse Molinaccio.

Bear left (actually straight on) at the first fork, in about 100 m.

Follow along the road until you come to an intersection **J**, with a blue metal bridge on the left-hand turn. Cross this bridge and immediately turn right on the farm track here, paralleling the railway track on your right.

This track parallels the railroad track for about 15 minutes, then bends away, uphill to the right toward Podere Bagiane. You'll reach this farmstead in 5 minutes (good views of rolling fields and woods).

Fork left off the main path here, passing to the right of a brick shed and going down into a field with a line of telegraph poles crossing it. Bear left across the field, ignoring a fork to the right that appears as soon as you enter it.

In another 10 minutes this peaceful farm track leads you through lovely open countryside to the abandoned farmhouse of Podere Carcerelle, where you bear left, downhill.

After 200 m the path forks; go right, staying on the main path until you come out on the asphalt road in another ½ km or so. La Befa is 5 minutes up to your right, where you can connect to the Murlo walk. (To go to the train station, turn left here.)

Addendum: La Befa (Stazione Murlo) to Murlo

Directions

From Stazione Murlo, with the tracks to your left, follow the dirt road away from the station. At the T-junction **V** turn left. (Right leads in 5 minutes to La Befa.)

Cross the railroad tracks and follow the road, ignoring

minor deviations to the right and left, and soon passing between the two farmhouses of Podere Molinello. Continue along the road, ignoring a left-hand turn by a large, solitary oak about 100 m after the houses.

About 1 km after the farmhouses the road forks; take the right branch **W**, which crosses over the railroad tracks.

When the road forks again shortly after crossing the tracks, take the downhill left fork.

Shortly the road forks again. Take the right uphill fork **X**.

About an hour from the start, you'll pass through the ruined hamlet of San Giusto.

When you reach a T-junction about 10 minutes after San Giusto, go left.

In another 10 minutes or so, you'll come to the abandoned homestead of Podere Campotrogoli. The path forks; take the right branch, around the back of the house.

The road will begin to climb; stay on it, continuing to climb and ignoring deviations.

As you pass a little pond on your right at the approach to the hamlet of Olivello, there's a fork. Take a left. Wander up through the village, then at the top turn right, passing under an old passage between two buildings over the road—a kind of arch. Then bear left past an old well with a pointed conical roof, and so proceed onward out of town on the main (dirt) road.

Coming downhill from Olivello, at a rather steep downhill section of the road, the main road curves to the left, while three somewhat lesser paths fork off to the right of it. (Signed "CAI 6" on a telephone pole.) Continue on the main road (dirt) here, bending to the left.

When you reach the new blacktop road of Miniere Murlo, follow the blacktop road as it passes through the small village and leads out of it at the end, to the right.

After a fairly uninteresting uphill stretch—relieved however by the sound of tinkling sheep bells rising off the plain below—you'll reach Murlo, with beautiful wide views on either side as you approach.

PITIGLIANO

The sight of Pitigliano bristling up from its long, narrow rock of tufa is one of the most starkly impressive in Tuscany. Indeed the whole area, honeycombed with Etruscan tombs and the astonishing, canyon-like, sunken Etruscan roads, has a wild, secretive beauty like nothing else in the region, and we are glad to offer a walk here for the first time, in this edition.

Far fewer tourists come here than to other parts of Tuscany, though weekends do bring large numbers of visitors, especially to the picturesque little medieval village of Sovana, which not only boasts the exquisite church of Santa Maria and a major Romanesque cathedral (be sure to look at the Lombard-Romanesque carvings on the portal), but also serves as the gateway to a large area of Etrsucan tombs, including the famous Tomba Ildebranda. Anyone interested in the Etruscans and their tombs would do well to read D. H. Lawrence's extraordinary short book *Etruscan Places*. It's based on his visit to the tombs in Tarquinia and Cerveteri, and consists of a kind of visionary evocation of the world of these mysterious people. The tombs here are less spectacular than the ones Lawrence visited (there are none of the paintings he writes about so vividly), but the Ildebranda is well worth seeing.

Pitigliano itself is of great interest for its many fine medieval and Renaissance buildings, not to mention the splendid sixteenth-century aqueduct that connects it like an island causeway to the rest of the world. It had a thriving Jewish community from the fifteenth century until World War II (conflicting stories about exactly what happened at

that point suggest the need for a clear and candid history to be written), and the quiet old narrow-alleyed ghetto forms a particularly pretty stretch of this altogether beguiling town.

If you have a car, you may want to consider staying at Il Melograno. This *agriturismo* seems a bit like something from another time. They are a *biologico* (organic) farm and make their own wine and olive oil, but their agricultural production is not limited to those usual staples. They had a beautiful cherry tree in the yard, fruiting while we were there, where the proprietor and his father could be found late most afternoons. Our children, too, seemed to have based themselves around this tree, from which they were enthusiastically encouraged to pick as much as they wanted. The owners also have animals, including wild Maremma horses that stray into the yard from time to time. Their lodgings are quite rudimentary, but clean. There's a very big pool, wonderful, but also in a rather rustic state. If you're prepared to accept these somewhat primitive conditions, this is a peaceful, friendly place to stay (be warned that their English is minimal). The mother of the family makes a lovely cake for breakfast, served with their homemade

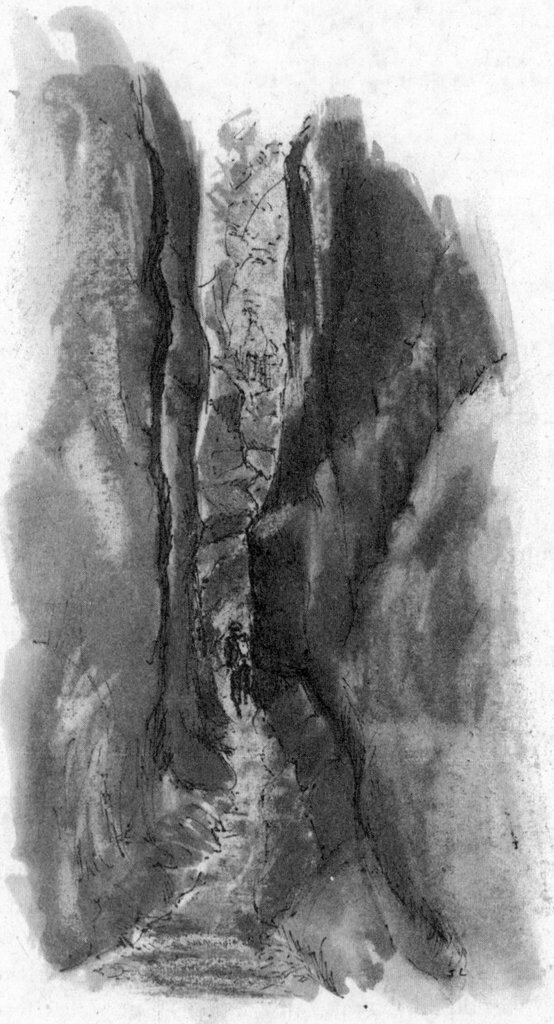

jams—cherry while we were there, which explained the presence of the proprietors in that tree's branches. (I tried to purchase some of this, but they don't make enough to sell.) They serve dinner too, upon request, which we regret having missed. Their (organic) wine is rough but eminently drinkable.

26 ■ PITIGLIANO TO FONTANA DELL'OLMO TO SOVANA

The walk takes you through the town down steep flights of stone steps to the old Etruscan alleys (currently not in very good shape) immediately below. After a brief stretch on the road (and you can cut out all the foregoing if you have a car) it enters a spectacular sunken Etruscan road—narrow lanes cut deep into the rocks (for reasons archaeologists have yet to agree on), leading to the pretty Etruscan carved fountain of Olmo. From here you can make a relatively short ring walk back to Pitigliano via an even more secretive path that cuts down through the rocks of a thickly wooded ravine.

Alternatively you can proceed through pleasant farmland to the beautiful village of Sovana, following dirt roads, more Etruscan paths and old cart-tracks worn into the rock. From Sovana you can visit the Tomba Ildebranda and numerous other tombs. If you're not staying over in Sovana, you can either take one of the (infrequent) buses back to Pitigliano, take a cab, or walk—about 1½ hours.

Food

Specialties of the region include *buglione d'agnello* (a robust lamb stew), wild boar with fennel seed, and various applications of *baccala* (salt cod). You can find all these, along with a great many other tempting concoctions, at the excellent restaurant Il Tufu Allegro, in the old Jewish quarter in Pitigliano. The menu here is elaborate enough to raise suspicions, but the cooking turns out to be equal to the ambitions, and if you're in the mood for something out of the ordinary (without being ridiculously expensive) this is the place to come. We had chicken liver with *vin santo* jelly, fabulous mixed *bruschetta, gundi* (giant spiced gnocchi), pasta with an asparagus sauce that actually tasted of asparagus, the aforementioned delicious *buglione,* and tender lamb ribs stuffed with sweetbreads and served with crispy artichokes. Desserts, equally good, included ricotta mousse and exceptionally fine homemade ice cream. There's also a serious cheese selection, including *guttus* (moldy pecorino)—sensationally pungent and not for the fainthearted. All this washed down with a bottle or two of a Morellino di Scansano from the producer Il Grillesino made for one of the better dining experiences of our trip.

In Sovana a newish place called the Ristorante dei Merli, the restaurant of the Hotel Scilla, was recommended. We had mixed feelings about it. The menu certainly looks exciting, boasting such things as a ricotta soup, *pici* with eggplant and pigeon, baked Tomino cheese and roast sucking pig with raspberry and apple sauce. Some of the dishes were very good (an excellent *magtagliata*—wide noodles with vegetables and herbs), but some were mediocre, and all were expensive. The rather large room feels set up for mass gastrotourism (a coach party dominated it while we were there), and the request of one of our friends for a certain soft beverage with his lunch triggered the only display of snotty waiter behavior we encountered on our entire trip.

All in all you would probably do better at the unpretentious Pizzeria and Trattoria La Tavernetta at the bottom of the piazza, featuring *buglione di agnello* at a modest 8.50 euros, as well as other local dishes.

There's also a very good *gelateria* (and we didn't find many of these, contrary to myth, that *were* very good) in the lane leading up between the piazza and the public carpark. They had a melon flavor that tasted of pure cantaloupe. Don't miss it.

LOGISTICS

PITIGLIANO– FONTANA DELL'OLMO– SOVANA:

Pitigliano–Fontana dell'Olmo, about 40 minutes (one way); Fontana dell'Olmo–Sovana, about 1½–2 hours; Pitigliano Ring Walk, via Fontana dell'Olmo, about 1½ hours; Pitigliano–Sovana, without Olmo, 1½–2 hours

NOTE: Allow another 20 minutes from Sovana to walk to the tombs.

ⓘ   Miscellaneous info

🚌   Transport

Ⓜ   Maps, guidebooks and trail info

🍽   Eating

⊞   Accommodation

ⓘ
PITIGLIANO

Piazza Garibaldi, 51
Tel./fax 0564 -617111
www.comune.pitigliano.gr.it
email: colledimaremma@tin.it or
pitigliano@laltramaremma.it
July–November open every day,
9:30–13:00 and 15:00–20:00

Winter open Monday–Saturday, 9:30–13:00 and 14:00–18:00.

The woman in the tourist office speaks English very well, so don't hesitate to phone ahead for information.

🚌
RAMA

The RAMA buses cover both the long-distance routes and the local routes between Pitigliano and Sovana. There are buses to Pitigliano from Orbetello (about 1½ hours), and from Grosseto (which you can pick up right at the railway station), just under 2 hours. If you don't have a car, the easiest way to get to Pitigliano from Florence or Siena is to take the train to Grosseto and then take the bus from there to Pitigliano.
www.griforama.it

GROSSETO
Four or five buses per day (not on Sunday)
Length of journey: An hour and 50 minutes

SOVANA
ATW there are three buses

PITIGLIANO

from Sovana to Pitigliano, at
7:30, 19:05 and 20:45.
Length of journey: About 10
minutes

TAXI

Ideal Viaggio di Luigi Biaggi
Tel. 0564-635424;
cell 335-7615602
  Taxi ride between Pitigliano
and Sovana will probably cost
about 20 euros.

(M)

ATW there aren't any IGM maps
for this area sold commercially. If
you plan to do more extensive
walking in this area than our
book covers, you can order one
ahead, on-line, from one of the
sources listed in the Hiking Maps
section, p. 31. As a last resort,
you can always ask someone at
the Comunita Montana office to
make you a copy of theirs. In any
case, if you're only doing the
walks in this book, you should be
okay without one.

Comunita Montana
Via Ugolini, 10
Tel. 0564-616039

(¶)

PITIGLIANO

Il Tufo Allegro
Vicolo della Costituzione, 5
Tel. 0564-616192;
fax 0564-617318
email: iltufoallegro@libero.it
Price: Moderate

Closing day: Tuesday all day and
Wednesday lunch

La Cantina Incantata
Piazza F. Petruccioli, 68 (next to
Magica Torre, just outside the
archway)
  This shop makes delicious
sandwiches of fresh ricotta.
Good place to provision for a
picnic at Fontana dell'Olmo.

SOVANA

La Tavernetta
Via del Pretorio
Tel. 0564 -616227
Price: Inexpensive
Closing day: Thursday

Ristorante dei Merli
Via Rodolfo Siviero 1/3
Tel. 0564-616531;
fax 0564-614329
www.scilla-sovana.it
Price: Moderate
Closing day: Tuesday
  The restaurant at the hotel
Etrusca is also reported to be
good; closed Wednesday.

⊞

PITIGLIANO

Albergo Guastini
Piazza F. Petruccioli, 16/34
Tel. 0564-616065;
fax 0564-616652
email:
htlguastini@laltramaremma.it
Price: Single room with
breakfast, 44 euros; double
room with breakfast, 78 euros

This is the only hotel in the town center.

SOVANA

Albergo-Ristorante Etrusca
Piazza del Pretorio, 16
Tel. 0564-616183;
fax 0564-614193
Price: Single, 44 euros; double, 80 euros; includes breakfast. It's possible the atmosphere is friendlier here than at the Scilla.

The Scilla's restaurant (Ristorante dei Merli), at least, did not score high marks on the friendliness front.

Scilla
Via del Duomo, 5
Tel. 0564-616531;
fax 0564-614329
www.scilla-sovana.it

Affittacamere in Sovana
Roberto, who you can find at the Bar della Taverna in the Piazza del Pretoria, 8/b.
Tel. 0564-614073;
cell 347-549-9972 or 328-224-1252

AGRITURISMO

Il Melograno
Loc. Formica

Tel. 0564-615536;
fax 0564-614108
www.melograno.to
email: il@melograno.to
Price: Apartment for four persons, 85 euros per night; extra bed, 15 euros per night; double rooms, 42 euros; breakfast, 3 euros per person

Sassotondo
Pian di Conati, 52. (See map.)
Tel. 0564-614218;
fax 0564-617714;
cell 348-9029125
email: sassotondo@ftbcc
Price: Double room, 42 euros per night, includes breakfast.

They don't serve dinners, though, so you either need a car or must be willing to walk ½ hour into Sovana to eat, or bring your own food: they have a three-room communal kitchen for guests to use. *Biologico* (organic) farm that produces several types of wine.

(i)

Pitigliano has its own local wine, Bianco di Pitigliano; don't forget to sample some of this local product. La Doganella vineyard is a quite visible producer of a *biologico* (organic) version.

Directions

NOTE: If you have a car, we recommend you drive to point **C** and begin the walk from there.

PITIGLIANO–FONTANA DELL'OLMO
(about 40 minutes)

From Piazza Francesco Petruccioli (standing next to Albergo Guastini and facing the archway into the old part of the city), go through the archway and turn left down Via Cavour, passing the Acquedotto Mediceo, through Piazza della Repubblica, and then bearing either right or left at the fork just after the piazza: bearing right onto Via Roma will take you past the Duomo in Piazza San Gregorio, bearing left onto Via Zuccarelli will take you past the Il Tufo Allegro restaurant, the Jewish synagogue, and further on, a bakery with good bread. In either case, about 5 minutes from your starting point in Piazza F. Petruccioli, you'll come to a very small triangular piazza, at the twelfth- or thirteenth-century Chiesa di Santa Maria.

Keep straight on until you come to a long flight of steps **A** on your right: take these steps.

At the bottom, turn left and then immediately right at a smaller stone road forking downhill. Fig trees grow along the left of the path here. In a minute or two the road forks where you face the mouth of a tufa cave in between the fork. Bear right downhill here. This part of the path is rather littered, and between that and the protective fencing (presumably to prevent the walls from falling down on you) one can't say this passage is particularly charming. Nevertheless, it is not without interest.

In a couple of minutes this path ends at an asphalt road **B**. Turn right onto this road.

In about 100 m, just before the asphalt road bends right over a bridge (crossing the Lente), there's an opening in the guardrail on the left side of the road. Here a stone road goes downhill left, while to the right is a small footpath running parallel to the road; take this footpath.

Cross over the Lente on the footbridge and turn left **C** at San Rocco. [If you have a car, you can drive to this point and begin the walk here. Instead of going through the guardrail mentioned in the previous paragraph, keep

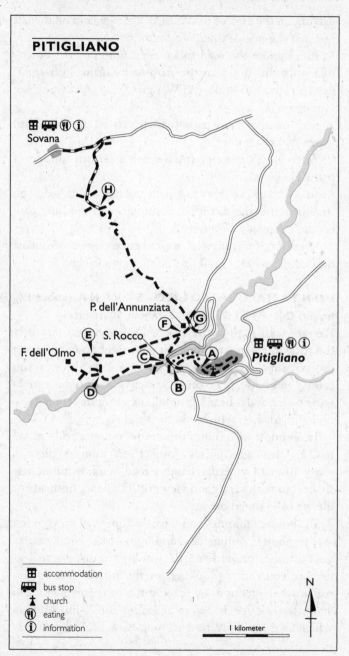

PITIGLIANO

Sovana

H

P. dell'Annunziata

F

G

E   S. Rocco

F. dell'Olmo

C

A

Pitigliano

D

B

▦ accommodation

🚌 bus stop

✝ church

🅿 eating

ⓘ information

N

1 kilometer

driving on the asphalt road over the bridge, and on the left just past the bridge there's room to park.]

In a minute the road forks, right uphill or left downhill; go right. In 15 m the path forks again: bear right, between the tufa walls (ATW signed "La via cava di san Giuseppe").

Stay on the main path (which can be slippery with leaves in wet weather).

After 20–25 minutes you'll reach a serious forking of paths **D**. Turn left.

In a minute or two the path crosses a dirt road: go straight across the dirt road, continuing on the little path on the other side of the road.

Another few minutes' walk brings you to Fontana dell'Olmo, where you'll find a few picnic tables.

FONTANA DELL'OLMO–SOVANA (about 1½ hours) OR PITIGLIANO (about 50 minutes)

Retrace your steps to the fork at **D**. Arriving at this fork, the path you came to Olmo on goes right downhill. For a shorter walk, you can simply go back here the way you came. Otherwise, to go on to Sovana or to do a longer Pitigliano ring walk, bear left uphill, in a minute coming out on a dirt road on which you turn right.

In a couple of minutes this comes out at a wide gravel road **E**. Turn right. This is a long (15–20 minutes) piece of dusty (though virtually empty) road walk, without any shade, but with very good views of Pitigliano, from an angle we hadn't seen before.

In about 20 minutes you'll pass a stone wall on your left and the house Annunciata, and come to a T-junction **G** with another gravel road. (If you'll be returning to Pitigliano, you can try looking for the turnoff before you reach this T-junction, by reading the next paragraph. But you may not see it before reaching the T-junction, in which case you'll just have to walk back 175 m or so.)

TO RETURN TO PITIGLIANO

About 150–200 m before the T-junction **G**, watch for a small turnoff—not a road, just a footpath—on your right. ATW there's a little sign here, and there is also a small log railing. But if these are gone, you can find the turnoff a different way: look for the farm track that goes off the road to the *left* (i.e., as you're coming from Olmo) uphill, about 10 paces *before* the turnoff you are looking for (which is on the right and downhill). Take this little footpath **F** by the railing, downhill into some woods. This path, which doesn't look very promising here at its entrance, turns into a rather spectacular "secret" path through *via cava,* these sunken roadways. Well marked once you get going.

In 10–15 minutes this path emerges onto an asphalt road. Turn right, and in 50 m or so you'll reach **C**. If you've left your car here, you're all set. Otherwise, you can continue on to **B** and return the way you came, or you can take a slightly different way back. If you want to go the different way, proceed as far as the break in the guardrail that you encountered on your way *to* Olmo. About 25 m further on, on the left side of the asphalt road, there's a dirt path leading off to the left uphill; take this path (ATW signed "Via cave di Poggio Cani").

Follow this to the top, where it comes out on a wider dirt road: turn left. In less than a minute you'll reach the steps up to Pitigliano.

Bear in mind when you reach the Chiesa di Santa Maria that you can take the streets to either side of it, as they both lead to the same place.

TO CONTINUE ON TO SOVANA

At the T-junction **G**, turn left (ATW signed for "Sassotondo," a *biologico* farm and *agriturismo*). Just beyond here, take the first left off this road, a narrower farm track (again signed for "Sassotondo").

After about 1 km you'll reach a gate across the road (the

turnoff to Sassotondo is to the left here). Ahead of you in the distance you can see the squat cathedral of Sovana; bear in mind that you're heading toward that.

Follow the well-trodden trail, watching for the CAI marks as you go.

In 15 minutes or so the path enters a shady, sunken-roadway-style stretch. In 4–5 minutes it passes an old stone arch with a CAI mark on it. Continue on straight ahead. Another 5 minutes or so past that, you'll cross an old bridge, hardly noticeable beneath the shrubbery, and emerge from woods into a field, with some caves visible across the field. There's a path straight across the field: don't take that; instead, turn left immediately upon exiting the woods, skirt the woods on your left for 20 m or so and you'll see a path leading back up into the woods (ATW marked with CAI marks): take this path.

The path here is well marked. Stay on it until it comes out on a dirt road **H**, on which you turn left. This dirt road conducts to an asphalt road in a moment; bear right onto this (and ignore smaller turnoffs to the right and left for the next minute or two beyond here).

Just before the asphalt road makes a sharp left-hand bend up into Sovana, you'll pass a small turnoff to the right, with steps, to Folonia (a necropolis reached in about 10 minutes, along pretty *via cava*). Continuing on past this turnoff, bear left at the city wall and so into town.

TO VISIT THE TOMBS FROM SOVANA

Facing the Palazetto Del'Archivio at the top end of the piazza, take either of the streets going up beyond it, to the cathedral. Drop down to the right of the cathedral, where you'll find another stone road leading downhill. At the bottom of this, some stone steps lead down to the asphalt road: turn left through the tunnel. There's a nice dovecote above the tunnel, visible after you've passed through the tunnel.

You used to be able to cut through the woods here to reach the tombs, but this is now blocked off. Staying on the road, in a little less than 10 minutes, just after crossing over the *fiume* (signed for "Sovana: necropolis di sopra ripa"), turn left onto a dirt track. Cross the bridge and come to the little shop where you buy tickets for the Etruscan tombs.

TO WALK TO SOVANA WITHOUT THE FONTANA PORTION

Follow the Pitigliano to Fontana dell'Olmo directions to San Rocca, the parking area **C**. Instead of turning left here, continue on the asphalt road for another 50 m or so, watching on your left for the path that conducts up to **F**. From **F** (where the footpath comes out on the dirt road, near the small log railing) turn right on the dirt road, reaching the T-junction **G** in about 175 m. Pick up directions to Sovana from **G**.

UMBRIA

UMBRIA

As mentioned in our introduction to the 1997 edition, Umbria presented special problems when it came to finding walks. Though much of it is considerably wilder than Tuscany, much of it has also been spoiled by development and industrial sprawl. This happens to be particularly bad around some of the towns where we would have most liked to create walks: Perugia, Orvieto, Assisi and Todi. We had nevertheless hoped to find walks in these areas for this edition, but alas, things have become even worse. We've left our Assisi walk in the book, but can't recommend it any more enthusiastically than we did last time around. The saddest news is that the beautiful Valnerina has been opened up by a vast road tunnel through the mountains from Spoleto, thereby ruining one of our most spectacular itineraries, the old railway walk from Sant' Anatolia di Narco to Spoleto, with the sound of roaring traffic drifting up from the valley. We considered leaving the walk in anyway, but it turns out that the two-kilometer railway tunnel that (along with crossing the long, narrow viaduct, whose rusted guardrails are either missing altogether or dangling off the edge, framing a view of the valley bottom a quarter of a mile below) gives this walk its peculiarly thrilling character has been locked shut. Signs direct the walker off along a rather tedious, featureless woodland detour, so you can still do some version of this walk if you're absolutely determined, but be warned that the new signs are not easy to follow. One day, after the age of the automobile has passed, the new road tunnel will no doubt make a thrilling stretch of its own along some new walk into this once magical valley. Until then, this immediate area is best avoided.

On a brighter note, Gubbio and the area around Norcia, Castelluccio and the Sibillini mountains remain as gorgeous as ever. In Norcia itself we've replaced our old ring walk with a new, far more interesting one that takes you up through beautiful countryside to the lovely abbey of San Eutizio, where there's an excellent little restaurant (which also happens to rent rooms). This is now one of our most highly recommended walks.

27 ■ GUBBIO DOUBLE RING WALK

Gubbio is one of our favorite places in this book, and this walk one of our favorite walks. On this trip we left it until the end, and in the end couldn't get there—a disappointment we can only mitigate by planning to make it our first destination next time.

There's an excellent new CAI map for this area that shows many promising walks in this beautiful countryside. Insofar as these trails are marked on the ground, you may find yourself crossing over them or following them at various points in the itinerary, especially CAI 253, with which we overlap at several points. We highly recommend availing yourself of this map before setting out.

Meanwhile, correspondence from readers indicates that the itinerary as we describe it hasn't changed much, except that CAI has marked a better ending to it now, one that avoids the stretch on the busy road at the end. We have revised the directions to incorporate this improved ending. Note that the CAI map doesn't show this new ending (which leaves the road just before reaching the cemetery), but readers report that it is marked on the ground.

We are deeply indebted to Luigino Brunetti at the Gub-

bio section of CAI, for his generous help in updating this walk.

The two restaurants that were our favorites last time (one was a Chinese restaurant) are gone now. In their place, we have asked various Gubbio residents to recommend their favorite restaurants, and have listed those choices in the Logistics section. We hope to receive feedback from readers on these new recommendations, and have kept our original reviews for the two restaurants that are still open, as local inhabitants seemed generally to concur that they are still excellent, if expensive.

Backing up against the windy slopes of the Umbrian Apennines, the hill town of Gubbio with its steep stone alleys and tightly-clustered medieval buildings has an austere splendor all its own. Legend and history agree on a certain quality of wildness and stony independence about the town, and a trace of this survives in the present-day atmosphere. Local folklore holds that it was one of the first five towns built after Noah's flood, and it's certainly true that the foundations go back to pre-Etruscan times. In the twelfth century, the emperor Frederick Barbarossa had a league of twelve towns poised to attack Gubbio. The town's bishop, Ubaldo, managed to persuade the emperor to restrain them, for which the good bishop was subsequently adopted as the town's patron saint. This act of diplomacy was echoed in the next century by no less a figure than St. Francis. This time it was wolves rather than the Imperial league plaging the town. One in particular was terrorizing the local populace, and the story goes that the saint simply went out into the countryside, found the animal, spoke to it, and worked out a settlement whereby in return for regular meals it would stop preying on the townsfolk. The deal was ratified by a shake of the paw, memorialized by a bas-relief over the door of a church in Via Maestro Giorgio. Recently (for what it's worth), the skeleton of a large wolf was discovered buried under a slab of stone by workmen repairing another church.

More recently the town was a center of resistance against the Nazis; tragically so: forty partisans were executed in the square at the entrance to the town, now named Piazza Quaranta Martiri in their memory.

Traditions from the Middle Ages survive in two important festivals. The Palio della Balestra is a crossbow competition held on the last Sunday in May, providing a nice occasion for the national civic obsession with dressing up in medieval costume. A larger event held earlier in the same month (May 15th) is the Festival of the *Ceri* (large wax candles used in churches), in which teams of men race through the streets and up the extremely steep lower slopes of Monte Ingino to the Basilica of San Ubaldo above the town, carrying colossal constructions that look something like vast and ornate wooden egg timers, each topped by a wax saint. These *ceri* are kept on display at the Basilica, as is the body of Saint Ubaldo himself, minus three fingers that were lopped off by his servant for a lucky charm.

The Walk

This is an exceptionally beautiful walk through the high pastures, woods and old farmsteads in the mountains above Gubbio. The beginning is certainly the most dramatic of any in this book; a ride up Monte Ingino to the Basilica of San Ubaldo on the scary *funivia,* something between a ski chair and a cable car, with stunning, wobbly, vertiginous views onto the town and plain below. From the Basilica, the walk continues along old farm tracks through increasingly remote and attractive countryside: meadows full of wildflowers and butterflies, thick hedgerows of blackberry bushes, rolling hills covered with yellow broom, white Chianina cattle grazing in the fields, and behind them the rugged mountains of the Umbrian Apennines. There's a particularly lovely old farm on the way that looks like something from a seventeenth-century painting, complete with pitched haystacks and piled bundles of twigs tied with strips of bark.

Food

High-quality white truffles grow in the fields above Gubbio and feature prominently on the local restaurant menus. If you've never tried them, probably the best way to appreciate their amazing (to some tastes rather overwhelming) flavor is in a simple dish of scrambled eggs sprinkled with truffle shavings. The Taverna del Lupo does this exceptionally well, though the restaurant is one of the more expensive in town. Another somewhat fancy place, with perhaps a more innovative menu though a rather stiff atmosphere (and the surreal practice of giving a *ledy*—i.e., "lady"—menu, on which the prices have discreetly absented themselves) is La Fornace di Mastro Giorgio, where two set menus are offered in addition to the à la carte menu. Dishes include marinated hare, grilled vegetables, fresh fusilli with a sweet pepper sauce, *strangozzi* (hand-rolled pasta) with a delicious buttery sauce of pigeon stock flavored with truffles, duck with green olives, *sformato* (a kind of souffle) of potato and snail with a porcini mushroom sauce, and an excellent creamy risotto with mascarpone and zucchini flowers. The food is presented hospital-style, under a china bonnet, by buttoned-up waiters who use a spoon and fork just to move your napkin.

There's a little cafe in the Piazza di Signoria where you might like to sit outside before dinner, sipping a Bellini made of *prosecca* (similar to champagne) and raspberry juice, and contemplating the exquisite Palazzo dei Consoli.

LOGISTICS

GUBBIO DOUBLE RING WALK,
2–4 hours

ⓘ Miscellaneous info

🚌 Transport

Ⓜ Maps, guidebooks and trail info

🍴 Eating

🏨 Accommodation

ⓘ

Piazza Oderisi
Tel. 075-9220693
e-mail: info@iat.gubbio.pg.it
www.comune.gubbio.pg.it

🚌

You can reach Gubbio by train on the Florence–Terontola–Perugia line (closest station is Perugia / Fontivegge, 40 km from Gubbio), or the Roma–Ancora line (closest station is Fossato di Vico / Gubbio, 18 km from Gubbio). There are bus connections between both these stations and Gubbio.

APM

Tel. 075-506781, or toll-free inside Italy 800-512141
www.apmperugia.it

TAXI

Tel. 075-9273800

Ⓜ

The Gubbio section of CAI has produced a new 1:25,000 map (*carta dei sentieri*) of the area. In addition to the CAI office, it's available at the stationery shop La Cartoleria Pierini, located at Via Reposati 53, and should also be available at almost any of the newspaper kiosks.

🍴

La Fornace di Mastro Giorgio
Via di Mastro Giorgio, 2
Tel. 075-9221836
Price: Very expensive
Closing day: Tuesday all day, Wednesday lunch
    Along with Taverna del Lupo, one of Gubbio's best.

Taverna del Lupo
Via Ansidei
Tel. 075-9274368
Price: Very expensive
Closing day: None
    According to some local inhabitants, this is the best restaurant in Gubbio, but you can't eat there for less than 100 euros.

Il Campanone
Via Picardi, 21
Tel. 075-9276011
Price: Moderate
Closing day: Wednesday
    Located in a medieval stone building in the town center. Local dishes.

Ristorante dei Consoli
Via dei Consoli, 59
Tel. 075-9273335
Price: Moderate
Closing day: None
Serving local typical dishes.
Central location, in a medieval
building.

Il Faro Rosso
Loc. Montanaldo
Tel. 075-9258010
fax 075-9258062
Price: Inexpensive to moderate
Closing day: None
Agriturismo located on top of
a hill just overlooking Gubbio
(with a breathtaking view). They
have their own cattle, their own
sheep and pigs and so on. The
cuisine is *eugubina* (from Gubbio).
They are located about 8 km
outside of Gubbio. If you don't
have a car, you might enjoy using
a combination of taxi and school
bus; the latter leaves Faro Rosso
for Gubbio at about 7:35 and
returns to Faro Rosso at about
13:30, from mid-September to
mid-June. If you have a car, take
route 206 toward Castiglione;
follow signs for "Montanaldo–
Villa Montegranelli–Faro Rosso."

ParcoCoppo
In the Parco di Coppo, behind
Monte Ingino, near the CAI
rifugio.
Tel. 075-9272755
Price: Inexpensive
Closing day: Wednesday
Open from the beginning of

April until September 30. Open
for lunch at 12:30 and for dinner
at 19:00. They also have good
pizzas. Located on top of the hill
in front of Mount Ingino. You can
see it from the Basilica di San
Ubaldo (starting point of the
walk) from which it is about 1 km
away. You can also ask for directions at the bar next to San
Ubaldo.

⊞

Check with the tourist office for
listings of *affittacamere* and
agriturismo.
Sport Hotel
Via Bottagnone
Tel. 075-9220753
fax 075-9220555
e-mail: info@urbaniweb.com
www.umbria.org/hotel/sporting
Price: Double, 68–100 euros;
double as single, 54–70 euros;
prices include breakfast

San Marco
Via Perugina 5
Tel. 075-9220234
fax 075-9273716
**www.hotelsanmarco
gubbio.com**
Price: Double, 68–88 euros;
single, 55–65 euros; prices include breakfast

AGRITURISMO

Il Faro Rosso
Loc. Montanaldo
Tel. 075-9258010
fax 075-9258062

Price: 30 euros per person, includes breakfast

See descriptive note in Il Faro Rosso's restaurant listing.

CAI, Gubbio
Piazza S. Pietro, I
E-mail: caigubbio@libero.it
**http://digilander.libero.it/
caigubbio**
(The Web site has a beautiful
"action" design at the top—
quintessentially Italian.)

Funivia opening hours
March–June:
10:00–13:15 and 14:30–18:30
Feriale (Mon.–Sat.)
9:30–19:30 Festivi (Sundays and
holidays)

July–August:
9:00–20:00
September:
Usually the same as the
March–June schedule, but occasionally on the October–March
schedule
October–March:
10:00–13:15 and 14:30–17:00,
every day except Wed., on
which it is closed.

This is the schedule ATW, but
if it's really important to you,
you might want to check ahead.
Meanwhile, you can always walk
up to San Ubaldo, about a half-
hour walk (but of course not as
much fun).

Directions

Take the funicular (*funivia*) from Porta Romana on the east side of the town. From the top, walk up the hill to visit Basilica di Sant'Ubaldo.

Standing in front of the church, with your back to it, turn right down the road, passing the intersection with the path back down to the *funivia*.

Follow this asphalt (but untrafficked) road, winding around, ignoring a left-hand turn **A** (also asphalt) after about 5–8 minutes.

The road winds through a little park/picnic area and passes the bar Tre Ceri, after which the asphalt gives way to dirt.

Pass to the side of a metal gate blocking the road to cars.

When the road forks **B** (the left fork actually goes straight ahead, and has a private property sign; the right fork goes more steeply downhill), take the left fork.

When the road forks again **C**, take the lower, downhill right fork, joining CAI 253. Continue downhill, following CAI 253 now, always staying to the main path. In just under 1 km from **C**, you'll come to a left bend in the road where a house, Casa Sasso, sits off to the right on a bit of a ledge, and the road forks **D** into an upper and lower branch, signed by CAI.

According to an e-mail we received recently, this part of the trail has been very "chopped up." This reader said to skirt around behind a garage just before the house, descend a steep hill, then pick up the trail. However, the CAI map shows two trails here, as was formerly the case, so while the paths may be slightly reconfigured, if they are now actually signed, you should have no problem here. CAI 253 (which is what you've been on) goes to the right, and CAI 256 is the upper left-hand fork (possibly still signed to "Scheggia" and "Costacciaro" and there may still be a drinking fountain here at the turn). If you are doing only one of the loops (though the second is beautiful, and we don't recommend missing it), continue on CAI 253 to the right. Skip to the end of the walk directions, where we return to town from Casa Sasso.

If you're going for the double loop, take the upper left-hand fork, CAI 256, following it past the abandoned (at the time of original writing) farmstead Casa Barco I, about ½ km past **D** on the right side of the road. (There's also an abandoned structure on the left side of the road here.)

About 10 minutes later you'll reach another house, Barca II, on the right side of the road. The road forks here; take the left, upper fork, CAI 256.

When you come to the next old farmhouse **E**, this one inhabited and working (note that only the buildings, and not the name, are shown on the CAI map, at altitude point 696), go to the right of the house. The path turns left here; do not take the right-hand turn downhill. The path begins to climb past the outbuildings of the farm.

About 300 m past the farm, ignore a smaller fork **F** to

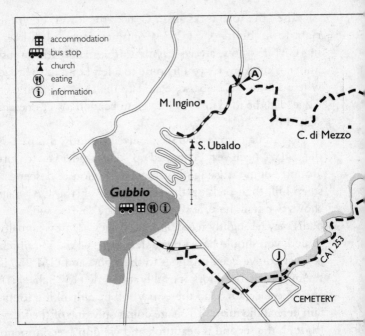

the right off the main path. Note that this smaller fork to the right is now CAI 256 (and it's also possible it's no longer *smaller*), which you will be leaving at this point. (Assuming you have the CAI map with you—and a lot of time for getting lost—you could add about 10 km onto the loop here by continuing on along 256 here, to Villamagna, then taking 255 back to **C**.)

Staying on the main path for the next 3 km or so, you'll pass through some of the prettiest unspoiled countryside in Umbria.

When you reach a T-junction with a similar road (CAI 255), go left **G**.

About 200 m past **G**, CAI 255 bears to the right **H**. Our path goes left here; however, you could take 255 for a somewhat longer route; it rejoins our path in another 1– 1½ km (depending which way you go), at **I**.

In about 15 minutes more, the path reaches a junction **I** with CAI 255; turn left here, rejoining CAI 255.

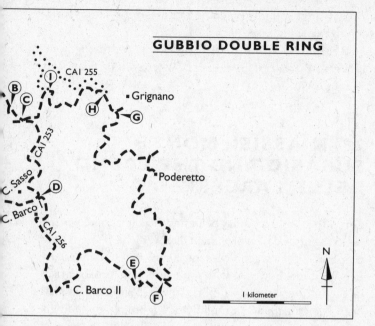

GUBBIO DOUBLE RING

CAI 255

Grignano

Poderetto

C. Sasso

C. Barco

C. Barco II

N

1 kilometer

Stay on this path, CAI 255, for about ½ km more, where the path forks **C** (that is, there's a path going off to the left, downhill). Here you can retrace your steps back either to the *funivia* (in which case you'd turn right here), or to Casa Sasso, in which case turn left here.

FROM CASA SASSO BACK TO GUBBIO

Standing in the intersection **D**, take the lower fork, down-hill, CAI 253.

In about 2 km (20–30 minutes), just before reaching the cemetery, watch on the right for the CAI trail to leave the road **J** at the little chapel by the stream just before en-tering the canyon.

Follow the trail, which will lead to a small road, Via del Crocifisso.

Walk down Via del Crocifisso, cross over the main road (Via della Porta Romana, a.k.a. S.S. 219), and pick up Viale G. Verdi on the other side of the main road.

Stay on that until you come to Via Cesare Battisti forking to the right: take that.

Reaching Via Isonzo, turn right. Stay on that for one block, to Via della Rimembranza, where you turn left, and so into town.

28 ■ ASSISI: MONTE SUBASIO AND THE EREMO DELLE CARCERI

Given that St. Francis has been unofficially adopted as the patron saint of the environmental movement, it seems only proper to offer a walk on the mountain sacred to his memory. We do so, however, with some reservations. Like much of the northern part of Umbria, the area around Assisi has been badly mauled by unsightly development, including a motorway running past the town of Spello, directly beneath Monte Subasio. You can hear the roar of traffic for some distance up the mountain on the Spello side, and you can see the suburban sprawl spreading for miles on the plain below you. The mountain has been a national park since 1983 when an American priest and ornithologist, Bert Schwarzchild, appalled by the sight of so many hunting cartridges on the ground and the corresponding absence of birds, launched an international campaign to protect the mountain from further devastation. Things may be better than they were then, but there are still a number of matters the saint would not have approved of. An unpleasant cluster of radio antennae greets you at the rounded summit, and some of the pathways around the hermitage are appallingly littered. Most of the old-growth trees on the slopes have been logged out and replaced by conifer plantations, while on the other hand the dense, ancient ilex forest around the hermitage itself—a source of pride to the present-day Franciscans—has, according to the naturalist Gary Paul Nabhan, been *over-*

protected by fire suppression and other static preservation methods, to the point that it has stopped regenerating itself and is in fact dying. For Nabhan the thousand-year-old tree in the hermitage, said to have shaded St. Francis while he preached to the birds and now held up by cables and iron stakes, is less a symbol of Franciscan solicitude for nature than of misplaced reverence and underlying neglect.

That said, the higher parts of the walk go through very pretty areas of grassy downland and offer enormous views over the surrounding countryside. Then, too, the little hermitage itself is still quite lovely. This was where Francis used to come on retreat and commune with the birds. His cell, the Oratorio Primitivo, is still intact, and his pillow is allegedly among the relics held in the chapel. A few Franciscans still occupy the hermitage today, living off alms from visitors. This walk takes you within view of the summit, which you can continue on to if you choose, though it's not a particularly charming spot.

Directions

From Piazza Matteotti (now a car park) at the top of Assisi, go to the upper left corner of the piazza, and walk up the road (Via Santuario delle Carceri) to the old city gate, the Porta Cappuccini. Just outside, take the cypress–lined stone track that leads to the left (trail marked 50 and 51). Steep climb. Bear right past the ruins of a fort (Roccacciola) after 200 m.

After about 20 minutes (a little more than ½ kilometer), the road forks **A**. Take the middle prong (signed 50, also signed to the Eremo). The path narrows and begins to seem a little less tame here.

Views open onto the vast plain below—built up. Sound of the motorway constant.

Continue on up past a truffle reservation.

The path levels off, and is joined **B** by path 53 and another smaller path, both coming from the left. Go straight on. In 15 minutes, passing a horribly littered picnic site, you'll come out at the wide gravel road. Turn right **C**. (Now signed 60.)

In a few minutes the Eremo (Sanctuario delle Carceri) comes into sight, snugly situated in its wooded hollow. The road forks **D**; if not visiting the Eremo, take the left fork 50 m before the stone gateway, following the sign for San Benedetto—an asphalt road (also signed 50). To visit the Eremo, go right. There's a surprisingly modest kiosk at the gate, after which the peacefulness of a real sanctuary has

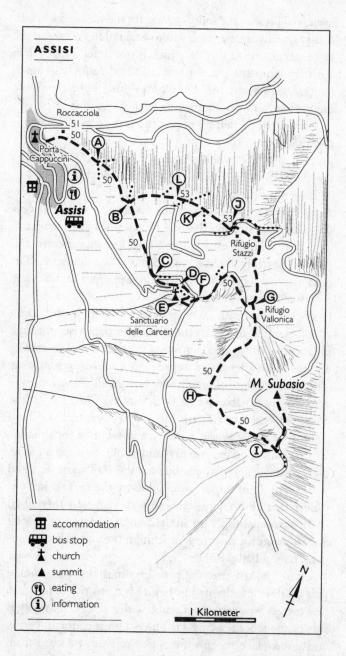

ASSISI

Roccacciola
51
50
Porta
Cappuccini
(A)
50
Assisi
(i)
(L)
53
(B)
(J)
(K)
53
50
Rifugio
Stazzi
(C)
(D)(F)
50
(E)
(G)
Sanctuario
delle Carceri
Rifugio
Vallonica
50
(H)
M. Subasio
50
(I)

accommodation
bus stop
church
summit
eating
information

N

1 Kilometer

been well preserved. Notices asking for silence are respected. A tiny stone staircase leads you to St. Francis's own minute stone cell, the doorway of which is not much bigger than a catflap. Squeeze out through this and follow the *uscita* (exit) signs, passing the white doves' little dovecote. Note the wall with ilex trees growing in and out of it.

Fork up to the left 30 m past the restrooms. The path is called Sentiero Sole e Luna.

The path crosses the ravine. After about 30 m there's a sharp left **E** leading uphill to the road; take this.

Reaching the road in about 50 m, turn left, go a few meters and at the crook of the hairpin turn you'll see a yellow sign indicating the trail to Vallonica to the right **F**. Take this trail (it's also marked 50). The entrance to this path is horribly littered, but things soon improve. The path narrows, climbs steadily through trees and bushes, and finally loses the traffic sounds.

Follow main path 50, watching for where it turns right at a fork after about 10 minutes. The path rises through pleasantly shady woods, crosses a streambed and soon after emerges into the grassy upper slopes of Monte Subasio. The path winds up to the pretty little Rifugio Vallonica— actually just an abandoned farm building. Just before the *rifugio* you come to a T-junction with a larger track **G**. Turn right, toward the *rifugio,* which is a good place for a picnic.

The path soon gets narrow and rather vague as it circles the summit—keep an eye out for the trail signs (red and white, 50). If in doubt, simply follow the central hollow. One rather ambivalent sign seems to suggest a turnoff to the right, but simply go straight ahead, keeping the long Subasio summit to your left. It might not be easy to navigate here in bad weather.

Over the first rise, the path becomes clearer, bringing you to a vast panorama just before it turns to the left. In a few meters you come to a fence with a stile. On the other side of the fence is a cross **H**. This is a great panoramic spot, and good place to end the walk. You can proceed from here to the top if you like; just keep following the path (it has a tendency to divide: keep to the upper level). You'll soon see a cluster of radio antennae. The path leads you to them, stopping at a fence beyond which is a gravel road. Turn right at the fence until you come to a gap with a CAI 50 sign on it. Go left on the road **I** for a couple of hundred meters and you'll see the summit on your right across the grass. It's very desolate up here, and in July it's swarming with flies. Frankly, it's not worth the effort, except perhaps for the view, which is impressive on a clear day. Go back to the cross the way you came.

From the cross, go back to the Rifugio Vallonica. A little beyond it, you'll reach the junction **G**. Instead of turning left the way you came, go straight on. In about 1 km, you'll see a road ahead of you, and the Rifugio Stazzi above you to the left. Either go to the road and turn left or else cut left across the grass to the right-hand side of the clump of trees at the right bend in the road. Just before the bend, you'll see a small sign marked 53 pointing down to the right **J**. There's no actual path at first, but follow the brow of the hill about 40 m above (and parallel with) the wooded hollow to your left and you'll soon find a stony track. Keep on this track; after 200–300 m the path enters the woods, meeting a larger stone track where you turn right **K** (trail mark).

In 5–10 minutes from where you just turned right, the path is joined by another path coming from behind and right, and a few meters later it forks. Take the right fork **L** (marked 53 to Assisi).

Ignore a path off to the right after 250 m. But look for a sign (53) pointing down to the right about 300 m beyond that, and follow this path.

Coming out at a T-junction **B** where trails 50 and 53 intersect, turn right (ignoring the smaller path immediately to your right). This is the way you came: trail 50.

In 20 minutes you'll reach Roccacciola. Continue on past here, returning the way you came, into town through the Cappuccini gate.

This isn't one of the wildest or loveliest of the walks. You seldom feel very remote from civilization—whether in the form of traffic noises wafting from the thruway, or the sight of the suburban/industrial sprawl on the plain below, or worst of all, the litter on parts of the path. But it's worth it for the lovely Eremo (you can drive there, but it feels more appropriately Franciscan to walk), for the pretty area up near the Rifugio Vallonica, and for the sheer scale of the views up there.

29 ■ SOUTHEAST UMBRIA

Eastward from Spoleto to the border of the Marches lies some of the wildest and most ravishing countryside in Umbria, and the gastronomic pleasures of this little-known region are also among the most varied and interesting.

Immediately east of Spoleto lies the Valnerina, an upland valley running for about 40 km between steep limestone ridges with superb views, flower-filled meadows and beech woods where wild boar are common and even the Apennine wolf makes an occasional appearance. The quick, clear Nera itself is one of the main tributaries of the Tiber, flowing down from the Sibillini mountains in the east. Fortified villages, hermitages, abbeys and churches in a variety of styles including Lombardian (San Pietro in Valle), Romanesque (San Felice di Narco), Renaissance (Santa Maria della Neve) and hybrids (San Eutizio) dot the valley in a beguilingly picturesque manner.

East of the Valnerina, winding above the pleasant town of Norcia (which happens to be one of the great gastronomic centers of Italy), a small road climbs through the foothills of an austere, wild range of mountains called the Sibillini, to a vast Alpine plateau known as the Piano Grande. In June this sixteen-square-kilometer meadow blooms with a succession of wildflowers that paint it one brilliant color after another. Perched on a hill at the end of the plateau is the little farming village of Castelluccio, the highest—and probably the most isolated—settlement in peninsular Italy. Though visitors here have certainly increased in number since the original edition of this book, the atmosphere is still one of wild remoteness (especially if you venture into the Sibillini themselves) extremely unusual in modern Europe. It's easy to understand why the popes, who once ruled this area, used to ban traveling across the plain in winter: even to-day when the fogs come down, the bells of Castelluccio are rung to guide shepherds through the deceptively vast distances.

Rising high above the hilltop of Castelluccio are the great peaks of the Sibillini themselves, forming a natural amphitheater around the Piano Grande. Named for the three ancient sybils, one of whom is supposed to have de-livered her oracular prophecies here (it was the sybils, among others, who foretold the coming of Christ), these stark mountains retain a hieratic and slightly sinister aura. On the far side of Monte Vettore (at 2476 meters the third highest peak on the Italian peninsula and providing, along with its neighbors, wonderful opportunities for long ridge walks) is a curious bright blue lake called Lago di Pilato. Allegedly the body of Pontius Pilate was buried here when the oxen transporting his body from Rome to his birth-place refused to go any further. There's evidence that the ancient Norcians used to sacrifice animals and possibly hu-mans, too, up here. Between them—Pilate, the sybils and a large crag of rock with a distinctly diabolic profile—the area has not surprisingly acquired some notoriety as a place of devil worship. Judging from one or two of the individ-uals we saw drifting around this strange, desolately beauti-ful spot, the practice continues.

Food

Aside from Perugia (where heavy suburban sprawl makes walking rather unsatisfactory), this is gastronomically the most rewarding part of Umbria, in terms of both quality and variety.

Like most mountainous areas, where there is more pasturage than cultivatable land, the cuisine is built around meat. According to Waverley Root, the Umbrians eat more meat than the people of any other Italian region; beef and lamb around Perugia, mainly pork and its multitudinous by-products here in the southeast, where thick oak woods provide the acorns that give the meat its rich flavor.

Simple cooking methods prevail: charcoal grilling, spit-roasting (the local *porchetta* is often spiced with fennel), stewing with wine and herbs in the form of a *salmi*. A local roasting technique known as *pilottati* involves wrapping lard in oiled paper and letting it melt over the meat as it cooks. Lamb is sometimes seasoned with salt, pepper and a little vinegar and cooked *all'arrabiata,* "angry"—i.e., over an intensely hot flame.

But what truly distinguishes Umbrian cooking, and this region in particular, is the black truffle (*tartuffo nero*) that grows in the hills above Spoleto and Norcia, and is probably the best in Europe. These two towns are the joint truffle capitals of Italy, and certainly the places to visit if you want to indulge in the peculiar gastronomic luxury of consuming your dishes—everything from simple pasta to cheese, roast lamb, pâté, liqueurs, and even chocolate—flavored with sprinklings of the intense and aromatic fungus. Norcia holds an annual truffle festival in November. This is the beginning of the season, which extends to April, though there are some rare varieties that mature later in the year. Truffles can be preserved reasonably well under oil, or in the form of a paste, so don't despair if you miss the season. A measure of the high quality of the Umbrian truffle is the use of the Umbrian dialect word for truffle, *trifole* (rather than the Italian *tartuffo*), to describe a kind of cooking— *trifolati*—whereby other foods such as kidneys, mushrooms and pasta are prepared so richly as to suggest truffles, particularly the Umbrian variety.

The chalky soil that plays its part in the delicate alchemy of the truffle also helps create an olive oil low in acids and rich in flavor, and the Spoleto olive oil is rightly considered one of the best in Italy. Excellent mushrooms such as the milky and orange agarics, honey mushrooms and cèpes grow in the beech and chestnut woods. For the sweet-toothed, local specialties include *attorta* (a kind of apple strudel), a sweet gnocchi prepared around Christmas, various fried pastries such as *frappe* and *castagnole,* and a chocolate cake known as *crescionda* served during the February carnival.

Moving east, the Valnerina has exploited its resource of clean, fast-flowing water to farm not only trout but also a particular kind of crayfish found otherwise only in Turkey, and most recently sturgeon. Meanwhile, Norcia's reputation for gastronomic excellence, especially in the area of sausages, hams and other pork products, is such that high-quality pork butchers all over Italy refer to themselves as *norcinos.* Unshaven boar hams, salamis, fresh and cured sausage, rolled pig-cheeks, cervelat, brawn made from the heads of hogs fed on horse chestnuts, *mazzefegati* (liver sausage seasoned with garlic, pepper and coriander), as well as a variety of sheeps' cheeses and cone-shaped, rich ricotta cheeses eaten fresh or aged (the aged being much harder and used for grating like Parmesan) and often rolled in bran—all these fill the windows of the amazing *norcinerias* of Norcia.

Two dishes described by Root, which you may have better luck finding than we did, are *testina di vitello alla norcina*—pieces of calf's head coated with a mixture of ham, pork fat, mushrooms, butter, parsley and bread, wrapped in pig's membrane, rolled in breadcrumbs and fried in olive oil—and *fagiano alla norcese*—pheasant stuffed with truffles a day before being roasted and served with a *grappa*-flavored gravy.

Even tiny Castelluccio has its claim to culinary distinction, in the form of the appropriately tiny Castelluccio lentil, grown exclusively around the Piano Grande and richly flavored. It's usually served in the form of a thick soup, or stewed with sausages, either of which makes an extremely hearty and satisfying meal.

Finally, the ancient grain known as spelt is still grown in this region and forms the basis for a delicious savory porridge-like mush called *farro,* served in many restaurants and well worth trying.

NORCIA TO SAN EUTIZIO: BOTH WAYS

The handsome town of Norcia lies on a sloping, earth-quake-prone plain under the Sibillini mountains. With its low, tiled buildings and flowery balconies, it has a curious Spanish air, and one half expects to see bulls being run through its circular piazza. What one does in fact see is a statue of St. Benedict, who was born here in 480 (as was his twin sister St. Scholastica), a fine church and *communale* building, and several *norcinerias*—the fabulous butcher/delicatessans whose mouth-watering merchandise is the main reason Italians visit this town, and the basis for the local economy.

We've replaced our old Norcia ring walk with a new, longer, far more interesting walk, which we now consider one of the best we have to offer. Connecting Norcia to the mountain abbey of San Eutizio, it follows a fifth-century pilgrim path (used by St. Benedict) through farmland, small villages and high, forested hills. There are many superb views, and an abundance of wildflowers in the meadows and woods along the way (in the stretch between Campi and Acquaro alone, thirty-six different species of wild orchids have been identified). Being a pilgrimage route, the walk naturally enough also passes many splendid churches—some of them with wonderful primitive frescoes—and some ruined hermitages. The abbey of San Eutizio itself was founded on the tomb of its namesake, who died around

540. It flourished for a couple of hundred years in the medieval period, largely on the reputation of its monks for curing illnesses with herbs from the Sibillini mountains. Thereafter a slow decline set in, and the place was abandoned in the 1700s. It was reopened in 1956, and extensively (and rather beautifully) restored over subsequent years. Since 1989 it has been a spiritual and cultural center.

At about four hours each way—and that without counting any time for stopping to look at the many churches along the way—the best plan is to take two days and go there and back. Right by the abbey there's a delightful restaurant that also rents out pleasant, basic rooms. If you prefer something more upscale, there's a hotel with a pool close by in Preci (itself an extraordinary little hilltop village). If you only have a day, we suggest taking a cab one way (for about 15 euros) or else taking one of the infrequent buses between Preci and Norcia.

We did the San Eutizio to Norcia portion first, and for the first half hour the walk was so well signed we thought it was going to be superfluous to give directions. Eight hours later, as we stumbled into Norcia, we realized this was not the case. There were numerous places where the signs are infuriatingly absent. The area around Campi Vecchio was particularly time-consuming, as the signs have been either moved or taken down; we've tried to be especially careful to use landmarks that are more or less permanent.

Norcia is famed for the quality of its drinking water (tap) and there are many fountains along this route where you can fill up. This walk is a perfect occasion for a gourmet picnic, for which Norcia is of course the ideal place to shop.

NOTE: Although we didn't have time to do it on this trip, the next time we go we will walk CAI trails 20 and/or 21 (see a 1:25,000 trail map) which lead off the Norcia–San Eutizio walk at **F** (CAI 20) and ½ km north of **F** at altitude point 1015 (CAI 21) and connect with CAI 22 or 19A

(which is part of our Castelluccio Ring Walk) on into Castelluccio. This would make a great Norcia to Castelluccio walk; if you opt to try it, make sure to bring an IGM map (obviously) and a compass (available at the hiking store in Norcia), and allow *lots* of extra time: we have found that CAI trails are almost never as straightforward as the confident red line on the map would have you believe.

Food

In Norcia there are almost as many *norcinerias* as churches, a happy circumstance as it's in these that you'll find some of

the best food in town. Also not to be missed are the truffle shops on the main street, one of which resembles a high-tech laboratory more than a food shop, such is its appropriately reverent attitude toward its merchandise. The restaurants are a little hit and miss, though the hits comprise some of the best meals to be had in either Tuscany or Umbria. *The Cadogan Guide* lists Dal Francese as one of the ten best restaurants in either province. It was possible to eat well there nine years ago (their homemade *panna cotta* with a sauce of wine, honey and hazelnuts was especially memorable), though even then the place had clearly seen better days. We can't answer for it now, but it's probably outclassed by the restaurant in the pleasant hotel called the Grotta Azzura. This is still excellent, despite its air of a fine old institution working somewhat on autopilot. You can splurge on an entire *tartuffato* menu featuring among other things a sublime roast lamb with truffles; or you can sample such things as *papardelle alla norceria rossa*—thick ribbons of pasta with local hams and mushrooms in a creamy tomato sauce—or cannelloni stuffed with spinach and ricotta in an unusually *piccante* tomato sauce, followed by very fresh grilled trout with chard sauteed in lemon; or *salsicce* served in a bowl of delicious Castelluccio lentils, rounding it off with a *tiramisu* that ranged from terrible to sublime over the course of our stay there. The oven-roasted tomatoes are delicious, the salads are lackluster, and avoid the Steak Surprise unless you're in the market for some souvenir crockery (the "surprise" is a decorated plate of purest kitsch). The service is exceptionally friendly despite the large numbers of people eating here. If you're not eating outside, try to get a seat in the dungeon-like restaurant proper, where the grill is, rather than in one of the large-scale banqueting rooms.

Up in San Eutizio, the low-key, utterly charming Biancofiore restaurant with its fine view onto the abbey is a great place to eat (especially if you've just walked 14 km from Norcia). It's amateurish in the best sense—just a family and some friends interested in cooking good food in a beautiful setting. There's no menu, but the daily specials on our visit featured a sublime dish of gnocchetti with porcini mushrooms, *chicoria* (bitter greens) and truffles, as well as a plateful of tender lamb cutlets from the grill. Vegetables included excellent white beans with onions, and they also serve uncommonly good *gelato,* all at a very moderate price.

LOGISTICS

NORCIA–SAN EUTIZIO: BOTH WAYS,
4 hours each way

- (i) Miscellaneous info
- 🚌 Transport
- (M) Maps, guidebooks and trail info
- (🍴) Eating
- ⊞ Accommodation

(i)
NORCIA

Via Solferino, 22
Tel. 0743-828173
www.comune.norcia.pg.it
e-mail: info@norcia.net
Hours: 9:30–12:30, 15:00–18:00
Mon.–Fri.; weekends 9:30–12:30
and 15:30–18:30

Norcia also has a Casa del Parco office, which has information on

the whole area comprising the Sibillini Park.
Via Solferino, 22
Tel./fax 0743-817090
e-mail: cpnorcia@yahoo.it

PRECI (CASA DEL PARCO OFFICE)

Via Madonna della Peschiera, 1
Tel. 0743-99145 or *tel./fax* 0743-937000
e-mail: cppreci@tiscalinet.it

🚌

Norcia is well served by buses from Spoleto as well Perugia, Assisi, Terni and Foligno.

SSIT

Tel. 0743-212211
www.spoletina.com
Spoleto
From Spoleto railway station, or Piazza Vittoria
About five buses per day, two or three on Sunday
Length of journey: Just under an hour

Norcia (Porta Ascolana)–San Eutizio (stop is Piedivalle)
Norcia–Borgo Cerreto
bus
One bus per day each way: Norcia–Piedivalle: 1:35, Piedivalle–Norcia: 7:59
There are two more per day between Piedivalle and Ancorano, if you want to pick up the walk at point **F**.

Length of journey: About 20 minutes

TAXIS

15 euros between Norcia and San Eutizio
Tel. 338-747-1411 (24 hours a day), or 368-3833455 or 0743-816930 or 0743-816226 or 0743-816455

On the San Eutizio end of the walk, if you're staying at Hotel Agli Scacchi, you can arrange with them for transportation between San Eutizio and the hotel (just a few minutes distant). See their listing in the Sleeping section.

Ⓜ

Parco Nazionale dei Sibillini. There are a few versions of this, a Multigraphic version and one put out by CAI. Any version is fine, as long as it is in 1:25,000 scale and includes the town of Preci; check before you buy. (The old Multigraphic we had did have Preci on it, but you had to turn the map over.)
There is a very good store in Norcia for hiking supplies, maps, guidebooks, etc. See the Misc section below.

🍴

NORCIA

Grotta Azzurra
Ten meters off the main square
Tel. 0743-816513

fax 0743-817342
www.bianconi.com
Price: Moderate
Closing day: None

There is also a very good *rosticceria* next to the taxi stand, across from the bus stop. It also has an entrance on Via Legnano on the inside of the city walls. You could stock up here for a picnic.

SAN EUTIZIO

Biancofiore
Loc. San Eutizio–Piedivalle (it's right next to the abbey)
Tel. 0743-939319
cell 335-8350413
or 338-4634379
Price: Inexpensive
Closing day: Monday

⊞

NORCIA

Hotel Grotta Azzurra
Ten meters off the main square
Tel. 0743-816513
fax 0743-817342
www.bianconi.com
Price: 41–100 euros for a double room with breakfast. The less expensive rooms are in a different building, nearby, called Les Dependances. Double rooms in the hotel itself begin at 50 euros. They also have single rooms.

Ostello per la Gioventu "Norcia"
Via Ufente 1/B
Tel./fax 0743-817487 or 828616
cell 349-3002091

www.montepatino.com
e-mail: ostellonorcia@montepatino.com
Price: B&B, 13 euros; dinner, 8 euros

This is a hostel with 52 beds in rooms for four, six or eight people. Open all year.

Monastero San Antonio
Via delle Vergini, 13
Tel. 0743-828208
fax 0743-828241
Price: Double room, 47 euros; single room, 25 euros; half pension (sleeping, breakfast and dinner), 35 euros per person

For a very peaceful, different kind of place (all the rooms have desks) run by nuns, this working convent comes complete with pigs, bees, rabbits, an orchard and a garden. The nuns make their own pesto (from basil, mushrooms and anchovies), honey and various other sundries. The monastery is in a very nice area just inside the city walls.

PRECI / SAN EUTIZIO

Biancofiore
Loc. San Eutizio–Piedivalle (it's right next to the abbey)
Tel. 0743-939319
cell 335-8350413 or 338-4634379
Price: Three double rooms, each with bathroom, 50 euros. One room with two single beds. (A single person could make a deal.) Full pension, 55 euros per

person (lunch and dinner); half pension (lunch or dinner), 45 euros per person.

No breakfast, but bar opens around 9:00.

Agli Scacchi
Quartiere Scacchi, 12
Tel. 0743-99221
fax 0743-937249
www.hotelagliscacchi.com
Price: Double room, 60 euros, includes breakfast; single room, 39 euros, includes breakfast

They also have a restaurant and a pool. They will arrange round-trip transportation from San Eutizio to the hotel; just let them know (it's only a few minutes away).

Il Collaccio
About 10 minutes from Preci
Tel. 0743-939005 or 939084
fax 0743-939094
www.ilcollaccio.it
Price: They have a wide range of accommodations (including camping) at a wide range of prices. They list weekly prices for their bungalows and apartments, but when available they also rent these for shorter periods. Rooms are 40 euros per person (30 euros in low season), or 55 with half-board (i.e., includes dinner).

Il Collaccio is only useful if you have a car. It's a nice place for kids, and an easy place to be, with its two kiddie-pools and two regular pools (in one

of which, somewhat inexplicably, bathing caps—available for purchase at 3 euros in the office— are required), restaurant and friendly atmosphere. (And for the parents, Nastro Azzurro on tap.)

ⓘ

There is a very good hiking store in Norcia that has an excellent selection of maps and guidebooks. (They also provide faxing and copying services.)
Geosta
Via Foscolo, 10
Tel./fax 0743-828470
e-mail: info@geosta.net

The Cioccolateria Vetusta Nursia, at Via della Stazione, 41/43, sells some extremely good chocolate cookies called Biscotti San Benedetto.

If you've got some extra time to stay on the San Eutizio end, you might be interested in four ring walks that are marked from the abbey. Contact the Casa del Parco in Preci for more information.

#1 San Eutizio, San Marco, Collescille, San Fiorenzo, Valle, San Eutizio

#2 San Eutizio, Acquaro, San Marco, Valle, San Eutizio

#3 San Eutizio, Acquaro, San Macario, Fonte della Liniera, Collescille, San Eutizio

#4 San Eutizio, Collescille, Casale Viola, Valle, San Eutizio

Directions

NORCIA TO SAN EUTIZIO

Leaving Norcia through Porta San Giovanni, cross the main road and take the smaller asphalt road slightly to your right.

In about 70 m a smaller gravel track forks straight off the main road where it (the main road) bends to the left: take this track **A**.

Follow this track along the right side of a wall, and in a couple of hundred meters you'll come out at a small asphalt road which you cross over, continuing forward, your path now a small asphalted lane.

In about 100 m more, this asphalt lane ends at a gated driveway. Immediately to the right of the gate is a grassy—somewhat overgrown—track, passing between the gate and a chain link fence. Take this track.

In about 150 m this grassy track comes out at a gravel road **B** (and to your right is the main asphalt road, which is making a hairpin right bend). ATW there is a big sign here for "Sentiero Norcia–San Eutizio." Turn left (basically straight) on this gravel road.

In about 10 minutes the gravel path turns left; straight ahead is a grassy track (which is part of the CAI 58 trail marked on the Carta dei Sentieri map). You can go either way here **C**, as the tracks rejoin shortly at **D**. As the official *sentiero* goes left, we will too: stay on the path as it turns left here, then in another 100 m turn right again, in front of Casa Cupa.

In about 5 minutes, as the path bends gently left, you'll pass the grassy alternate coming in from the right **D**. Be alert here, as you're going to have to look for something unsigned.

In about 175 m (or about 2 minutes), there's a big gap (about 10 m wide) in the hedge you've been following on your left. Turn left through this gap and follow along the left side of another hedge that climbs up the hill here

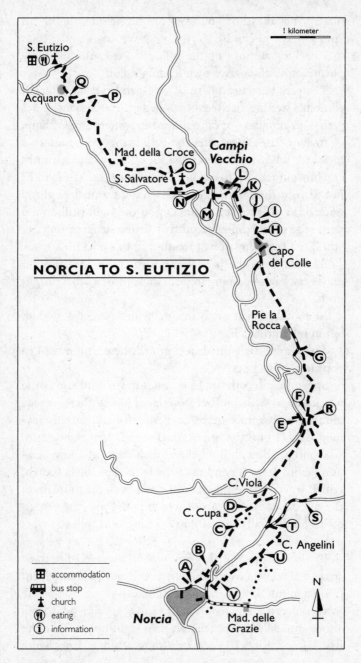

! kilometer

S. Eutizio

Acquaro

Q

P

Mad. della Croce

Campi
Vecchio

S. Salvatore

O

L

N

M

K

J

I

H

NORCIA TO S. EUTIZIO

Capo
del Colle

Pie la
Rocca

G

F

R

E

C. Viola

C. Cupa

D

S

C

T

B

C. Angelini

A

U

accommodation

bus stop

church

eating

information

V

N

Norcia

Mad. delle
Grazie

(Casa Viola ahead of you now on the hillside, slightly to your left as you climb).

Reaching the top of the hill, cross over the main asphalt road to the grassy path leading uphill.

The path becomes a narrow, well-defined stone footpath climbing steadily between two hedges—a pleasant secret path with glimpses out onto mountain scenery as you climb.

In about 20–25 minutes the path brings you out into a meadow, following its left edge for 50 m, where it climbs an embankment up to a point on the main asphalt road **E**. Just to your right here as you're facing the asphalt, a gravel track forks off the asphalt road up to the right (still on the same side of the asphalt road that you're standing on; i.e., you don't cross the asphalt road): take this track.

At the top of the hill (about 30 m) you meet another gravel track (also coming in from the asphalt road): go right on it.

In another 75 m or so this path forks (right downhill, left uphill): go left **F**.

There are little ruined hermit cells here in the field to your left, amid trees.

Stay on main path for 15 minutes or so, until you come to a junction with another stony path (ATW there's a picnic table across from here) **G**. Turn left here, coming immediately (10 m) to a small asphalt road: turn right.

Continue downhill on the asphalt road, in a few minutes (about 300 m) coming to the hamlet of Pie la Rocca, which you pass through. (Good water from the fountain in the middle of hamlet, from which point you can also go off to Madonna Bianca if you're so inclined, signed across from the fountain.)

Past town the asphalt gives way to a gravel/dirt track again. Stay on the main track, which leads in about 1 km (10–15 minutes) into Capo del Colle.

Coming to a T-junction with a small asphalt road (there's a fountain ahead of you here), turn right uphill. Take the first left off this (20 m or so) onto a single-lane white paved road leading into a hamlet (still Capo del Colle) of small buildings, the first of which on your right (Chiesa di San Antonio) has the remains of a fresco on its front.

Coming out of "town" the path becomes a gravel track again. Be alert along the upcoming stretch. As you start climbing uphill on this track you'll pass a cement water trough (and ATW a picnic table). The path bends right past here, and then climbs up in another 25–30 m to a small fork **H** (right smaller and uphill, left somewhat bigger and also uphill). ATW signed here, right for the ruins ("Ruderi"), left for "Campi Vecchio." There is also a red and white paint blaze on a rock to your right. Bear left here.

The path bends left, and in a moment wide views of the valley open up on the left. Continue to be alert along here. ATW there are signs, but if they go, it will be very easy to miss the next turnoff.

Stay on the main path now, ignoring deviations, and in another couple of minutes the grassy path gives way to biggish stones in an open area **I**. It looks like the path would bear right uphill here, because it's wider, but if you did that you'd find it doesn't really lead to much of anything. The actual path here is a narrow left downhill path consisting of more of these big stones. Take this path.

Follow this path, which soon levels off and comes to a dry streambed (*fosso*) where it makes a sharp left-hand turn just after crossing. (The old CAI 58 trail on IGM leads up to the right here between rocky walls—unusable now, and fenced off up near Campi Vecchio.) About 3 m beyond the *fosso,* the path forks into two tiny paths (left downhill, right uphill). Go right uphill **J**.

Follow this very narrow footpath that ascends gradually, then begins to gently descend, following the contour of the hill. About 3–5 minutes after the path begins to descend, it suddenly descends sharply for about 50 m (little log steps here to help you down), and then comes out on an asphalt road **K**. Turn right here.

Passing a stone fountain on your right, the road forks; ignoring the steep uphill right, bear left. Pass through the open archway. (Above you is the church of Sant'Andrea, whose lovely loggia frames a nice view over the surrounding countryside. To see inside the church, walk down the lane off the piazza to the caretaker's house, about the fourth on the right; a small tip is appreciated.) After passing through the archway, bear left, finding some steps leading down; take them all the way down to the bottom. Reaching a stone fountain at the bottom of the steps, bear left downhill, soon reaching a T-junction with an asphalt road: go right **L**.

In about 5 minutes you'll come to a crossroads **M** with Chiesa San Antonio on your right; turn right, passing in front of the church.

In 125 m you'll come to a small asphalt road: turn left downhill.

Take the first right option you come to (in about 75 m), a hairpin right downhill **N**.

This little gravel path comes out in a minute or two at an asphalt road: turn left downhill.

In about 5 minutes you'll come to the church of San Salvatore on your right; bear right off the asphalt road onto the gravel path of its "driveway" and follow this as it passes diagonally in front of the church and down to a little gravel track to the right (main asphalt road immediately to your left here), which you take.

Ignoring the first left-hand turn off here (a farm track after about 150 m, take the second left **O**, a good-sized farm track between hedges, near a large iron cross.

Follow this track as it passes through beautiful fields, and in nearly ¾ km goes back into a lightly wooded section. As you come into the wooded section, the path forks where there's another large iron cross to your left. Bear right here to see the Madonna della Croce a moment's distance away, otherwise bear left.

Stay on the main path, which after a rather arduous—but fairly brief—climb turns into a beautiful woodsy contour footpath. After about 20 minutes, when the path makes a hairpin bend left as you cross the narrow valley between two hillsides, there is an old roman bridge (Porta Romana) **P** underneath you, which you won't know you're crossing unless you look underneath.

Another 5–10 minutes past Porta Romana (about a half hour past the fork at Madonna della Croce), the path turns left downhill **Q** (ATW signed, and there's a right uphill path with big stones, signed to San Macario). In a few minutes you'll pass a little ruined hermitage on the right and just beyond it a little pink chapel also on the right. Continuing downhill you'll pass a stone trough at a spring on your right, just before reaching the hamlet of Acquaro.

At Acquaro go down the steps, pass through the hamlet and, as you get to the bottom of the hill and a T-junction (black metal railing to your left), take the hairpin left downhill.

Bear right onto the stone steps going downhill, then pass underneath a house and a stone arch there. Bear left downhill just past the arch, on a tiny footpath—somewhat overgrown—that leads you in another 2–3 minutes of sharp descent to the trailhead and San Eutizio just beyond.

SAN EUTIZIO TO NORCIA

Walk up the main road from the church and on your right by the parking area is a big wooden sign about the *sentiero*. The path begins just to the right of this.

After climbing up steeply for 5 minutes you'll come to some stone steps at what looks like someone's house. Climb up the steps, which bend left, and at the top of the steps go straight, uphill, in about 25 m coming to another fork: go right, steeply uphill. This is Acquaro.

Keep climbing up, in another minute or two coming to a chapel and more steps. On the far side of the chapel, passing it on your right, the pavement gives way to gravel path.

Pass a little pink ruined chapel building on your left:

bear left uphill here (a beautifully stepped path, ruins of old hermitages, birdsong in the morning and increasingly spectacular views).

Coming to a T-junction after quite a climb, turn right **Q** (ATW signed left to San Macario, one of the four ring walks signed from San Eutizio by the Comunanza agraria Guaita San Eutizio). The path is a bit overgrown in this first little part, but beautifully clear after that, with fragrant wild honeysuckle.

In another 5–10 minutes, where the path makes a hairpin turn to the right as you cross the narrow valley between two hillsides, there's an old Roman bridge (Porta Romana) **P**, which you won't know you're crossing unless you look underneath you.

In 20–25 minutes past Porta Romana you'll pass on your left the "driveway" up to the Chiesa Madonna della Croce, marked by a large metal cross on the right just beyond the driveway. (Don't be deceived by an obvious gravel fork to the left 100 m before this, which is a less felicitous approach.)

Stay on the main path past the Madonna della Croce driveway. After about ¾ km on a beautiful stretch along fields, you'll reach a T-junction with a similar-sized (small) gravel road **O**. At this junction there are fields just ahead of you, with Campi Vecchio on a hill behind them; to the right and downhill from Campi Vecchio is the village of Campi, and about 300 m to your right is the Chiesa San Salvatore. There's also another large metal cross on the left side of the path at this junction. Go right.

Come to the church of San Salvatore and cemetery. There's a T-junction with the main road: don't go quite down to the main road, just circle around the right side of the church and take the smaller, single-lane asphalt road that goes up behind it.

In a minute or two you'll come to a house on your left with a stucco wall (topped with terra-cotta tiles) running along the road. Following along the wall and the road, when the road bends left just at the end of this wall, there's a large iron cross on your left and a farm track to your right: take this farm track.

This track climbs in another minute to a T-junction with a small asphalt single-lane road; turn left here **N**.

In about 75 m you'll come to an intersection with another small road: go right. In another 125 m you'll come to a crossroad **M** with the Chiesa di San Antonio on your left. Turn left here.

In about 5 minutes, as the asphalt road bends right, you'll see a steep fork left uphill **L**, a white paved road at a light-colored stone wall. Take this left (the light-colored wall will be on your right once you make the turn).

Climb up to the top (about 75 m), where there's a fork (left downhill, right uphill) with a stone fountain on your right; bear right, coming almost immediately to some steps on your right. Take these and climb all the way to the top.

At the top of the steps you'll be in a little piazza. (Above you is the church of Sant'Andrea, whose lovely loggia frames a nice view over the surrounding countryside. To see inside the church, walk down the lane off the piazza to the caretaker's house, about the fourth on the right; a small tip is appreciated.) Pass across the piazza and go out through the archway.

Follow the road around as it bends right, coming to a stone fountain on your left and a rocky gravel road down-hill to the right. (Note: CAI 58 as marked on the IGM Monti dei Sibillini Carta dei Sentieri is no longer viable. It's fenced off where you'd pick it up at Campi Vecchio. You can notice it reconnecting with your route in about 15 minutes from here, at a *fosso*.)

About 75 m past the fountain, watch carefully on your left for a little path going uphill, made of small log steps: take this **K**.

This is truffle country; the next stretch passes alongside

truffle reserves. About 10 minutes after embarking up the little log steps, the path crosses a *fosso* (where we reconnect with CAI 58) and bends around right.

Soon the path begins to climb up a stony path; when it emerges from the woods into an open area with big stones **I**, turn right downhill, along a grassy path (ignoring a right fork in about 30 m). CAI paint blazes along here.

In another 3–5 minutes the path forks **H**. ATW this fork is signed, but if the signs are gone it could be easy to miss. Both forks are small; the uphill left fork (basically straight ahead) is slightly smaller, and signed "Forca di Giuda" and "Roveri" (ruins). If you're interested in visiting the ruins of Castelfranco, you can make this detour. Otherwise, take the downhill right.

Another minute downhill you'll pass some kind of water trough on your left, and shortly beyond that enter the hamlet of Capo del Colle.

At the end of the hamlet, pass the little fourteenth-century Church of San Antonio. The road bends right, then comes to an intersection with a small asphalt road. Turn right on the asphalt road (you can see the ruins of Castelfranco on a hill above Capo del Colle), then take the first left after about 20 m (across from another stone water trough).

Continue straight on this road, ignoring deviations, straight through town and beyond.

Bear left uphill at a fork a minute or two out of town.

This wide dirt and gravel track leads in about 15 minutes to the hamlet of Pie la Rocca. Pass straight through Pie la Rocca (you'll pass a fountain on your left, nice cold water, in the wide asphalt area in the middle of "town" signed "Belvedere di Pielarocca").

Bear left uphill at a fork at the end of town.

Climb steadily on the asphalt road, watching on your left in about 5 minutes for a wide gravel fork to the left uphill, which itself immediately forks again with a big metal cross between the two forks: take the fork to the right of the cross **G**.

The path gets much nicer again here, more tranquil. Stay on the main path for about 15 minutes, ignoring deviations. (You may be relieved to know that there's not a lot more climbing from here.)

There are little ruined hermit cells to your right amid small trees in the field along this stretch.

Come to a T-junction with a gravel path **F**: turn left, coming in about 50 m to a stone fountain on the left and a farm track cutting through the middle of a field on the right, downhill, just before it. Take this farm track **R**.

Stay on the main track, ignoring deviations, basically descending all the way.

In about 20–25 minutes you'll pass a farm on your right; the track becomes paved and soon meets a small asphalt road: turn right **S**.

Continue downhill on this road for about 10 minutes.

About 20 m before a fountain/trough on the left of the road, and about 30 m before the intersection with a bigger asphalt road, there's a gravel fork to the left **T**, which itself then immediately forks again (left fork level, right fork downhill): take the right fork, steeply downhill.

This path goes downhill for about 100 m, crosses a *fosso* (no stream here) and begins to climb. About 10 m past the fosso, as the main track bends left, take the lesser fork to the right uphill.

This climbs up through a very dark wood, then comes out and passes just to the right of a big stone house (C. Angelini). Continue straight on, going back into a secret tunnel of green passage. (If it's 100° out, like it was when we were doing this, bet you're glad you didn't choose the asphalt option.) Wish we could say this wide and comfortable track conducts all the way back to Norcia.

After about 5 minutes, watch for a lesser fork to the right **U**, where the main path bends left. Take this lesser right downhill (ATW there's a chain link fence along the right-hand side of this track). This path is a bit overgrown with grass, but looks like it will remain.

(However, if this path is ever closed off or disappears in the future, you can stay on the main path here at **U**, which comes out in about 200 m on a small asphalt road where you turn right. In about ½ km you'll meet another small road, where the church of Madonna delle Grazie will be off to your left; go right here. After another 600 m, turn right by a stop sign and a small old building which ATW has a small address plate reading "#9 Viale E. Lombrici," and so into town.)

About 5 minutes from **U** you'll pass a couple of modern houses on your left (the track is a single lane of asphalt here) and in another 2–3 minutes come out on another small, single-lane asphalt road; bear left (basically straight).

Follow this road downhill for another minute or two until it curves left into the middle of some stucco houses; as it is curving left, there's a fork off to the right (basically straight ahead) that almost immediately becomes long grass: take this, downhill, soon following to the right of a cement wall, and coming out in a minute or two on a farm track crossing your path (there is also a farm track going on ahead of you across a field; ignore that one); turn left **V**.

When this meets with the little asphalt road in a minute, turn right.

Another minute and you'll reach a T-junction at a stop sign. Turn right. At the next T-junction turn left, and so into town through Porta Palatina.

PIANO GRANDE AND CASTELLUCCIO RING WALK

The beautiful Piano Grande lying below Castelluccio is unique in all of Europe, an upland plain of sixteen square kilometers that in early summer is covered in flowers. You can walk more or less at will here (avoiding the wildflowers) without danger of getting lost, as this vast alpine plain is almost completely flat. With Castelluccio sitting snugly on its hill at the far end, it would be difficult to lose one's bearings except in thick fog (and for this reason we're not supplying a map). It's actually more interesting to look down on from the surrounding mountains or from Castelluccio itself—and presumably even more so from one of the myriad hang gliders and parascenders riding the thermals over it on clear days—than to walk in, as the extreme flatness and deceptive distances can be a little wearying. Mountain bikes or horses, both of which you can rent, might also be more fun. On a cool day, though (there's no shade), it's pleasant to wander down along the west side and cross to the east, between the two hills of La Rotonda and Monte Guaidone. If you look back across the plain after you've crossed it, you'll see a clump of trees on the opposite hillside that have been cut in the shape of Italy and Sicily—a bizarre conjunction of forestry and patriotism.

A shifting preponderance of buttercups, poppies and daisies deck the piano out in a succession of colors throughout June. In mid-June you can be fairly sure of a fine blaze, with blossoms of the Castelluccio lentil illuminating the sloped fringes of the plain with broad stripes of pale yellow. Narcissi, fritillaries, wild peonies and tulips, and rarities such as the Apennine alpine star, Apennine potentilla and a species exclusive to the region, *Carex buxbauni,* all bloom here over the course of the year. Set off by the ring of mountains rising steeply around it, it's an amazing sight. Zeffirelli used it as the setting for *Brother Sun, Sister Moon.*

The Castelluccio ring walk is an exceptionally pretty walk, leading through the rugged, beautiful Valle di Canatra adjacent to the Piano Grande, up through woods to high pastures with gorgeous views of distant mountains, and returning along the slopes above the Piano Grande: one of the best ways of viewing it. There are plenty of shady spots for picnics, and if you come in June you'll see wild peonies blooming on the hillsides, along with fields full of purple, white and deep yellow wildflowers, and the lighter, brighter greenish-yellow of the lentil flowers. Sheep and a few cows dot the route, and snow was still in the crevices of the nearby mountains in June. The rare Apennine partridge is also said to frequent the Valle di Canatra.

As with all walks up here, the weather can change rapidly; you might consider taking a waterproof jacket. As always, bring your own water.

Food

Since we last came, The Taverna has evolved into a really excellent, bustling restaurant, and is probably the better place to go. The owner has a serious interest in the old *cucina povera* of the region. He uses wild greens when they're in season, grows his own organic lentils and has even started cultivating the special peas required for *farecchiata,* a strange, greyish variation on polenta that looks a little daunting but tastes wonderfully wild and earthy. A certain earthiness pervades the menu, which is heavy on mushroom, sausage, truffle, mutton (*castrato*), *strangozzi* (thick homemade pasta) and cake-like bread, all of it delicious. The pièce de résistance is the *polenta tris*—a platter of yellow polenta topped by a trinity of wickedly good sauces: mushroom, *ragu,* and lentil. Hard to improve on this, especially when washed down with a nice Sagrantino di Montefalco, with the velvety green mountains of the Piano Grande fading into twilight around you.

LOGISTICS

PIANO GRANDE AND CASTELLUCCIO RING WALK,
about 3 hours

ⓘ   Miscellaneous info

🚌   Transport

Ⓜ   Maps, guidebooks and trail info

🍴   Eating

🏢   Accommodation

ⓘ
NORCIA

Via Solferino, 22
Tel. 0743-828173
www.comune.norcia.pg.it
e-mail: info@norcia.net
Hours: 9:30–12:30, 15:00–18:00 Mon.–Fri.; weekends 9:30–12:30 and 15:30–18:30

Norcia also has a Casa del Parco office, which has information on the whole area comprising the Sibillini Park.
Via Solferino, 22

Tel./fax 0743-817090
e-mail: cpnorcia@yahoo.it

🚌
SSIT

Tel. 0743-212211
www.spoletina.com
Norcia (Porta Ascolana)–Castelluccio
Norcia–Castelluccio bus
Two buses per day, but they only run on Thursday; Norcia–Castelluccio, 6:25 and 13:30; Castelluccio–Norcia, 7:20 and 14:20.
Length of journey: 50 minutes

The people at the hotel Grotta Azzurra may be able to arrange a ride up to Castelluccio. The first time we went, they got us a ride with the postman. We gave the postman a tip, which was appreciated. You could also ask at the tourist office. And of course, you can always hitch, rather easily.

Ⓜ
Parco Nazionale dei Sibillini. There are a few versions of this,

including a Multigraphic version and one put out by CAI. Any version is fine as long as it is in 1:25,000 scale.

There is a very good store in Norcia for hiking supplies, maps, guidebooks, etc. See below. Maps are also generally available at the bars in Castelluccio.

🍴

Taverna Castelluccio
Via Dietro la Torre, 8
Tel. 0743-821158 or 821100
e-mail: tavernacastelluccio
@libero.it
Price: Inexpensive
Closing day: Wednesday
   They have pizzas, too, at night. Their amazing wild local

greens are available from May to mid-June.

⊞

NOTE: Always book ahead for Castelluccio; there aren't a lot of options.
Taverna Castelluccio
Via Dietro la Torre, 8
Tel. 0743-821158 or 821100
e-mail: tavernacastelluccio
@libero.it
Price: Double room with break-fast, 42 euros high season; 36 euros low season

Hotel Sibilla
Castelluccio
Tel. 0743-821124
Price: Double room, 55 euros, includes breakfast

Directions

With the Albergo Sibilla on your left, take the main road out of town; you'll pass three left-hand turns before you get to the last buildings of town. The main road bends left as you reach the last buildings of town, and on your left (only a minute past the Sibilla) is a small uphill road that begins as asphalt but becomes dirt in about 10 m or so: take this road **A**.

Walking parallel to the main road but above it, stay on this dirt road (CAI 22), ignoring deviations. The Valle di Canatra is to your right as you walk. About a half hour from the start, this road goes by an open area used for camping, and soon thereafter turns into more of a farm track. In June the valley bottom along the right here is filled with the yellow blooms of lentil flowers. Also along here, the track gives out and forks into two grassy paths. Take the right-hand one **B**, which re-enters a patch of woods in about 50 m and becomes more defined.

The path will soon begin to ascend gently, with a grassy slope to the right and a wooded slope with lots of flowers to the left. Staying always to the main path, in about a half hour it begins to ascend gently into woods and is quite well defined again. About 10 minutes later, in a wooded section, it starts to climb steeply.

After about 5 minutes of steep climb, the path emerges from woods and becomes very grassy again. Gently ascending, flanked on both sides by grassy hillsides, you are effectively walking along the bottom of a small valley. Continue following the path, which stays in the valley all the way up to the top—a 10- or 20-minute climb. ATW the path is grassy but easy to follow; should you have any doubts, merely stay in the crease, following it up to the top, where you'll find a rutted track—a serious cart track. Turn left here **C**. This area is a great picnic spot, with shade and lovely views.

From here you begin the very gradual descent back to Castelluccio. The path is easy to follow. After about 45 minutes to an hour of easy walking, you'll reach a T-junction with a gravel road **D**, and a view over the Piano Grande and surrounding mountains. Go left on this gravel road, which takes you back into Castelluccio.

TWO-DAY SIBILLINI WALK: FORCA DI PRESTA TO FOCE TO CASTELLUCCIO, via Monte Vettore and Lago di Pilato

We didn't redo this walk for the new edition. We haven't had any reports of difficulties with it, so we've simply updated the Logistics section. We emphasize again that you need a 1:25,000 hiking map for this one. When we were last there, CAI Perugia was in the process of marking routes, so you may find the walk quite a bit easier to follow

CASTELLUCCIO RING

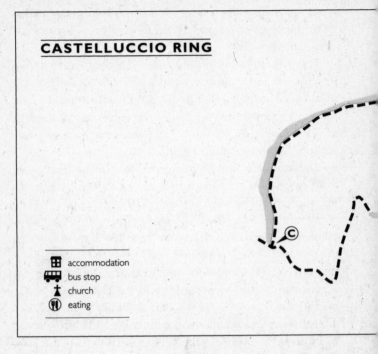

- ▥ accommodation
- 🚌 bus stop
- ✝ church
- 🍴 eating

than it once was. Get a recent CAI map in Norcia or Castelluccio (see map on p. 378).

If you're in good physical shape and find the prospect of a strenuous but exhilarating two-day walk through some of the wildest scenery in Europe enticing, then this is an adventure you shouldn't miss.

Forca di Presta is about ten kilometers from Castelluccio, and if you have a car it's worth driving out there just to look around even if you're not doing the walk. The ride over, along the Piano Grande, is stunning, and the sheep and the big white Maremma sheepdogs (many of whom appear to be out of work) are a great sight under the colorful wings of the hang gliders. On the other hand, if you don't have a car, you should still be able to hitch a ride

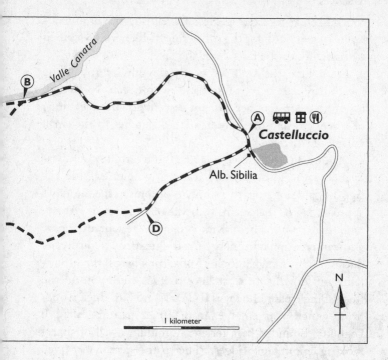

from Castelluccio (or the crossroads two kilometers below it) pretty easily.

The Rifugio degli Alpini in Forca di Presta is a well-run little mountain refuge where you should stay especially if you don't have a car, as you'll need to start early in the morning. It's very bare-bones lodging, but it's worth staying the night there for the sound of the howling wind alone.

Rising steeply from the Rifugio Alpino, the trail climbs the wind-battered flank of Monte Vettore. Our route veers away a little short of the summit, but if you're ambitious enough to climb it, both the Adriatic and Tyrrhenian seas are visible from there on a clear day. Descending into the crater-like valley brings you to the curious double pool of the Lago di Pilato (see p. 345), glinting among the barren stones of the valley bottom. The lake is home to a rare and protected species of shellfish, so swimming is not allowed. Look for the sinister devil-like profile formed by the cliffs on the far side of the lake.

From here the walk is mostly downhill through the lovely harebell-covered moorland, with beech woods and, toward the end, a rather difficult descent down a steep slope of scree, crossing the border of the Marches to the small village of Foce.

"Mountain resort" seems a grandiose term for this mysterious, rather otherworldly and nearly deserted little village; but judging from the numbers of tents in the meadows approaching it, that seems to be its main function. At any rate, there's a hotel here, with a tolerable restaurant, where you can recoup your energy for the next day's equally arduous (and somewhat longer) hike back across the mountains and down into Castelluccio. This takes you up the steep shingle path known as Il Canale and into thick woods from which you emerge at the high pasture called Il Laghetto, bounded by a terrific, forbidding wall of sheer-looking mountain ridges. The path—reasonably well marked by CAI up here—leads you through a remote, craggy landscape dominated by the triangular rocky peak

of Sasso Borghese, and over the ridge, where you'll see Castelluccio in the distance below you. Climbing down, you'll come to the Rifugio Capanna Ghezzi, where you can stay if you've had the foresight to get the key from the CAI office in Perugia. Otherwise it's another four or five kilometers back to Castelluccio, primarily on the most rudimentary of dirt roads along which the occasional adventurous car may offer a hitching opportunity if you want it.

This is serious hiking country. The winds can be formidable at the higher elevations, and the weather can change rapidly. Bring a windbreaker or sweater on this walk in high summer; in other seasons wrap accordingly.

Our map tries to take account of the disparity between CAI paths marked on the official hiking maps, and actual paths on the ground, *but you should not embark on this walk without a hiking map.*

Food

If you've got a car you'd be better off eating at La Taverna, but the Rifugio at Forca di Presta will prepare a simple evening meal and provide you with snacks for breakfast if you're planning to leave at the crack of dawn. The restaurant in Foce serves reasonable pastas and grilled meats. The food is substantial if not exactly gourmet, and the atmosphere is friendly.

LOGISTICS

TWO-DAY SIBILLINI WALK,
about 5 hours each day

ⓘ   Miscellaneous info

🚌   Transport

Ⓜ   Maps, guidebooks and trail info

🍴   Eating

🏢   Accommodation

ⓘ
NORCIA

Via Solferino, 22
Tel. 0743-828173
www.comune.norcia.pg.it
e-mail: info@norcia.net
Hours: 9:30–12:30, 15:00–18:00 Mon.–Fri.; weekends 9:30–12:30 and 15:30–18:30

Norcia also has a Casa del Parco office, which has information on the whole area comprising the Sibillini Park.
Via Solferino, 22
Tel./fax 0743-817090

e-mail: cpnorcia@yahoo.it

🚌

The nearest bus is the Thursday Castelluccio bus from Norcia. (See Norcia to San Eutizio walk Logistics section for more information.)

TAXIS

See Taxi listing in Norcia to San Eutizio walk.

If you haven't got a car, you can hitch a ride from Castelluccio (or the crossroads about 2 km below it—see your IGM map), or even from Norcia. Alternatively, you might consider walking the 10 km or so the day before you begin this walk.

Ⓜ

Parco Nazionale dei Sibillini— There are a few versions of this, including a Multigraphic version and one put out by CAI. Any version is fine, as long as it is in

1:25,000 scale. The Universo Montevettore map used to come with a supplement showing the latest stretches that CAI has marked, but if CAI has a new map, this may no longer be so important. The CAI Monti Sibillini map used to come with an excellent sew-on wolf decal of the Parco Nazionale Monti Sibillini. If it still does, take a peek inside to make sure your map contains one; they were often missing. The best bet might be to ask which map is the most recent.

There is a very good store in Norcia for hiking supplies, maps, guidebooks, etc., called Geosta, at Via Foscolo, 10.
Tel. 0743-828470
E-mail: info@geosta.net
Maps are also generally available at the bars in Castelluccio.

🍴

See The Piano Grande and Castelluccio Ring Walk. If you don't have a car, you can eat at the Rifugio degli Alpini.
In Foce, the Taverna della Montagna has its own restaurant.

🏨

For Castelluccio or Norcia, see the respective Logistics sections.

Rifugio degli Alpini
Forca di Presta
Tel. 0736-809278
fax 0736-809600 (Write "Attention Gino" on any fax you send. He also speaks English.)
Price: Mezza pensione (sleeping, dinner and breakfast), 26 euros; sleeping only, 13 euros. Add 4 euros to these prices if you don't arrive with a sleeping bag.

Bear in mind you may be bunking with other people in this *rifugio*. It's quite a place though, definitely an interesting experience.

Open every day between June 15 and September 15. Closed November and December except Christmas week. The rest of the year, open weekends only.

Rifugio Taverna della Montagna
Foce di Montemonaci
Tel. 0736-856153 or 0736-856327
Price: Double, 45 euros; single, 30 euros

Directions

DAY ONE

From Rifugio Alpini, walk down the road north toward the mountains.

The path is just at the base of the mountains, where the *rifugio* road T-junctions with the road from Castelluccio **A**.

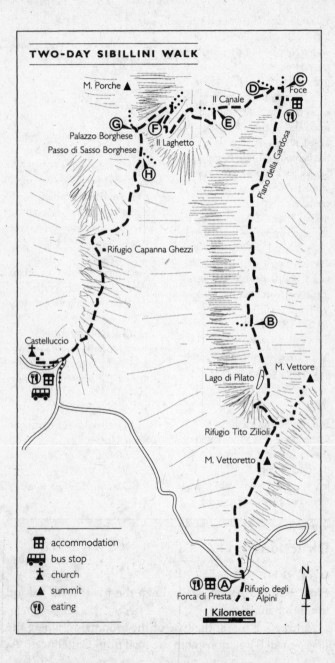

TWO-DAY SIBILLINI WALK

M. Porche ▲

Il Canale

Ⓓ

Ⓒ Foce

Ⓔ

Ⓖ Ⓕ

Palazzo Borghese

Il Laghetto

Passo di Sasso Borghese

Ⓗ

Piano della Gardosa

Rifugio Capanna Ghezzi

Ⓑ

Castelluccio

M. Vettore ▲

Lago di Pilato

Rifugio Tito Zilioli

M. Vettoretto ▲

🔲 accommodation

🚌 bus stop

♁ church

▲ summit

🍴 eating

Ⓐ

Forca di Presta

Rifugio degli Alpini

N

1 Kilometer

You can see the path as it crosses the hills from the roads below. Take it.

There are old red marks along parts of the trail. The wind can give you quite a battering along here.

After an hour and a half of climbing, you'll arrive at Rifugio Tito, which is a shelter with a bench—not much more. The shelter is badly littered, having become, as the old CAI plaque posted there warned, a testament to man's stupidity.

From Rifugio Tito, to the northeast the big peak is Vettore and there's a path to it if you want to climb it.

Otherwise, head north over the ridge/hillock (to the left as you stand facing the door of the *rifugio*) and drop down the grassy hillside toward the chasm and facing the big cliffs on the other side. Soon you'll see some red paint marks, an arrow, for the path, which begins again just before you come in sight of Lago di Pilato down in the valley.

When the path forks about 1½ km (15–30 minutes) after the lake, CAI path #2 will be on the left, and CAI path #3 on the right; bear right onto #3 **B**.

The paths straggle and diverge a bit, but basically you're just following the valley line, staying on paths.

Another 45 minutes or so will bring you to a steeper descent into the Piano della Gardosa and Foce. (This descent is rather difficult, and you may want to take it quite slowly.)

Reaching the bottom of this descent, pass a stony area with a picnic table and some wood post fences. Keep on until you come to a little stone road on which you turn left, and so into Foce.

DAY TWO

Continue on through town (i.e., heading north) on the road you entered it by yesterday.

After about ½ km you'll come to a little wayside tabernacle on the left; the path is immediately beyond it, also on the left. Take it **C**.

At a fork in the path after 5 minutes, take the left fork,

climbing steadily **D**. In another 5 minutes the path converges with another path coming from the left.

You are in for quite a long, steep climb here, hard work on the soft shingle path.

(After 10–15 minutes of steady and more or less straight climbing, another similar size track joins you from the right. Continue straight on.)

The path enters a wood (about 30–45 minutes after leaving Foce), having been shadeless until now, and soon starts to zigzag.

When the path comes to a clearing, go on through it, ignoring a fork up to the right **E**. In 5–10 minutes the path comes out at the high pasture of Il Laghetto and the staggering sight of the mountain wall beyond.

From here the path climbs steeply toward the ridge, then it levels out, passing after a few hundred meters a little corrugated iron shepherd's hut. Shortly after this you come to some metal drinking troughs **F**. Climb up to the left here, and as you come to the first clump of trees you'll pick up the red marks signing you up toward the Passo di Sasso Borghese. Rather a scramble at first, and toward the top you have to keep a careful eye out for the red paint marks, but on the whole it's well signed, and as it flattens, you pick up the red and white CAI marks.

Extremely high-velocity winds up here. Be careful.

Marks give out toward the top of the ridge. Simply follow the main path as it zigzags toward the top.

Just before the very top, join the path that goes left around the inside of the ridge **G**, toward the triangular rocky peak. You will have seen this path from below as you climbed.

As the path climbs over the ridge, bending around to the right, you'll see Castelluccio below you. Amazing craggy landscape up here. CAI signs resume.

A little below the ridge (on the Castelluccio side) the path divides, left going around along the next ridge, right going down. Take the right **H**.

The well-marked path descends toward Castelluccio. After about 40 minutes, where the path makes a fairly marked turn to the right, following around the side of a round hill, you'll see a building below you with a path leading from it to another building with a tin roof. This latter is Rifugio Capanna Ghezzi, run by CAI Perugia. Go down to this. From here a dirt road takes you into Castelluccio, another 4 km.

Bibliography

Angiolini, Sandro, and Monica Naef. *Agriturismo in Toscana.* Rome: ITER srl, 1997.

Antinori, Andrea. *I Sentieri del Silenzio.* Folignano: Societa Editrice Ricerche, 1997.

Ardito, Stefano. *Backpacking and Walking in Italy.* Bradt Publications, 1987.

————*A piedi in Umbria.* Rome: Edizioni ITER, 1989.

Arrighi, Antonio, and Andrea Mancinelli. *A piedi nel Chianti.* Rome: Edizioni ITER, 1991.

Arrighi, Antonio, and Roberto Pratesi. *A piedi in Toscana,* 2 vols. Rome: Edizioni ITER, 1987.

Arrighi, A., A. Bertogna, S. Naef, and P. Pusceddu. *Chianti: Le piu belle escursioni e il trekking Firenze–Siena.* Torino: Vivalda Editori, 1998.

Buckley, Jonathan, Mark Ellingham, and Tim Jepson. *Tuscany and Umbria.* London: Rough Guides, 1994.

Casoli, Curzio. *Trekking and Mountain Biking around Florence and Siena.* Florence: Apice Libri, 1993.

Cecconi, Giovanni, and Stefano Rensi. *Dolce campagna, antiche mura.* Florence: Ed. Libra, 1993.

Cori, Enzo. *Umbria: Le Piu Belle Escursioni.* Folignano: Societa Editrice Ricerche, 1995.

Facaros, Dana, and Michael Pauls. *Cadogan Guides: Tuscany, Umbria and the Marches.* London: Cadogan Books, 1992.

LeFavour, Bruce. *France on Foot: Village to Village, Hotel to Hotel: How to Walk the French Trail System on Your Own.* St. Helena: Attis Press, 1999.

Guidotti, Simone. *Guida alla natura di Toscana e Umbria.* Milan: Mondadori, 1994.

Jepson, Tim. *Wild Italy.* San Francisco: Sierra Club Books, 1994.

Lawrence, D. H. *Etruscan Places* (first published 1932), New York: Viking Press; London: Penguin Books.

BIBLIOGRAPHY

Let's Go, Inc. *Let's Go: The Budget Guide to Italy 1993*. New York: St Martin's Press, 1993.

Marani, Orazio, and Rita Masci. *Passeggiate Fuori Porta*. Pitigliano: Editrice Laurum, 2002.

Montori, Marco, and Fabio Pellegrini. *Sulle orme di Bacco*. Cortona: Editrice Grafica L'Etruria, 1991.

————*Viaggio a piedi dalle Crete Senesi a Montalcino alla Val d'Orcia*. Cortona: Editrice Grafica L'Etruria, 1990.

Nabhan, Gary. *Songbirds, Truffles, and Wolves*. New York and San Francisco: Pantheon Books, 1993.

Panerai, Marco. *Treno natura*. Florence: Stampa Nazionale Firenze, 1991.

Price, Gillian. *Walking in Tuscany*. New York: Interlink Books, 2000.

Root, Waverly. *The Food of Italy*. New York: Vintage Books, 1992.

Slow Food Editore. *Montalcino e Montepulciano, Val d'Orcia e dintorni*. Bra: Slow Food Editore srl, 2001.

Spender, Matthew. *Within Tuscany*. New York: Penguin Books, 1994.

Index

INDEX